de Gruyter Studies in Organization 22

Redding: The Spirit of Chinese Capitalism

de Gruyter Studies in Organization
International Management, Organization and Policy Analysis

An international and interdisciplinary book series from de Gruyter presenting comprehensive research on aspects of international management, organization studies and comparative public policy.
It covers cross-cultural and cross-national studies of topics such as:
- management; organizations; public policy, and/or their inter-relation
- industry and regulatory policies
- business-government relations
- international organizations
- comparative institutional frameworks.

While each book in the series ideally has a comparative empirical focus, specific national studies of a general theoretical, substantive or regional interest which relate to the development of cross-cultural and comparative theory are also encouraged.
The series is designed to stimulate and encourage the exchange of ideas across linguistic, national and cultural traditions of analysis, between academic researchers, practitioners and policy makers, and between disciplinary specialisms.
The volumes present theoretical work, empirical studies, translations and 'state-of-the-art' surveys. The *international* aspects of the series are uppermost: there is a strong commitment to work which crosses and opens boundaries.

S. Gordon Redding

The Spirit of
Chinese Capitalism

Walter de Gruyter · Berlin · New York 1993

S. Gordon Redding
Professor of Management Studies and Director, University of Hong Kong
Business School, University of Hong Kong, Hong Kong

♾ Printed on acid free paper which falls within the guidelines of
the ANSI to ensure permanence and durability.

Library of Congress Cataloging-in-Publication Data

Redding, S. G.
  The spirit of Chinese capitalism / S. Gordon Redding
    p. cm.-(De Gruyter studies in organization : 22)
  Includes bibliographical references and index.
  ISBN 0-89925-657-0 (cloth : acid free)
  ISBN 3-11-013794-1 (pbk)
  1. Capitalism–Asia–Social aspects. 2. Family–Asia. 3. Family
  corporations–Asia. 4. Chinese–Foreign countries. I. Title.
  II. Series.
  HB501.R33 1990   90-37134
  306.3'42'089951–dc20   CIP

Die Deutsche Bibliothek – Cataloging-in-Publication Data

Redding, S. Gordon:
The spirit of Chinese capitalism / S. Gordon Redding. –
Berlin ; New York : de Gruyter, 1993
  (De Gruyter studies in organization ; 22 : International
  management, organization, and policy analysis)

  ISBN 3-11-013794-1
  NE: GT

This book was originally published in hard cover in 1990 by Walter de Gruyter & Co. Berlin

Typesetting: Asco Trade Typesetting Ltd., Hong Kong. – Printing: Gerike GmbH, Berlin. –
Binding: D. Mikolai, Berlin. – Cover Design: Johannes Rother, Berlin. –
Printed in Germany.

For Philip and Peter
and for the
family of Han Hwa

Preface

The title of this book pays tribute to Max Weber and suggests that what is being attempted lies in the shadow of *The Protestant Ethic and the Spirit of Capitalism*. That is so, and Weber's influence is humbly acknowledged. In doing so, however, it is important to state that much has happened in the worlds of practice and theory since 1904 when Weber's thinking first appeared. The cynic might observe that we still have no clearer understanding of the linkages between societal values and economic activity despite the best part of a century's research but at least we have a far richer set of conceptual frameworks with which to think about organizations and societies. This book is, in a sense, a test of whether these extra frameworks can produce more enlightenment or whether we really are stuck with Bonini's paradox that our models, as they get closer to the real world and thus more complex, begin themselves to be as incomprehensible as reality.

The simple notions guiding this book begin with the idea that the way managers see the world affects economic systems via the organizations those managers create. Secondly, this is especially so when the managers are owners at the same time. It is even more so when they come from a society with a strong set of values about cooperation and authority.

The particular group of interest here is a set of owner-managers among the Overseas Chinese people of Hong Kong, Taiwan, Singapore, and Indonesia.

Those are the countries in which long conversations were held with 72 senior executives about their belief systems. At the same time, research from Malaysia, Thailand, and the Philippines is brought into account, to produce a hopefully comprehensive picture of how, and more particularly why, the Overseas Chinese operate as they do, to dominate the economies of the countries surrounding the South China Sea, and in turn to play a significant part in international business generally.

That this set of people is economically important in world terms is occasionally acknowledged. It is however difficult to align recognition with their true significance, as their impact is spread across so many national boundaries that they cannot as a total be represented in any national statistics. Even adding together Taiwan, Hong Kong, and Singapore is grossly inadequate, as it leaves out so much going on in Malaysia, Indonesia, Thailand, and the Philippines, to say nothing of China, or of Vancouver, Toronto, New York, San Francisco, London, Sydney, etc.

This book begins with some attempt to place their power in perspective, and then to examine its origins and its workings. That they produce large numbers of

successful business people is beyond doubt; how and why is still remarkably
obscure, as if they had deliberately avoided publicity. The number of books on
them is minimal, and detailed research in short supply. They get on with it quietly, but to remarkable effect. As their influence and their power continues to
grow, it is becoming increasingly important that their approach be understood,
and long overdue.

Such understanding as may emerge from this still somewhat pioneering introduction, rests on the work and help of many people. Especially instrumental in
this project has been the support of the Institute for the Study of Economic
Culture, at Boston University, and the encouragement of its director Peter Berger. Many of the ideas were formulated and sharpened in meetings under its
auspices, and the practicalities of writing were made much easier by a period of
six months residence at the Institute in Boston. During that period Maria
McFadden and Susan Leftwich were most helpful and Brigitte Berger most hos-
pitable. So also were the staff of the Boston University Library.

During this period I also benefitted from visits to the Fairbank Center for East
Asian Studies at Harvard, and would like to record my thanks to its director Rod
McFarquhar and the staff of the Widener Library.

That leave was from the University of Hong Kong where I have been teaching
Chinese managers since 1973. To those managers, and especially the DMS and
MBA classes, as well as to the university generally, a large debt is owed and
gratefully acknowledged.

Working with me on this project, conducting fieldwork in Taiwan and Singapore, have been Dr. Michael Hsiao and Dr. Theodora Ting Chau, and their
contributions are also gratefully acknowledged. It is sad to record that Mr. Lie
Han Hwa, who began the fieldwork in Indonesia, died during the work, and this
book is dedicated to the memory of his polite intelligence and helpfulness.

Among the many people at the University of Hong Kong who have assisted in
the project have been my research assistant Monica Cartner and departmental
staff Diane Law, Vienna Li, Henrietta Yim, and Christina Siu. Sirwinnie
Cheung, Toto To and Sabrina Li of the Mong Kwok Ping Management Data
Bank have also provided invaluable support, as has the Data Bank facility itself.
My colleagues Gilbert Wong and Simon Tam have provided many stimulating
conversations and Arthur Yeung provided valuable help with Aston data. Wang
Gungwu provided early and welcome encouragement in hosting a workshop at
Australian National University. The Indevo company provided welcome help
for one part of the study.

In Hong Kong also, I have greatly benefitted from the encouragement and
practical help of George Hicks, and from the friendship of a large range of
practising businessmen, notably among them Stan Cheung and Peter Tsang.

The generosity of the Euro-Asia Centre, INSEAD and, in particular, that of
its founder and director, Henri-Claude de Bettignies, has always been of great
help in facilitating my study of Asian business, and conversations there with

Philippe Lasserre and Hellmut Schutte have provided consistent stimulus and help.

There are many other contributors of ideas, including researchers and academic colleagues in Asia and the West, and large numbers of managers whom I have talked to and visited over the past seventeen years throughout East and Southeast Asia. They will remain anonymous here, but their help is greatly appreciated.

The respondents in this study who were kind enough to join the interview process were promised anonymity. This was necessary to protect confidences and to tempt out their versions of the truth. I regret, therefore, that I cannot thank them by name. I would nevertheless like to thank them by initial, whereby they can in turn decide whether to disclose their involvement. This is thus a gesture of sincere thanks for the universal courtesy, frankness and sincerity of:

Hong Kong   AC, AC, PC, SC, WC, CF, AH, RH, SH, WH, AL, CL, CL,
              FCL, GL, HLL, JL, ML, NL, PL, SL, TL, HTL, KWP, KNT,
              KYT, PT, RT, ST, TT, DW, PW, JY, NY, VLW, YCW,
Singapore   JNC, SG, FHH, KPH, MCL, CHL, AM, JT, TWT, SPT, WST,
              KKT,
Indonesia   BHH, IYS, TU,
Taiwan   SSB, FC, YMC, NC, BTH, TH, MHH, DK, HK, CHL, JL, GTL,
              BL, AS, RT, CKW, AW, CTW, YLW, CW.

The book has benefitted greatly from the advice of many academic colleagues. Most significant has been the detailed and helpful scrutiny of Gary Hamilton, but similar debts extend to Peter Berger, Bob Dernberger, Richard Whitley, Bod Tricker, Brian Stewart, Bob Garratt, Adam Lui and Stewart Clegg. Derek Pugh's instrumental help in facilitating the organization structure research is also gratefully acknowledged. Nevertheless, and particularly in a study in a new field, it is important to state that final responsibility remains my own.

Contents

Chapter 1
Introduction: The Overseas Chinese as an Economic Culture

It is a common observation that on returning to Hong Kong after a short absence you will find yet another tall building which was not there before. This somewhat complacent cliche takes on more force when you realize that that is what actually happens, and that it is possible to see the growth taking place, not so much like watching the grass grow but more like the speeded-up film of a flower opening.

The growth of the economies of East Asia is a new phenomenon not just in the sense that it is happening for the first time in the region, but more significantly in the sense that no previous burst of economic activity has been so dramatic anywhere in the world, recently or historically. Europe's economic growth unfolded slowly, North America's perhaps more dramatically but still not in the same league table as that of East Asia which has for three decades maintained annual growth at figures between seven and ten percent.

The search for an explanation of such events must come to terms with three sets of questions. Firstly, what kinds of business people and what kinds of businesses are operating in the region and how different are they from those in other areas? Secondly, how do such organizations manage to generate such apparent effectiveness and efficiency? Thirdly, what else, as well as managerial behavior, has to be brought into account to explain what is going on? This book attempts to examine such questions for the Overseas Chinese, particularly from the standpoint of their own theories of management. This chapter begins by placing the Overseas Chinese in perspective within the region, and in doing so to explore the notion of economic culture.

The use of the convenient phrase East Asia (first made familiar in Orwell's *1984* where he described the area as distinct for the fecundity and industriousness of its peoples) carries with it an implication that the region is homogeneous. At a superficial level it is. These are the "chopstick" cultures, and their peoples are universally mongoloid, as well as being universally in debt to ancient Chinese civilization, just as Westerners are to Greece and Rome.

To understand economic life, however, requires acknowledgement of substantial variations within the region. More particularly, given the managerial power of Japan and the vast amount of attention recently given by Westerners to understanding it, it is necessary to observe that Japanese and Chinese ways of doing things, despite common cultural origins, are now very different indeed. As Joseph Needham once observed, Japan is as different from China as if it had been towed away to Europe and anchored off the Isle of Wight.

The performance figures point to three leading contenders for respect and attention in understanding East Asian success. The first and most obvious is Japan, now so well studied that further analysis would be redundant here. The second is South Korea, currently developing very fast and still relatively little studied.

The third group is that of the Overseas Chinese. In East Asia, as it is normally thought of, this would include Taiwan and Hong Kong, plus for most observers Singapore. This puts together three countries dominated by people originally from China, all of whom still think of themselves as unquestionably still Chinese. It should however also include very significant numbers of ethnic Chinese in Thailand, Malaysia, Indonesia, and the Philippines.

We must therefore re-focus away from East Asia to a larger sphere which encompasses Southeast Asia also. The Chinese diaspora has been until very recently the region to the south of them, surrounding the South China Sea. The Americans historically went west, the Russians east, the Chinese south. For the Chinese, this is an ancient migratory tradition, and it contains a feature unusual in such migrations: the Chinese who moved have remained in some deep and significant sense still Chinese; the majority of them have not psychologically left China, or at least not left some ideal and perhaps romanticized notion of Chinese civilization. This is the feature which unites them, and which provides them with one of their most distinct strengths—a capacity to cooperate. That it has not often been displaced by other forms of identity, of the kind experienced when, for instance, a Pole becomes an American, says something about the vitality, validity and fundamental good sense of the set of traditional beliefs and values which unites Chinese people. To label this civilizing value-system Confucianism is convenient but simple. I propose for the moment to accept the convenience, and to remove the simplicity later. Directly Confucian ideals, and especially familism as a central tenet, are still well enough embedded in the minds of most Overseas Chinese to make Confucianism the most apposite single-word label for the values which govern most of their social behavior. This does not imply that they are unusually devout, consistent, or narrow. It is simply a convenient label for a complex and changing set of values.

A variation on it is "post-Confucian," used to extend the idea to other cultures, notably Korea and Japan, and to allow for the idea of modern re-interpretation of the original ideas, and also for variations in interpretation. For the Chinese themselves there is less need to explain re-interpretation, and the simpler notion of Confucianism will be retained.

No treatment of things Chinese, even though focussed on the South China Sea and its borders, and not aiming directly to discuss current events on the mainland, can totally ignore China itself. An understanding of present-day forms of business behavior among the Overseas Chinese will owe much to Chinese history, both social and economic. An understanding of the Overseas Chinese psyche will owe much to knowing what has happened to China over the last hundred years as well as to its earlier cultural heritage.

It is however important to draw a line and make clear that this book is not about China now, and will only make passing reference to what is happening there. There will be more substantial consideration, at the end, of possible implications for, even possibly strong influence on, a notional future China, but our agenda here is the Chinese as capitalists, not as communists or socialists.

A rather startling justification for such a focus of attention comes from adding up some indicators of economic power. The GNP of China is somewhere in the order of US $ 300 billion, with 1,008 million people. An estimate of the equivalent for the Overseas Chinese, taking account of their officially unacknowledged power in the ASEAN economies, would be somewhere in the region of US $ 200 billion GNP, with around 40 million people. With only one twenty-fifth of the manpower, the Overseas Chinese are playing in the same league-table economically as the whole of China. Even though this contrast is heightened by the massive and very fundamental poverty of China, the significance of the Overseas Chinese in world terms may perhaps now be glimpsed. Their significance for China is also now more starkly obvious, even though the question of putting it to good effect is as complex as its import is great.

A further reason for treating them as one group, despite the variety of environments in which they operate, is that the Overseas Chinese have developed one particular form of organization—the family business—and kept to it. Admittedly there are refinements of it, a wide range of sizes and technologies in use, a great variety of products, services, and markets, and an adventurous set of new variations on how to spin it out to larger and larger size, but certain common denominators seem never to be departed from. It remains in essence a family fortress, and at the same time an instrument for the accumulation of wealth by a very specific set of people. It is guarded against incursions from outside influence, and its workings are not publicly known. It is usually run nepotistically, with a benevolent paternalism throughout. Much of its effectiveness derives from intense managerial dedication, much of its efficiency from creating a work environment which matches the expectations of employees from the same culture. It is, in a very real sense, a cultural artifact.

It has, of course, much in common with family business elsewhere, with what is normally described as the first stage of organizational evolution. A question thus arises—what is special about it? Is it not already understandable from the literature on family business generally? The answer as to its special nature is that it retains many of the characteristics of small scale, such as paternalism, personalism, opportunism, flexibility, even to very large scale. It does not follow the Western pattern of professionalization, bureaucratization, neutralization to anywhere near the same extent. Nor does it follow the Japanese pattern of the powerful but informal trans-organizational bonding found in the *sogo-shosha* or *keiretsu*. It is capable of extending its transactions and influence by complex external networking, but the basis and mechanisms of this process seem quite distinct. It is its own animal, and seemingly unique.

Nor can this be argued to be a matter of time. The Chinese family business has had plenty of time to develop new forms. Sophisticated Chinese organizations have flourished both in and out of China for as long as Western organizations, perhaps longer. They have interacted with powerful markets for just as long and have been accessible to modern managerial technology had they wished. The fact remains that a traditional form of control is retained, and a particular form of legitimacy seen as appropriate. It is the purpose of this book to examine that perceived legitimacy, to seek its sources and to understand its results.

An underlying theme will run through much of what follows. It is that this special form of organization is peculiarly well adapted to its socio-cultural milieu and is thus not replicable elsewhere where that milieu is different. It is also peculiarly effective and a significant contributor to the list of causes of the East Asia miracle. At the same time, there are certain lessons which may be learned from it, for application in other parts of the world. Just as the West, stimulated by the example of Japan, has been recently rediscovering the significance of organizational culture, so may there be some lessons from the Overseas Chinese about paternalism, flexibility, and networking. Theory Z may be joined by Theory C. Their application will remain frustratingly difficult out of context, and the non-Chinese practising manager will perhaps eventually come to accept that he is likely to benefit more from the process of understanding his adversary than from trying to copy his tactics.

Such understanding is likely to increase in value over the next few decades. The organizations of Japan, Korea, and the Overseas Chinese will inevitably extend their impact on Western companies and markets. Western companies in devising appropriate strategic responses, whether those responses are to compete head-on, or to engage in some form of partnership, will need to understand what makes the other organization tick. This is equally valid within Asia itself, as the Chinese family business is likely to be just as opaque to a Japanese from Komatsu as to an American from Caterpillar.

That it has remained such an enigma is due to a number of forces. Firstly, Chinese businesspeople mind their own business. They have learned to be secretive because they have had to. This is a long-standing historical legacy. We shall see later that many of the environments in which they are accustomed to operate have not been notable for their hospitality to business enterprises or to Chinese entrepreneurs. Such entrepreneurs have developed a well-justified wariness in the face of officialdom and a well-honed set of defensive weapons to ensure their survival in an uncertain world. One of these is to keep information in the family.

A second cause for the relative neglect of them by the world of management theory is their dispersion over so many countries, and the lack of a critical mass in one place sufficient to justify the luxury of research institutes devoted to their study and perhaps sponsored by an interested government.

Thirdly, their organizations tend to take a low profile in the wider commercial world. You may go into Bloomingdales, or Selfridges or Matsuzakaya, and find an intriguingly large number of labels saying "Made in Hong Kong" or "Made in Taiwan." They will not however be on garments sporting a brand identity which you could associate with Overseas Chinese. They will say "Yves St. Laurent" or something reassuring in Italian. Except for Wang, it is hard for most people to think of an obviously Overseas Chinese brand name, and that exception itself appears now under threat. The contrast, in this respect, with Japan is dramatic. Overseas Chinese power is thus hidden. They operate in the interstices of the trading world, back down the channels of distribution, making components, manufacturing for others, sub-assembling, wholesaling, financing, sourcing, and transporting. They keep well away from copying the huge organizational hierarchies which coordinate supplies, designs, production systems, marketing needs, and distribution systems to finish up with a Sony TV or a Westinghouse fridge or an Olivetti typewriter. They appear to have an instinct for avoiding such an option, and the significant ramifications of this, and the understanding of why it is so, will become key themes later.

Reference has been made a number of times so far to the organization as a cultural artifact, a response to what form of cooperation a particular set of people either want or are willing to accept, depending on their negotiating position.

Before proceeding further with this assumption lying vaguely in the background, it would be proper to bring it out for close examination, and in doing so take the opportunity to outline the investigative framework which lies behind the research for this book [1]. Needing clarification also is the more general notion of economic culture and where it fits into explaining business success and national economic success. Lastly, it will be necessary to explain what information this book is based on.

Explaining how particular patterns of economic growth develop is fraught with difficulties both practical and theoretical. Significant among the practical difficulties is the tendency among theorists doing the explaining to operate from one discipline, such as economics, or sociology, or history, and to have the greatest difficulty coordinating an explanation across disciplines. It is perhaps understandable that we do not have many theorists truly competent in more than one field, but it is regrettable if they refuse to acknowledge alternative perspectives and insist on the dominance of one theme. I would wish to avoid such intellectual imperialism, and even though the focus of this book on socio-cultural values and organizational behavior will at times make it appear biased towards one standpoint, the occasional tentative venturing into economics, psychology, or history may at least stand as symbolic of a wish to acknowledge the value of alternative perspectives.

Problems to do with theory itself arise because of the complexity of the issues faced and the number of strands to be gathered together. Another factor making life more difficult for the theorist is that history, despite rumors to the contrary, does not repeat itself. The human race learns too much, especially technologically, as it goes along, for one total societal experience to replicate an earlier one (Popper 1957). It seems only in the micro field of individual human judgement that the often regrettable repeat performances occur. In facing these two issues, complexity and constant new circumstances, E.L. Jones, having attempted the task of explaining the "European Miracle" came to the view that it was like unpicking a giant combination lock for which there is no one key and no unique combination, yet with parts which fit together well enough to work (Jones 1981: 238). The whole developmental process will not fit into any simple model as "too many parameters shift and dissolve." Compromise is inevitable as it is not possible at the same time to derive generality, realism, and precision. His claim is that the particular combination of circumstances which made for Europe's very long-term development was sufficiently fortuitous to be in the category of miracles. A replica of that pattern, and particularly the "invention" of modern capitalism over the same period in Asia, would have been super-miraculous. Our concern now is with how certain groups in Asia this century, and one in particular, have beaten the laws of probability to move from the virtual impossibility of pulling off a super-miraculous feat to the just possible circumstance, aided to some degree by borrowing, of pulling off a miraculous one.

The complexity of explaining economic success, then, has two aspects: firstly, the number of possible influences is very large; secondly, the way they are connected together does not make for easy explanation. In regard to the first issue, it is possible to find plausible explanations for the recent economic success of East Asia in terms of (a) economic policies adopted by governments, (b) worldwide shifts in the processes of industry and trade, (c) socio-cultural factors operating at the individual and organization levels, (d) structures in the society which support business such as banking, capital raising, etc. (Hicks and Redding 1983). In each case, there is apparent logic. In no case has a single cause won universal acceptance. At the same time, almost no one has attempted to put the various contributing causes together. The dominance of intellectual specialization may have made that now impossible, or at least only attempted by the risk-prone.

The use of the word "cause" also raises more fundamental problems. Social science is not physics, and even so, physics is not what it was in the simple days of cause-and-effect. What the layman thinks of as cause-and-effect must give way to a whole complex of chains of factors, each one, if it is separated out for analysis, being determined by others, and being influenced in return by its results. Let me illustrate with the notion of family ownership of business. This simple fact of almost universal relevance to the Overseas Chinese
results from

(a) the Confucian political philosophy of designing a state based on the stable family;
(b) a set of values instilled in consequence over centuries of socialization;
(c) facts of Chinese history which have made it sensible for the Chinese family to act as the main source of identity and succor;
(d) psychological characteristics of dependence and loyalty;
(e) patrilineal and patrilocal kinship structures;
(f) more recent politico-economic environments which have encouraged family business units;

is a determinant of

(a) high levels of identity/loyalty/commitment in key organizational roles;
(b) paternalistic organizational climates and worker dependence;
(c) a narrowly defined set of stakeholders in the organization;
(d) nepotism, together with its accompanying tension;
(e) common economic outcomes of increasing family wealth;

and is affected in reverse by these results which tend to reinforce the established pattern by

(a) releasing motivation in key organizational areas and thereby promoting efficient performance;
(b) perpetuating the welfare of the key stakeholders, both practically and psychologically.

To understand fully this stream of connections would also require some incorporation of ideas from what might be seen as parallel streams of explanation; looking at, for instance, political factors, institutional structures, social psychology, history, economics, etc.

It is necessary then to abandon any notion of "mechanical" cause, that one thing results from another in a simple linear way like one billiard ball pushing another. Instead, we are faced with a vast net of connected elements, none of which is especially dominant, and all of which have somehow to be acknowledged, even though they may be only seen with peripheral vision.

It is in this context that the argument is placed for the notion of economic culture; in other words, that there are, within a certain geographical boundary, sufficient connections between socio-cultural values and economic behavior to make for a distinctive and unique constellation of features, identifiable both by particular economic characteristics and results and by overlapping social values (Berger 1986, Granovetter 1985). Japan is an obvious example, so too is South Korea; so too, beyond any single national boundary, is the realm of the Overseas Chinese. Others (e.g. Lodge and Vogel 1987, Morishima 1982, Rodinson 1974, Wiener 1981) have argued for the value of such a notion in understanding the behavior of many specific countries or cultures, and although the analysis is often carried across political boundaries, the most common envelope in which to place a particular economic culture is the nation-state.

Such an idea does not, of course, solve the problem of explanation, as causes and effects still remain ambiguous, but by drawing boundaries around successful cases, and by implying the combination of two main forces, the economy and the culture, it can facilitate the intellectual effort of untangling the connections within the object of interest.

Lying behind such literature, as an *eminence grise*, is the still authoritative statement of the core idea, Max Weber's *The Protestant Ethic and the Spirit of Capitalism*. The way in which he traced the connections between the behavior of modern capitalists in Western Europe and the precepts of seventeenth-century Protestantism, and the way in which he attempted to place religion alongside other factors in the formulation of a spirit of capitalism, need not be considered in detail, but some brief account of the Weberian position is justified.

The Spirit of Capitalism

Weber began in an intellectual milieu where much explanation of economic behavior made the common enough theoretical assumption that people were rational economic actors. His perspective was that this should not be simply assumed but, instead, explained. Although the import of what he proposed has been subsequently seen as highly significant, partly at least for its capacity to counterbalance the materialist explanations of Marx, in fact his agenda was carefully bounded.

Put at its sharpest (Poggi 1983: 83), what Weber is saying is: no capitalist development without an entrepreneurial class; no entrepreneurial class without a moral charter; no moral charter without religious premises. This contains a number of important implications. In the first place, it treats the ideas contained in the "spirit" of capitalism as parts of a more complex explanation. They are necessary components but not sufficient in themselves to produce the result in question. Secondly, the context of his study was European capitalism of the early twentieth century the forms of which were, in his view, influenced critically by an ethic shared by businessmen and traceable to the doctrines of seventeenth-century Protestantism. The arguments are not designed to transfer out of that particular time or place.

Given those reservations, however, a number of forces have conspired to make Weber's analysis attractive to many of those dealing with questions which are in fact located in different places and different times. In the first instance, the notion of ideas as moving societies in certain directions continues with all its intuitive appeal to have a narcotic attractiveness. Secondly, the sheer power of

modern capitalism has extended massively the size and significance of the phenomenon Weber tried to explain and embedded it deeply into other cultures
since then, causing them in turn to change significantly. Thirdly, the progress of
social science, by encouraging multidisciplinary and complex forms of explanation, has confirmed the salience of such belief systems as necessary although not
sufficient components of the understanding of economic behavior.

   The understanding of Chinese capitalism, which this book makes a start at,
begins with an assumption that there is a distinct and bounded phenomenon to
be explained, that it is the culmination of a set of processes which need to be
seen historically, and that the beliefs and values of businessmen have a part to
play in the understanding of it. To set the scene for such an analysis, it will be
salutary to look at the Weberian model as exemplar, although in doing so to
acknowledge the impossibility of matching the monumental scholarship which
formed the original. Instead, the emphasis in this study will be quite deliberately
empirical, an element notably lacking in the Weberian literature and its critical
progeny (Marshall 1982: 132).

   Modern capitalism, as Weber saw it, has the following components (Marshall
1982: 56, Poggi 1983: 23):

(1) Fixed capital invested in the production of goods on which depends the satis-
    faction of everyday mass needs;
(2) rationally capitalistic organization of formally free labor, including disci-
    pline;
(3) separation of business and household capital;
(4) rational bookkeeping and accounting aimed at long run, ever-renewed
    profitability;
(5) rational structures of law and administration;
(6) the rationalization of economic life in a shared "spirit" or ethic;
(7) orientation to opportunities open on the market.

The power of the modern capitalist system over others that had gone before
(but not necessarily, we must note, over others that have emerged since) was
based on the persistent theme of rationality. This releases the efficiency derived
from compelling businesses to operate via the most accurate calculations possible about the results or potential results of their activities. In the use of information for the pursuit of profitability, and in the peculiarly strong commitment to
the objective selection of the most appropriate means for given ends, sharpened
also by the capacity to foretell the equally rational behavior of others, this system has imposed a matter-of-factness and a capacity to rise above more "local"
considerations, which largely explain its transcendence. In the process, in treating the world as a set of objective arrangements "to be continuously and ruth-
lessly tinkered with" (Poggi 1983: 91), it has made marginal the irrationalities of
superstition, and deprived the world of much of its enchantment.

   The prior, more "traditional" world, with its superstitions and magics was also characterized by attitudes which ran counter to the accumulation of wealth. The traditional peasant would work to provide himself with enough to satisfy basic needs and had no ambition for further riches. The doubling of wages could result in the halving of work if needs were the same. This changed in parts of Europe after the seventeenth century and a new spirit, justifying hard work and the accumulation of wealth, began to spread and work its effects.

Weber was not so much concerned with explaining how the spirit of modern capitalism affected its day-to-day workings, as he was to explain where the spirit came from in the first place (Marshall 1982: 18) [2]. He traced it to the ascetic versions of Protestantism which grew up after the Reformation broke the monopoly held by the Roman Catholic church over the rights to worship. When these rights were dispersed to individuals, new ethics grew up and were reinforced by new sanctions to compel adherence. The main Protestant ethics of significance in this case were

(1) diligence in worldly callings or vocations, including business;
(2) asceticism;
(3) the systematic, i.e. non-wasteful, use of time.

The sanction which compelled adherence was founded in Calvin's doctrine of predestination, the force of this stemming from the following horrific logic:

(a) You are either elected as a child of God or condemned as a sinner to eternal damnation.
(b) You cannot know which you are.
(c) The distinguishing feature of the elect is that they trust through faith and live the godly life.
(d) The systematic and relentless practice of appropriate worldly activity therefore allows the individual to conclude that his or her faith is true and thus that he or she is "elected."

In consequence, a great deal of diligent and ascetic worldly activity ensued. The assiduous pursuit of efficient transactions became a way of demonstrating faith. The rationality which was arguably inspired, or at least strongly reinforced, by such an ethic then in turn contributed, along with a multitude of other determinants, to the increasing power of the system which emerged as modern capitalism.

A Spirit of Chinese Capitalism?

A plethora of questions surrounds the notion of a spirit of Chinese capitalism. Is that capitalism in itself distinct? Is its way of working the result, at least in part, of an identifiable set of people acting out a certain set of beliefs? Is that spirit coherent and internally consistent? What are the components of such a world-view? How did they come to crystallize out in this form? Where do they come from? How are they maintained and reinforced? How do they affect behavior? This book is about those questions, and in beginning a process of answering them, it must present at the outset some conditions for the analysis, and some assumptions about how causation will be viewed. The questions will serve to focus the discussion.

Is Chinese capitalism distinct? The seven components of modern Western capitalism listed earlier only partially describe Chinese capitalism. The separation of business and household capital is not complete in the Chinese case, certainly psychologically. Financial control practices are still so clandestine that they are only partially rational. The surrounding structures of law and administration are not entirely indigenously derived. In sum, a different list of characteristics would be needed to encapsulate the Chinese form.

This still does not justify its classification as distinct, as it may well be simply an example of more traditional business forms which have many variants. One needs to consider how different it is from Jewish business, from Armenian, from Marwari, before concluding that it is in fact a distinct type. This latter question can only be answered by implication later, as it is too large an issue for this text to address specifically. It will however be argued that, although there is much overlap with these other types, the combination of features in the Chinese case leaves it in a separate and distinct category.

A coherent spirit? For there to be an affinity between business behavior and the spirit which infuses it, assuming consistency of behavior requires also consistency of the notionally independent spirit. It will be argued that Overseas Chinese businessmen think sufficiently alike, and differently from others, for such consistency to be proposed. Internal consistency is a matter of the parts of the belief system making sense as contributing components to a sensible overall framework. This will be argued to be the case, and will strengthen the case for the distinctiveness of the belief system. The role of Confucianism as the bedrock set of beliefs is crucial in this regard.

Components of the world-view. These will be reconstructed from the statements of the businessmen in such a way as to interpose as little as possible between their expressions and the description of them. It is their categories which are sought and their reasoning. The method of research for this book paid particular attention to gaining access to deeply felt, but rarely articulated, beliefs.

How do the beliefs form? As a sum of the individual accounts of 72 businessmen in four countries, the description here focusses on typical processes of socialization and sources of influence in a person's own experience.

Where do beliefs come from? It is taken that the traditions of Chinese society, going back into mainland Chinese history are transmitted and maintained in the Overseas Chinese subculture, and that the beliefs come from such social and historical experience.

Maintenance and reinforcement? It is taken that there are forces which play on individuals, in the specific Overseas Chinese context, which reinforce adherence to the basic tenets of their ethic, and serve to renew and perpetuate it.

Beliefs and behavior? At the individual level, the connection between beliefs and behavior is loose and variable. At the societal level, doubtless it is more so. Nor can cause be seen to be going one way. The suppositions in this research are that understanding how the spirit of Chinese capitalism influences the practice of Chinese capitalism requires acceptance of the following caveats about causation:

(a) the determinants of a pattern of business activity are multiple and not analysable within one discipline;
(b) some will be more salient than others but not necessarily following precedents in other areas or other times;
(c) they will be interconnected among themselves;
(d) they will be influenced reciprocally by their effects.

We must now move on to claim in summary that the Overseas Chinese have an apparently distinct economic culture, that it is describable, and the outline of its determinants can be drawn. It is still necessary to place it in a larger framework of explanation if the question of macro-economic performance is to be a consideration.

In taking culture as a principal theme in this book, it is necessary to reassert that it is not seen as *the* dominant cause of economic success, obliterating or ignoring other factors like economic policy. Culture is one of several key features, deserving of a respectable place in any account. No more than that, but no less either. That this claim is necessary is in part due to an intuition that economics particularly has tended to (a) be accorded a form of automatic right to initiate explanation, but (b) has forfeited that right by staying somewhat disdainfully within its own cautious boundaries. No more embarrassing indicator of this can be found than the supercilious treatment by Samuelson in the textbook which so dominates that field of enquiry (Samuelson 1979: 718). In a section headed "Superficial Theories of Development," the question of custom and culture is granted 35 lines (in a text of 828 pages, double-column). Paradoxically he lists a range of cultural traits which are acknowledged to be influences on material progress. These include

(1) a replacement of a belief in magic and superstition by discernment of and belief in the cause-and-effect relation of engineering and science;
(2) the work ethic;
(3) materialism as opposed to other-worldliness or emphasis on the hereafter;
(4) tolerance of dishonesty and corruption;
(5) tendency toward thrift;
(6) ideological battles over the distribution of wealth.

Having acknowledged their influence, he says, somewhat obscurely, that "putting stress on these non-economic factors does not solve the problem of *explanation*. It poses new problems." Samuelson's solution to this apparently frustrating untidiness is to remove such issues from the account! Such epistemological naivete fits well with someone who then goes on to dismiss Weber's work with insulting curtness claiming that the Protestant ethic thesis "proves nothing, because there is almost nothing to be proved."

More recent thinking has seen economists beginning to deal with some of the more intangible features of life which sociologists have always dealt with. The work of Morishima (1982) on Japan for instance and Morawetz (1980) on Colombia are indicators of a desire to range more widely in search of answers, to respond to complex questions with complex explanations.

To see the culturally based explanation in context, it may perhaps be useful to summarize briefly the set of key approaches found so far in the literature.

Two recent reviews of the literature on East Asian success have categorized the approaches used, and may serve to introduce the field. Chalmers Johnson who is concerned to explain Japanese performance at the national level sees the main schools of thought in the following terms (Johnson 1985). There are three main approaches:

(a) the "MacArthurian" explains the country's success as the result of being like a child protected, and to some degree spoiled, by a rich uncle, and so far still able to behave self-indulgently;
(b) the "Nihonjinron" view explains Japanese success entirely in terms of cultural uniqueness, stressing such features as cooperativeness and identity with the work group, intergroup competition, sacrifice for common goals, etc.;
(c) the "Venetian" model explains the success in terms of the structural underpinnings of the trading nation, these being: stable rule by a political-bureaucratic elite immune from the kind of political pressures which would undermine economic growth; cooperation between public and private sectors within some understood strategy; heavy investment in education; equitable income distribution; sensitive use of intervention by the price mechanism.

Johnson comes down clearly in favor of the "Venetian" model, arguing that the successful economies of East Asia share the same structural features. For the purposes of the argument of this book, however, it is worth noting that in arguing the significance of the infrastructure, Johnson is also aware of a closer-grained reality. He faces the title-page of his distinguished book *MITI and the Japanese Miracle* (1982) with a quotation from Peter Drucker: "It is only managers—not nature or laws of economics or governments—that make resources productive!"

An alternative review is provided by Gary Hamilton and Nicole Biggart, although their approach differs from that of Johnson by making organization and management the centerpiece of their inquiries (Hamilton and Biggart 1988).

As this accords with the perspective taken in this book, perhaps their review will set the scene appropriately.

They distinguish three main approaches, within the social sciences, to the study of organizations:

(a) The *market* approach looks at the issues in a fairly mechanical way, attempting to draw up laws of market behavior, and analysing economic decision making in relation to market-mediated transactions. Thus the development of multi-divisional corporations is seen in terms of the efficiencies they bring to the reduction of the costs of transacting economic activities.
(b) The *cultural* approach takes it as a starting point that cultural beliefs and behavior patterns in the society will shape economic behavior, as deep-seated "character traits" of the society come to the surface.
(c) The *authority* approach concentrates on "principles of domination," which, although clearly related to culture, are not reducible to it, as historical, political, and economic elements also get involved. A more commonly understood title for this field is political economy, and it rests mainly on the foundations set by Marx and Weber.

As Hamilton and Biggart point out, the market approach suffers from the central problem of its mother-discipline, economics, in that it uses too simple and restricted a notion of cause-and-effect. It is difficult using it to explain the *variety* of organizational types in East Asia. It is, for instance, not convincing to explain large Japanese corporations, many of which pre-date the period of modern industrialization, without some incorporation of historical elements, or of societal attitudes to cooperation. It is not convincing to explain the Chinese family business in purely market-transactional terms and ignore the pressures on family survival and internal support which were common through Chinese history, related as they were to political control structures, and reinforced by a powerful set of social values.

The culture explanation, on its own, is equally unconvincing unless it, at the same time, acknowledges the reality of economic life and the inevitably powerful influence of market forces in reinforcing successful formulae.

And there is still something crucial left over, which is that organizations qua organizations are cooperative systems which imply domination and (perhaps more crucially) the acceptance of domination by the majority of people in them. Neither culture nor market can explain this totally, and resort must be made, in understanding this decisive central component, to the wider context of authority relations in the society.

One is led to three conclusions:

(a) economic explanations are more convincing if they acknowledge culture;
(b) cultural explanations are more convincing if they acknowledge the market forces of economics;

(c) the explanations which have most effectively stood the test of time have started with the society's view of authority and then attempted to incorporate the other features.

This latter approach, if taken too far, suffers from the danger of a permanent trap—that of saying simply that everything is connected with everything else. While this may end the nail-biting over choice, it produces no consolation for the enquirer looking for guidance through the swamp. A degree of risk is involved in making any model of reality, and one must trade off the waspishness of specialists who will attack what they see as an approach which is either biased or too general, against the extra illumination which simplicity will provide for the newcomer to the question.

That there is movement to reconcile these tensions is suggested in a review by Richard Whitley (1987). In this he argues that economic analysis would be better informed by acknowledging the significance of the fact that firms develop different characteristics which in turn affect subsequent resource allocation and use. They have, in other words, borrowing a notion from Spender (1980), different "recipes." Looking at the matter by industry, one could note that there are many similarities in the organizational behavior of say airlines, department stores, software houses. These could be argued to be responses to certain common technical and market forces. The point is that the form of organizational behavior, the "recipe," becomes an important part of any understanding of what is going on in an industry.

Similarly, and crucially for the concerns of this book, the cross-national understanding of why and how organizations behave as they do must take account of the possibility of "recipes" varying by culture, or country. Within the economic cultures of East Asia, such as the Japanese, Korean and Overseas Chinese, have emerged certain dominant organizational "recipes": the Japanese *keiretsu* and *kaisha*, the Korean *chaebol*, and the Chinese family business. To see them as relatively stable configurations, answering the need for coordination in quite specific contexts with quite specific impulses, constraints, and material to work with, is to see them in a way which connects the institutional approach of Hamilton and Biggart, with the organization-based approach of Whitley, while at the same time allowing culture into the explanation of why and how the recipe stabilized in its present form. Thus an informed sociology of firm behavior would enrich the study of economic logics with the study of the social processes and conditions for those logics. The notion of economic culture becomes a vehicle for that endeavor.

The main platform for the study of economic culture in this book will be the depiction of the beliefs of Chinese chief executives which together constitute a spirit of Chinese capitalism. It is intriguing in this context to note a significant point about the workings of capitalism, made recently by Peter Berger (1986: ch. 9). This is that it is essentially taken for granted, and in fact "has a built-in incapacity to generate legitimations of itself." In contrast with the "mythic potency" of socialism with its seemingly never-achieved and arguably never-achievable ideal state, capitalism is essentially prosaic. The economic and social outcomes are its *de facto* justification, and the source of its legitimacy, but they are not overtly inspirational.

The values to be teased out of any analysis of the statements of Chinese capitalists are thus likely to be buried below the surface of the day-to-day activities which they discuss. There will be no readily packaged philosophical system, perhaps no obvious logics, no creed. Instead, one might reasonably look for coherent thoughts only when pressed (and thoughts which, as a number of respondents remarked, had not normally been near the surface) about the nature and sources of their authority, and about the validity of the total economic system into which their roles are fitted.

Before examining such components of the spirit which animates so much of Asian economic life, it will be necessary to set the scene, and provide some understanding of the circumstances in which the Overseas Chinese have developed their business systems. More particularly, this requires a closer examination, firstly, of who they are, where they are, what they do, and where they came from; secondly, a look at the broader set of social values which have shaped Chinese life, and which still influence much economic behavior. A closer understanding of the way the typical Chinese family business works and why will then be built up gradually as the entrepreneurs themselves explain their ideas and ideals.

Footnotes

[1] A more detailed treatment of this question is given in Redding (1982b).
[2] The discussion given here is a very simple treatment of Weber and cannot do justice to his complexity. He is, for instance, accused of being unclear as to whether the spirit of modern capitalism is (a) a unique and distinguishing feature of such a system, (b) a necessary but not sufficient cause of it, (c) an attitudinal complex which may under certain conditions result in certain patterns of behavior, or (d) the behavior itself. For more complete discussions of such issues, see e.g. Marshall (1982) and Poggi (1983).

Chapter 2
The Sojourners

This chapter is concerned with scene setting: to understand who the Overseas Chinese are, how they came to their present position, what they do, and at a simple level why they do it. The emerging themes will be ethnic and more particularly subethnic identity, and networking, as means of dealing with the real or latent insecurity of their environments.

A portrait of the "typical" Overseas Chinese may be drawn as a composite, each component of which is visible in a real-life instance. Take thus a hypothetical Mr. Lim living in Semarang, an industrial port on the north coast of Java and a base for Chinese power for some centuries past. His family came to Indonesia from China at the turn of the century and in the 1930's adopted the Indonesian name of Hartono. He is Hokkienese by area of origin, and his family and friends still use the dialect among themselves. He has never been to China but members of his family have visited the ancestral village. He has a brother in Singapore, another in Hong Kong, and a sister who is an Australian citizen married to a Hokkien engineer in Sydney. His wife is Hokkienese also but they met in Semarang through the Protestant Christian church of which they are both members. He owns and manages a factory making plastic household goods. This relies on machinery transferred to second generation use after its first six years of life in a Hong Kong factory owned by a cousin. He purchases raw materials from a major multinational chemical company, in which two of his nephews are employed, one of them in the pricing department, the other in sales. He sells to three wholesalers in different parts of Java, two of them Hokkienese and one Cantonese by origin. His banker is a large Indonesian bank owned by an Indonesian Chinese of Hokkien extraction, and which employs one of his nephews and two nieces. He is now considering an expansion of his business in partnership with a Singaporean friend of his brother, who would in turn bring in capital raised from a Chinese-owned Singapore bank which has strong connections into Hokkien regional networks. His elder son works for him and has been groomed to succeed him with an engineering degree at California Institute of Technology followed by a Berkeley MBA. The middle son is a professional accountant attached locally to a Chinese-owned consultancy company but intending to set up his own practice in time. A third son is in Australia training to be a doctor.

He meets regularly with other members of the Chinese community socially: firstly, as a board member of a local hospital funded largely by Chinese business support; secondly, through the church which has a large Chinese membership; thirdly, with a group of close friends, all businessmen, who play mahjong together weekly; fourthly, at a series of social occasions such as weddings, dinners for new-born sons, and various other forms of celebration which bring the Chinese community together, almost always to tables of twelve in a restaurant where the occasion might justify anything from one table to fifty.

Mr. Lim travels about twice a year around the region, in each place renewing friendships and acquaintanceships in a round of business-oriented socializing. He normally stays with relatives, travels economy class, and spends frugally except in entertaining when he can be a lavish host. On these trips be accumulates information on new products, new technologies, new market possibilities, alternative sources of finance, of supply and continues to investigate the possibility of exporting goods from Indonesia. Most of this information is gathered in conversation with his sources rather than via any formal reports, and he keeps most of it in his head.

Mr. Lim has over 40 million compatriots, people with a common heritage, many common ideals, shared norms of social behavior, similar strengths, and similar weaknesses; in sum, a distinct cultural type, and one moreover which has remained consistent and true to itself for centuries.

In the year 1621 an English merchant venturer, Sir Thomas Herbert, was reporting home on his journeys in the East Indies, and provided the following vignette about the town of Bantam in West Java:

The town of its own growth affords little save rice, pepper, and cotton-wool; albeit pepper for the greatest part brought thither by the infinitely industrious Chyneses, who each January come to anchor in multitudes at this port, and unload their junks or praws from Jamby in Sumatra, Borneo, Malacca, and other places, making Bantam their magazine; out of which for *rials*, or by exchange for other commodities, they supply the English, Dutch, and other nations. The Chyneses are no quarrelers, albeit voluptuous, venereous, costly in their sports, great gamesters, and in trading too subtle for young merchants, oftimes go wedded to dicing, that, after they have lost their whole estate, and wife and children are staked; yet in littel time, Jew-like, by gleaning here and there, are able to redeem their loss (Purcell 1965: 394).

Such an account could have been rendered of virtually any of the major trading stations around the South China Sea, and would doubtless have characterized the Chinese similarly—there is strong accord in so many accounts that they are "infinitely industrious," "no quarellers," "great gamesters," subtle, and frugal.

Their penetration into the coastal regions of the South China Sea began with small excursions in the Tang dynasty, a thousand years before the account just quoted, when Chinese businessmen would trade porcelain, silk, and tea for cloves, pepper, and other local products (Wu and Wu 1980: 59).

As seen by Fernand Braudel, in the millenium between A.D. 500 and 1500, before Europe burst out of its "tiny but supercharged space," the Far East was a huge self-sufficient "world economy" (Braudel 1984: 397). With power balanced between China, Islam, and India, the center of gravity eventually settled down in the East Indies, in the Malay peninsula, in ports such as Bantam, Atjeh, Malacca, and later Batavia and Manila. This crucial crossroads had been penetrated between the first and fourth century by Hinduism, and the fifth-century arrival of the Chinese dragon had been too late to secure cultural dominance of these central locations (Curtin 1984: 158–178).

It is worthy of note, at this point, especially in view of the common assumptions about sophisticated business practice being developed in the West and then being gradually dispersed elsewhere as a benevolent transfer of organizing technology, that trading in the Far East in this early period was already a matter of skill and professionalism (Curtin 1984: 177). Braudel's view on the matter is:

We can challenge the traditional image of Asiatic traders as high class pedlars hawking about in their small packs tiny quantities of valuable merchandise—spices, pepper, pearls, perfumes, drugs, and diamonds. The reality is rather different. Everywhere, from Egypt to Japan, we shall find genuine capitalists, wholesalers, the retailers of trade, and their thousands of auxiliaries—the commission agents, brokers, money-changers, and bankers. As for the techniques, possibilities, or guarantees of exchange, any of these groups of merchants would stand comparison with its Western equivalents (Braudel 1984: 486).

The attitude of China to external trade was, for most of that period, either ambivalent or officially negative. Only rarely was a conscious effort made to extend influence to the south. In the years between 1400 and 1430, there was an extraordinary wave of maritime expeditions under the auspices of the newly invigorated Ming dynasty, but these tailed off, and for reasons which still remain obscure to historians, long-distance expeditions were abandoned for good. In succeeding centuries, China operated a "sea-ban," and withdrew inside its self-sufficiency. Such a ban could not easily be policed and, in any case, the political will to impose it would vary from time to time until events in the nineteenth century overtook it and it was abandoned.

An important trade connection throughout the seventeenth and eighteenth centuries was the link with the trans-Pacific Spanish galleon trade operating between Manila and Acapulco in Mexico. Each year some 30 to 50 Chinese junks would transport silk to Manila for onward transmission. So many Mexican dollars were brought west in consequence that they eventually became the principal silver currency of the China coast (Fairbank, Reischauer, and Craig 1965: 25).

A useful summary of the main historical periods and the types of activities typical of the Overseas Chinese at various times has been provided by Wu and Wu, and represented in Figure 2.1.

From this it is clear that initial trading was seasonal both by land and sea, but eventually gave way to long-term settlement of Chinese in the region. This was partly due to the gradual consolidation of trading activities, but also, significantly, an escape option for refugees from various forms of strife in China. Settlers

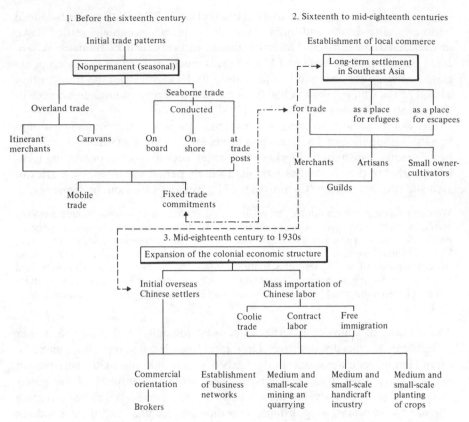

Figure 2.1: Evolution of ethnic-Chinese economic activities in Southeast Asia

Source: Wu and Wu (1980: 131)

were merchants or artisans, who would link into guilds, or small farmers. As the colonial economies developed extractive industries and plantations from the mid-eighteenth century onwards, the numbers of Chinese settlers were swollen by the mass import of laborers. This reached a flood towards the end of the nineteenth century as the final collapse of the Manchu dynasty was presaged by gradual disintegration of the social fabric of China.

It would be misleading to suggest that all Chinese migration was to the south. In fact, large numbers went north into Manchuria, or east across the Pacific. Some also went further south to Australasia. The fact remains, however, that the borders of the South China Sea attracted most. These regions were more accessible, more climatically benevolent, and footholds had already been established in which their social networks could flourish (Hamilton 1977).

The legacies of the past century of unrest, both social and psychological, remain with the Overseas Chinese today, and the period will bear a little closer scrutiny.

Movements of people from north to south in China have been a regular part of Chinese history. So too has been the tendency for the north to dominate politically and militarily, and the south to be an area of potential, and sometimes actual, rebellion, requiring firm control and at times great harshness of treatment.

A population drift to the south may be accounted for partly by the tendency for military pressure to arise in the north and expel people. It may also have been due to the generally more benevolent southern climate and the lower likelihood there of suffering from the once traditional disasters of famine or flood. In the major famines of 1846, 1849, and 1877, 23.4 million people died, in powerful testimony to the inability of the last imperial dynasty to cope with the government of a country undergoing a massive population explosion (Fairbank 1987: 66).

Movements of people in from the north would then put the south under more pressure, such that they in turn would move out from the coastal provinces. In the nineteenth century, approximately three million people are thought to have left Fukien and Kwangtung provinces, a drift which has continued well into the twentieth century with people fleeing political turmoil in the 1930's, war in the 1940's, and communism continuously since the 1950's.

Testimony as to why is provided by Wu and Wu (1980: 129), who report a 1934 survey of 905 families in the Swatow area. A list of their principal reasons for emigration is as follows:

Table 2.1: Principal reasons for emigration from near Swatow, 1934
(Source: Wu and Wu 1980: 129)

Reason given	No. of Families	% of Emigrants
Economic pressure	633	69.95
Previous connections abroad	176	19.45
Losses from natural calamities	31	3.43
Plan to expand specific enterprise	26	2.87
Bad conduct	17	1.88
Local disturbance	7	0.77
Family quarrel	7	0.77
Other	8	0.88
	905	100.00

The economic pressure, in a mainly farming community, was reported to be due to a combination of high population density, the uneven distribution of farmland, and the prevalence of tenant farming. These forces were exacerbated

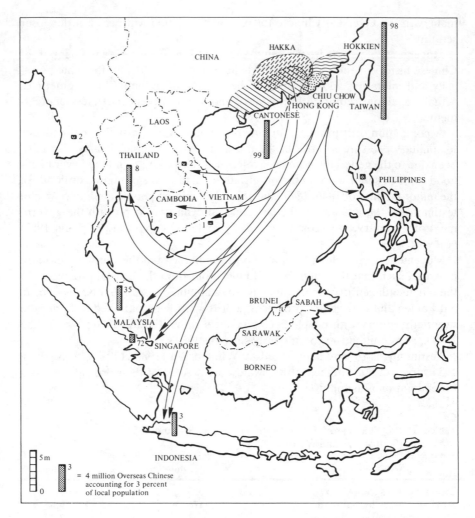

Figure 2.2: Historical migration patterns and estimated present distribution of Overseas
             Chinese around the South China Sea

Sources: Purcell 1965; Wu and Wu 1980

by flood or drought occurring on the average once every six years. The more
specific symptoms complained of were individual unemployment, a lack of
assets, limited income, and overcrowded households.

People who left China at any period to go abroad did not generally do so with
the blessing of the state. The sense of China as the middle kingdom mediating
between heaven and the remainder of humanity, fanciful though it may seem, is

a very influential underpinning to much Chinese thinking, either historically at
the political level, or psychologically for individuals. The name given to those
who left was, and is, *nanyang hua ch'iao*. *Hua* signifies Chinese and *ch'iao* signifies a short-term visitor, a sojourner. The fact that many have sojourned for
centuries does not change the expectation that they would eventually return to
the motherland. The other half of the name, *nanyang*, means southern ocean or
the South China Sea. Again this takes its meaning from China, which it is south
of, rather than referring to the sovereign nations which form the region, such as
Thailand, Malaysia, Indonesia. The sense is of *our* people, temporarily away,
not really settled, and bound eventually to return.

Two intriguing paradoxes ensue from this. Firstly, many of the Overseas
Chinese do genuinely still feel bound to China even after centuries of family
settlement elsewhere, and the flow of movements of *nanyang* visitors to China is
enormous. This is despite the passing of much time, and despite the need to
return to a regime for which little sympathy is expressed. Secondly, it is only in
recent years that China has been prepared to protect the interests of the Overseas Chinese. For some hundreds of years, the emigrants were seen as having
abandoned the protection of China, whose concerns were decidedly introverted,
and they were left unprotected to suffer whatever fate had in store for them.
When, for instance, repeated racial massacres in Manila and Batavia in the first
half of the eighteenth century took 70,000 Chinese lives, China itself showed no
interest in protecting them, a pattern repeated in the nineteenth and twentieth
centuries in both Indonesia and the Malay peninsula.

It has been noted that those who departed came mainly from the southern
provinces. Although there was a supplementary exodus after 1947 of people
from other regions, and especially from Shanghai and the east coast provinces,
the vast majority of Overseas Chinese have moved out from the southern regions. Figure 2.2 provides a simplified map of where they came from and where
they went, with some indication of the numbers concerned, and what those numbers have now grown to throughout the region.

Some attempt must now be made to indicate the economic significance of the
43 million people whose demographic distribution is an inadequate index of
their real consequence.

Hong Kong, Taiwan, and Singapore

In Hong Kong, with 99% Chinese population, one might reasonably attribute
the entire economy to them. The foreign-based firms which are there are normally run with only a tiny handful of expatriates, and the economy is effectively
in Overseas Chinese hands as far as business activity is concerned. So too in
Taiwan, although foreign and notably Japanese influence is evident, the coun-

try's economy is very much a matter of a Chinese polity running a Chinese-dominated economy.

It is occasionally a matter of controversy to include Taiwan in a list of Overseas Chinese areas, but it is seen as appropriate here on the following grounds. Firstly, many of the most significant business people there are refugees from China, and the majority of the population have moved there from the mainland over the same historical period as was applied to the earlier analysis of those going further south. Secondly, their business behavior and general economic support systems, despite a still perceptible Japanese influence from the colonial period of 1905–1945, are similar to those of the rest of the Overseas Chinese, as are also their basic social norms. They are Chinese, and they are out of China; they are therefore, for our purposes, Overseas Chinese.

Singapore presents a somewhat less straightforward case than perhaps first appears, given the inclusion of so much externally dominated industry in its make-up. In the manufacturing sector, for instance, 55% of the workforce is employed in foreign-owned (although not entirely foreign-managed) companies. Even so, the body politic owes much of its basic ideology to Chinese traditions, and the population is 72% Chinese ethnically. Mandarin is an official language, Confucianism is on the curriculum of schools, and most foreigners are kept clearly to the status of visitors. Even if it is not a totally Chinese city-state, it is certainly overwhelmingly so, although its development has taken it further than any other Chinese enclave technically and economically from its roots in the traditional civilization of the mainland. It is proposed to treat it here as an Overseas Chinese bastion, but one with a more cosmopolitan flavor than others, with Indian and Malay influences evident, and with extensive absorption of managerial and technical influences from the West and Japan. It is thus something of a special case.

In the cases of Hong Kong, Taiwan, and Singapore, it is not, then, too fanciful to treat the national statistics as representative of Overseas Chinese efforts and skills. In acknowledging the partial absorption of Western and Japanese techniques and capital, one is still left with the fact that the structure into which they are absorbed is that of a fundamentally Chinese economic system.

In the cases of Indonesia, Malaysia, Thailand, and the Philippines, the nature and extent of the ethnically Chinese portion of the economy is very much more difficult to discern, and therefore these countries deserve closer scrutiny. It will be seen that Chinese economic power is very much more significant than one would first suppose from the population figures alone. National statistics say nothing about it. It is normally in the interests of the governments concerned to conceal, as much as possible, the extent of Overseas Chinese economic power, in the pursuit of social stability. The Chinese themselves are diffident about claiming economic achievements. Their low profile is part of their survival kit. In consequence, hard data are rare.

Indonesia

The largest of the ASEAN economies is Indonesia, whose population at the last census in 1980 was 147.5 million. This had probably grown by the late 1980's to around 170 million and, given that two-fifths of Indonesians are under the age of 15 by the end of the century, the population could reach 220 million. A recent estimate of the ethnically Chinese component of the population is 3.5 million or 2.1% (The Economist 15.8.87).

Consider now this statement from Richard Robison's study of what he sees as a post-1965 capitalist revolution in Indonesia.

Suffice it to say that the Chinese own, at the very least, 70%–75% of private domestic capital and that Chinese business groups continue to dominate medium and large-scale corporate capital. The domestic capitalistic class remains predominantly Chinese (Robison 1986: 276).

There can be no more dramatic manifestation than this of the Overseas Chinese capacity to work themselves into a commanding and yet unobtrusive position in a host economy. From a population base of 2.1% to move to ownership of 75% of private domestic capital requires business and political acumen of a remarkably high order. And we shall see the pattern repeat itself in other countries, perhaps not so dramatically as in Indonesia, but certainly still sufficiently to suggest that this is an unusual group of people whose economic behavior sets them apart from many of their neighbors. It is the clearest *prima facie* evidence in support of the notion of distinct economic cultures.

To understand this phenomenon, it is necessary to take account of certain other features of the Indonesian context, particularly the encouragement of Chinese during the colonial period and, more recently, their relations with the military and with government bodies.

The founding of the Dutch East India Company in 1602 ushered in a period in which a pattern was established of Chinese acting as economic intermediaries between the colonial monopoly of foreign trade and the indigenous concentration on primary, mainly agricultural, production. The Chinese commercial activities of wholesaling and retailing became well established at this time, and they later also spread into farming and manufacturing. The influx of Chinese labor for plantations in the late nineteenth century also increased the dependence of the ruling colonialists on key Chinese intermediaries who could be relied on to keep the peace, to gather taxes, and to manage business activities which linked the lower orders to those in power. The role of *kapitan*, responsible for law and order, would often be combined with that of *comprador*, or business supervisor [1].

Thus the Chinese became accustomed early to reaching an accomodation with a ruling power which would still leave them free to pursue their own activities.

This is a key requirement both for survival and prosperity, and it will be visible regularly over time and throughout the region.

In more recent years, and despite the severe setbacks they suffered during the Japanese occupation and then during the Sukarno regime (when, for instance, 90,000 Chinese left Indonesia in the first three months of 1960), this capacity to work within the power system has been one of the principal causes of their current quiet ascendency.

The Indonesian economy is the preserve of four powerful groups: the state corporate sector, groups owned by the military, Chinese-owned capital, and indigenous capital (Robison 1986). Because most foreign and domestic investment was committed to trade and primary production, the government, in pursuing a policy of industrialization since the early 1970's, made heavy investments itself. Building from an initial base of the nationalized enterprises inherited from Dutch rule, state enterprises are now slightly ahead of the private enterprise total in contributing to the economy.

This state sector is, however, deeply penetrated by Chinese influence. As an example, one might cite the raising of US $ 552 million in 1980 by the Liem Sioe Liong group to create a joint venture with government in the Krakatau Steel complex. Indonesian Chinese capacity to raise capital on this scale is an indicator not just of prosperity within the country but of the international financial linkages which are part and parcel of their ethnic network system, and a significant source of negotiating leverage for them.

The inner workings of state capitalism are also visible via Robison's description of the National Logistics Board (BULOG), the institution whereby state monopolies are managed:

A significant aspect of BULOG's operations has been its capacity to facilitate access by private companies to a sector of the economy which embraces the whole range of trade in basic commodities: import, distribution and purchase, and the manufacture and distribution of some basic footstuffs, notably flour. BULOG is well placed to provide the monopolies which guarantee the growth of the domestic capitalistic class and, more specifically, to decide which companies gain monopoly positions and which are excluded. Under the patronage of BULOG, several private business groups have flourished, mostly those of Chinese capitalists with long-standing connections in KOSTRAD (Army Strategic Reserve Command), a prime example of the so-called *cukong* system under which Chinese businessmen fulfill the role of financiers to the military in return for access to licenses, credit monopolies and political protection (Robison 1986: 230).

The relevance of such protection will be enlarged upon later in considering under what circumstances Chinese organizations grow large. One must distinguish between firms and business groups which are networks of firms under a coordinating central focus. An example of the latter is one of the groups referred to in the above description, that of Liem Sioe Liong, which employs somewhere in the region of 30,000 people. The P.T. Astra group, also working from a similarly protected base, is of the same order of magnitude. These are the largest Overseas Chinese organizations, but an understanding of their size must take account of the slack an organization may be able to carry, given such security of tenure in a market. That such security might end overnight is perhaps an influence on end-game strategy, but is unlikely to exert pressure for day-to-day operating efficiency. Size here may be the result of the softness of an astutely managed environment rather than an indicator of what the Chinese family business would logically grow to without special protection.

The power of the military in Indonesia, perhaps as a means of co-opting its support by the ruling political group, has been allowed to seep into the economy, thus guaranteeing it a share of the nation's wealth. This dismantling of the normal barriers between military and civilian life, although not unusual in a number of third world countries, appears to have been taken further in Indonesia than in most other places. It is therefore an economic stakeholder to be reckoned with.

The main military-owned business groups were formed at a time of large-scale unrest in the 1950's, when various army commands sought extra revenue they could control themselves, and incidentally perhaps benefit from personally. This produced a crop of somewhat nefarious activities such as illegal levies on business, unofficial transport tolls, enforced peasant labor, smuggling, and enforced low-price purchasing of peasant crops such as coffee. In these kinds of activities, and later with more regular business activities, many Chinese businessmen proved to be reliable, efficient, and highly expedient extensions of military power.

In subsequent years, this has yielded political protection and in turn, by creating large conglomerates clustered around military/political power centers, it has served to deny access to many sectors by indigenous capitalists.

Thus the Chinese in Indonesia are close, if unobtrusive, allies of the two major sources of influence, the government and the military. It is also common to find them linked by joint ownership with the indigenous capitalist sector. This latter, although growing, is still, according to Robison, "far less important than state-owned, foreign or Chinese capital" (Robison 1986: 363).

The Philippines

There are many parallels between the situation in Indonesia and that in the Philippines. A colonial regime, in this case the long-standing one of the Spanish, could accommodate Chinese skills within an export-crop economy, and encouraged immigration in the nineteenth century. Since then, the Chinese have carefully built networks into the government and military power bases. Their numbers are tiny, in this case less than one percent of the population, but again their economic power is out of all proportion to such numbers.

In summarizing the route they have followed over the past century, Wickberg has observed:

The Chinese were able to expand their economic influence because of three factors: liberalized Spanish policies, new opportunities offered by the new export crop economy and Chinese business methods. Of the three, perhaps the last was the most decisive (Wickberg 1965: 121).

The business methods referred to are built around two principal areas of attention for the Chinese, and although they will be examined later in greater detail, it may be worth pausing to take brief note of them here. The first key characteristic is very astute management of cash and financing. This is evident from a study which demonstrated that compared with similar-sized Filipino companies Chinese turned over stock much faster, operated on lower margins, had much lower outstanding debtor figures, and generally used capital, their own and more particularly that of others, much more efficiently (Hicks and Redding 1982).

The second business method is the construction of networks of vertically integrated companies which control a total market process, but doing so by informal processes only. These networks of trust serve to reduce uncertainty and transaction costs, for instance over the risk of credit, and they can also serve to exclude competitors who would interrupt the system (Dannhaeuser 1981).

The end product of years of the application of such skills is revealed in the ownership pattern among the 259 largest companies in the Philippines. Lists of main shareholders were studied to identify (with informed local advice) those who were ethnically Chinese, and thus to establish which companies were majority-owned by which ethnic group, seen simply as Filipino, Chinese, and foreign.

If one takes sales volume as an indicator of economic power, the national figures are heavily influenced by the very large sales volume of foreign-owned oil companies. These occur in the 34% of national sales accounted for by foreign-owned companies. Of the remaining 66% of the economy representing that owned and managed within the Philippines by either ethnic Chinese or Filipinos, the Chinese control 35% of sales.

This figure has to be seen in the light of a long-running campaign by various Philippine governments to prevent Chinese from acquiring either economic power or citizenship. Republic Act No. 37 in 1947, Republic Act No. 1180 in 1954, Republic Act No. 3018 in 1960, labor regulations of 1961, exchange control legislation, and the Filipino-subsidizing work of the National Marketing Corporation were all clearly designed to protect Filipinos from Chinese competition, usually by proscribing alien Chinese activities while at the same time making it very difficult for ethnic Chinese to acquire nationality [2]. Although there has been relaxation in more recent years, this background is essential if the extent of Chinese penetration is to be properly understood.

In the commercial sector of the economy, where discrimination against ethnic Chinese has had less effect, there were 74 large companies studied, of which 68 were locally owned and only 6 foreign. 47% of the locally owned companies were under ethnic-Chinese control, and they accounted for 67% of the sales volume. Again, the significance of this figure becomes imposing against the fact that ethnic Chinese, whether citizens or not, represent at most 1% of the national population (Omohundro 1981).

Although the above data come from a study of the largest companies and must therefore be treated with some caution as small companies proliferate, it is nevertheless reasonable to suppose that in the field of small company operation the Chinese will be no less effective. This is in fact an area of substantial strength for them normally, and it would be surprising if their performance at that level were any less dominant (Amyot 1973, Omohumdro 1981, Weightman 1960).

The state of the Philippines economy has, of course, changed as the "crony capitalism" which marked the Marcos era has given way to an attempt at greater democracy. Now recovering from a substantial downturn in economic activity associated with political uncertainty over several years, there has been a great deal of jockeying for position as political and military alliances have had to be dismantled and rebuilt. The detailed story of these upheavals is not yet clear, but one might reasonably suppose that Chinese acumen in protective networking, and their capacity to keep options open, will have served them well. Nor should one forget the Chinese ancestry of Mrs. Aquino.

Malaysia

Proportionally much larger numbers of Chinese went to Malaysia to settle, in the nineteenth and early twentieth centuries, than went to the other countries of the *nanyang*. In consequence, they now account for 37% of the population, the remainder being 51% Malay and 12% Indian.

The traditional Chinese social progression was from coolie labor to small-scale entrepreneurship such as running a food stall or small retail shop, then by a process of patient accumulation of surplus, to investment in property and eventually into capitalizing of larger-scale industry and commerce. In following this particular route, they tended to leave politics to the indigenous Malays, the traditional rulers of the country which had, in any case, been constructed from a combination of old Malay princely states.

This tendency of the Chinese to be subservient politically, while being perfectly explicable in Indonesia and the Philippines where they make up such minute portions of the population, is less understandable in the case of Malaysia, and suggests that there might be a specially Chinese view of political power and how it should be dealt with. This becomes a focus for later consideration, but one might here hazard a few tentative observations on the theme, in preface to more revelations about disproportionately high economic power.

The understanding of Chinese political behavior in Malaysia has its roots in the colonial period, when the British encouraged the Chinese "middleman" in the same way that the Dutch did in Indonesia. This process created a clear role for the Chinese which since independence has simply been perpetuated. The political power which the British held has been assumed by indigenous Malays, in large measure re-establishing a traditional structure cloaked in modern form. It is perhaps not surprising under these conditions that the Chinese have not been inspired to carve out an entirely new role for themselves in the polity, and have retired to their traditional position of maintaining economic strength while co-opting political allies where possible (Jesudason 1989).

The relatively apolitical nature of the Overseas Chinese, which leaves them without open public debate of social issues in most of the countries where they live, is also noticeable. It is suggestive of a deeper layer of expectations about relations with the state, which are likely to have been forged in traditional China, and which linger in their present contexts, whether those contexts are the more or less benevolent autocracies of Taiwan, Hong Kong, and Singapore, or the sometimes overtly discriminatory societies of Indonesia, the Philippines, and Malaysia. One cannot help observing, nonetheless, that their instincts in avoiding public politics have not led to noticeable deprivation, and that whatever alternative accommodations they use have been effective. The case of Malaysia becomes a clear example.

In 1971, the Malaysian government, concerned at the disproportionate wealth of both ethnically Chinese Malays and foreigners, established a New Economic Policy which, over a long period, would redistribute wealth into the hands of the ethnic Malays (known as *bumiputras*).

In 1971, 62% of the economy was in the hands of foreign-based companies, reflecting in the main the colonial legacy. Malaysian nationals who were ethnically Chinese or Indian controlled the next 34%, leaving a mere 4% in *bumiputra* hands. The new policy was designed to give *bumiputras* at least 30% of domestic business, leaving 40% to Chinese and Indian Malays, and 30% to foreigners.

The way this was to be done was via controls on business ownership, the use of business permits to control ethnic involvement, the government-sponsored buying out of foreign businesses, employment quotas, and educational quotas.

Such measures could not help but influence events, and by 1985 *bumiputra* control had grown from 4% to 18% (The Economist 31.1.87). The foreign sector had shrunk from 62% to 25%. Significantly though, the Chinese/Indian portion had grown from 34% to 57%. Clearly the hoped-for inheritance of the original foreign sector by the *bumiputras* was not working out as well or as fast as had been planned. Where they had been successful in taking over was in the plantation and banking sectors where government influence had traditionally been strong, but in commerce and manufacturing, government support does not appear to have been enough to allow the *bumiputras* to compete with the Chinese and Indian groups. More recently, an economic recession has in turn slowed down the redistribution process, and as the Economist remarked "the gravy days for the *bumiputras* have come to an end." It is now expected that *bumiputra* control may reach 22% by 1990, rather than the 30% aimed for. Even so, this figure has to be treated with caution, given the ingenuity displayed in the creation of companies which are apparently Malay owned but whose real controlling influences remain with Indian or Chinese capitalists, sheltering behind a respectable local name on the notepaper and the share register.

What then is a fair index of Chinese economic power? If we leave out the 25% of the economy still under the control of foreign-owned companies, and consider the remaining locally-owned economy, then 76% of that lies with Chinese or Indian interests. Given that Chinese outnumber Indians by roughly 3 to 1, it is reasonable to suppose that of that 76% somewhere between 55% and 60% will be in Chinese hands. To this must be added the portion of Chinese influence hidden away in the Malay sector, a factor which is going to take the Chinese portion of the locally owned economy to somewhere between 60% and 70%. Let it be recalled that their population proportion is 37%.

Thailand

Perhaps because of an all-pervasive Buddhist tolerance in their culture, the Thais have never openly discriminated against outsiders. Their religion is not exclusionist like the Islam of Indonesia or Malaysia and instead provides a context for easy assimilation. Because of lower consciousness of ethnic separateness, it is difficult to assess how many Chinese have settled in Thailand, but Thomlinson in a demographic study puts the figure at between 5% and 10% of the population. His description of the assimilation process is insightful:

Despite . . . the consciousness of their separateness, there has never been harrassment of the kind frequently applied to the ethnic minorities in other nations. This lack of aggressive behavior is, of course, to the credit of both the ethnic Chinese and the Thais. One suggested, but unproven, explanation for this peaceful assimilation of the Chinese into Thailand may be the similarity of Thai and Chinese value systems, both of which are founded on paternalism and a reciprocal repayment of kindnesses between patrons and subordinates. Differing with this hypothesis, however, is the frequently stated contention that the Thai and Chinese attitudes toward work, enjoyment of life, and acquisition of money are very different (Thomlinson 1972: 34).

The benevolence of the Thais is not naive, and there is evidence that the Thai tolerance can reach its limits when it becomes obvious, as Skinner noted in an earlier study, that the "rich Chinese-Thai use intermarriage and the resultant interlocking family business associations to dominate the economic life of the country" (Skinner 1958).

The way in which such interlocking family groups burrow deep into the power-base of the economy is evidenced in a study by Hewison of the Thai banking industry (Hewison 1985). Given a predominantly rural economy, and given a long-established Chinese custom of operating from their urban bases into the countryside as itinerant rice brokers and wholesalers, it should not be surprising that the Chinese would gravitate over time into the field of banking, and especially the kind of banking which has small business and agriculture as its domain.

Allied to this natural outcome of steady economic progress was the government policy of limiting the introduction of foreign banks and preventing those already there from building branch networks. In consequence, domestic banking has flourished, recording a net growth between 1960 and 1982 of fifty times. The majority of these local bankers are Chinese-Thai. As well as a state-owned bank, there are five other major banks in Thailand, and they control 65% of total banking assets. Of these, one is associated with the Crown, the remaining four are all Chinese-Thai.

Out of these bases go extensive networks into other sectors of the economy; marriage ties and interlocking directorships serve, as elsewhere, to reduce the risks inherent in business by providing a stable foundation for trust. In a society where, as in most developing countries, the rule of commercial law does not saturate the fabric of business life, and the quality of information available for decision making is often poor, it may be seen that explaining networking in terms of *purely* ethnic reasons would be simplistic. There are reasons of hard economic and business expediency as well as ethnic loyalties behind much of this behavior.

The proportion of the Thai economy in ethnic Chinese hands can only be guessed at, but an estimate in the mid-1970's, cited by Limlingan (1986: 2), was that

The Overseas Chinese in Thailand (8.5 per cent of the population) owned 90 per cent of all investments in the Commercial Sector, 90 per cent of all investments in the Manufacturing Sector and 50 per cent of all investments in the Banking and Finance sector.

In an important study of what he termed "ersatz" capitalism, Yoshihara (1988) attempted to summarize the significance of the Chinese in Southeast Asia, concluding that

The superiority of Chinese capital over foreign capital is less clear than its superiority over indigenous capital. But as a whole, Chinese capital seems to be a more important element of Southeast Asian capital than foreign capital (Yoshihara 1988: 52).

In the absence of hard data, in turn a result of company data being unavailable, Yoshihara provides an impression of the relative position of Chinese capital in Southeast Asia in Table 2.2.

Table 2.2: The relative position of Chinese capital in Southeast Asia (ASEAN)
(Source: Yoshihara 1988: 51)

Industry	Foreign Capital	Chinese Capital	Private Indigenous Capital
Banking	moderate	substantial/ dominant	moderate/ substantial
Property Development		substantial	substantial
Construction	moderate	moderate	moderate
Mining	moderate	moderate/ substantial	moderate
Oil Exploration	dominant		
Plantation Agriculture	minor	substantial	moderate/ substantial
Export/Import Trade	substantial	substantial	minor
Manufacturing	substantial	substantial	minor
Light Industries	minor	dominant	minor
Machinery	substantial	substantial	minor
Metals & Petrochemicals	dominant	minor	

Note: Based on assessing the relative positions of (a) foreign, (b) Chinese, and (c) private indigenous capital, on a ten-point scale, such that
less than 1 = no entry
1.0 to 2.4 = minor
2.5 to 3.9 = moderate
4.0 to 7.4 = substantial
above 7.5 = dominant

The Nanyang

Throughout this account so far, the Overseas Chinese have been considered as if they were distinct from their host cultures in Indonesia, the Philippines, Malaysia, and Thailand. This is of course a simple view of such a relationship and needs to be qualified with an acknowledgement that their blending with local societies has taken varying forms and achieved varying degrees of inter-penetration from one country to another (Hamilton 1977).

A clear way of seeing this variety is presented by Wu and Wu (1980: 208) and given in Figure 2.3. It separates two categories of Overseas Chinese—broadly and narrowly defined—from those who are not. This latter category applies to people of multiple mixed parentage, but in doing so also indicates the dominance of the male line of succession. As long as the father is Chinese, the children may still come into the category. If the father is non-Chinese, it becomes much less likely.

Despite an often long process of assimilation, and despite the fact that a meeting of ethnic Chinese friends, or a family dinner table, might include nationals of

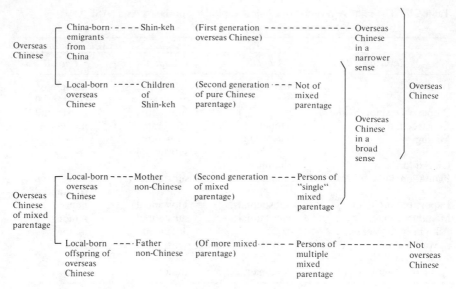

Figure 2.3: Overseas Chinese identity and the effect of mixed parentage

Source: Wu and Wu 1980: 208

Thailand, Indonesia, Singapore, Malaysia, the Republic of China (or the Taiwan Province of the People's Republic of China, depending on your point of view), or British national overseas citizens of Hong Kong; and despite the fact that there is nowadays a strong likelihood of the addition of an American, Canadian, or Australian, there is nonetheless an unbreakable sense of unity and a clarity of identity which seems always capable of overriding other gravitational pulls. The sense of Chineseness, based as it is on the immense weight of Chinese civilization, seems to diminish remarkably little over distance or with the passage of time. It is the cynosure of the Overseas Chinese, and also their definition.

Moving now to consider the region as a whole, and an attempt to define the key issues which characterize their relationship with their environments, it is possible, despite the variety of contexts, to identify a set of influences shared by many Overseas Chinese. Such influences have arguably moulded much of their present thinking and are necessary preliminaries to an understanding of it. They may be summarized, prior to explication, in the following contentions:

(1) They have commonly lived in social environments which were resentful of them, and at times openly hostile, thus forcing them defensively in on their own resources.
(2) This, in turn, has caused a heightened sense of cooperativeness within the Overseas Chinese group generally.

(3) This, in turn, has reinforced the natural tendency to identify with China and to derive a cultural identity from it.

(4) The formative experience of moving countries was often a time of great family hardship and fostered values related to economic survival, such as a work ethic, thrift, and pragmatism, these being natural extensions of traditional Chinese folk values.

The question of environmental hostility is not simply to be understood in terms of the sporadic outbursts of anti-Chinese rioting which have occurred throughout the region historically: they only serve to pinpoint periods of major stress often brought on by forces not directly connected with the Overseas Chinese. The more typical situation is one compounded of (a) a constant series of small but subtle reminders of separateness, and (b) an underlying strain of uncertainty about future stability. Because it is mainly a response to these latter forces rather than to the occasional cataclysm, whatever "siege mentality" may be discerned is not one characterized by paranoia, but more by caution, avoidance of publicity, and hedging of bets.

The subtle reminders of separateness, in some countries, would include ethnic control of access to universities, difficulty and cost in obtaining citizenship, government-sponsored economic favoritism shown to indigenous groups, occasional legislation aimed specifically at displacing Chinese business from certain sectors, and various clearly aimed prescriptions such as that on the publishing of anything with Chinese script in Indonesia [3]. These are more by way of irritants than threats, but they do serve to remind all who are involved in designing, operating, or being affected by them, that people are seen as belonging to two classes.

Such features do not, of course, occur in Hong Kong, Singapore, or Taiwan, which remain the most natural Overseas Chinese strongholds, but, at least in Hong Kong and Taiwan, the second feature, that of long-run uncertainty, continues to make the environment less benevolent than it might be. Even here, families do not take the future for granted. The nature of the threat being communism, and the eventual absorption of both states into the mother country, attitutes are predictably ambivalent, and very complex. The common factor of major uncertainty, however, turns the environment into one with which their cousins throughout the region can identify.

Except for Singapore: now guarding its citizenship access jealously, able to defend itself, and confident in its prosperity, this is the only Overseas Chinese state where the environment can be said to be truly benevolent for Chinese people, and free from fears about the future. It should be no surprise were we to discover that values there are beginning to diverge from those in the rest of the region, as the society to which values relate is beginning to diverge noticeably (Redding and Richardson 1986).

That people band together against a common enemy is an obvious and inevitable social fact. When they come from a society with a strong tradition of horizontal networking across the base of society, then the ground is laid for the weaving of a net of great strength and flexibility. Such nets are fundamental to an understanding of Overseas Chinese social and economic life.

We shall later examine a special feature of Chinese social structure but give it brief acknowledgement here as it has an important bearing on cooperation. This is that the networks are normally built of very specific personal relationships, many of which may have been initiated for their practical usefulness and then maintained to a point where genuine friendship has cemented them. The important point is that cooperation outside such linkages cannot be taken for granted (Baker 1979, Lau 1982). In a totally Chinese context such as in Hong Kong or Taiwan, the prevailing mood is the paradoxical one of competing families each one against the rest, working out pragmatic interconnections which have to be mutually self-serving.

Lin Yu-tang's metaphor is apposite here, when he speaks of Japanese society being like a piece of solid granite, whereas that of traditional China is like a tray of loose sands, each grain being a separate family (Lin 1977: 177). In the Overseas Chinese contexts of Indonesia, Malaysia, the Philippines, and Thailand, however, the sense of being an outnumbered minority is more likely to turn this competitiveness towards outsiders than towards those they see as their own people.

Networks are thus crucial, but one further dimension needs to be added to make more clear the nature of such a matrix. This is the tendency for people within one regional grouping, such as Hokkien or Chiu Chow, to stay within a certain range of occupations, thus reinforcing the tendency to cooperate by raising its value. Table 2.3 presents a summary of findings about this from a study by Wu and Wu (1980) of local materials on the subject in Indonesia and Thailand. Although not covering the entire region, it is nevertheless revealing of the subtle kind of solidarity which attaches to a sense of regional identity, and reveals some of the detail otherwise concealed beneath the broad title "Chinese." It is *prima facie* evidence also for the tendency of a subgroup to help its own members to get established in a business field where informed advice is easily available. This in turn raises questions about the business aspect of such cooperation and more specifically why new competitors may be encouraged to establish themselves.

The answer to this is threefold: firstly, the growth of these economies over recent decades has been such that livelihoods of those already in the field are unlikely to have been under threat; secondly, the idea of growing the Chinese business community at the expense of the remaining non-Chinese would counterbalance the disadvantages of internal sharing; thirdly, the Chinese notion of competition contains a provision for not cutting to pieces those close to you, and of letting all have a reasonable share. This does not apply to outsiders but would certainly enhance the willingness to help a clan member to get started.

If, as is also quite likely, many of these industries and trades were penetrated

Table 2.3: Occupational groupings of Overseas Chinese sub-groups in Indonesia and
Thailand (after Wu and Wu 1980: 61)

	Indonesia	*Thailand*
Hokkien	Rubber, copra, coffee, pepper, tobacco, import/ export, rubber & plastics, textiles, knitwear, weaving, garments, glassware, earthenware, tea processing, drugs, gold and jewellery, bicycles, trishaws, printing, hotels, entertainment, finance	Rubber, rice, import/export
Chiu Chow		Import/export, clothing, rice milling, native products, dry goods, canned food, cosmetics, hardware, jewellery, distilling, publishing, furniture, entertainment, finance, insurance, shipping
Cantonese	Rice milling, lumber, machine shops, soap, bakeries, food canning, furniture, hardware, tailoring, photography, coffee shop, truck farming, poultry, restaurants, clothiers, piece goods, dry goods, printing, plastics, entertainment	Machine repair, construction, food and beverage, printing, watches/clocks, sugar
Hakka		Leather and hides, weaving, banking, department stores, metal working, shoe manufacturing, tailoring, hairdressing, truck farming
Taiwanese	Transportation, hotels, restaurants, electronics, paper, lumber, engineering production	
Hainanese		Beverages, hotels, drugstores, furniture, hairdressing, fishing
Yunnanese		Jewellery
Kiangsu & Chekiang	Optical, clocks and watches, shoes, gifts, books	
Hupei	Dentistry	
Shantung	Piece goods	

by sponsorship of family members in setting up, then an extra factor comes into play. This is that family wealth is normally seen as a common pool. Thus the baker in one town who sets up his son, or even perhaps his nephew, in a neighboring town is simply extending and enhancing the basis of his own wealth.

Despite the obvious power of such regional affiliations for the Overseas Chinese at large, no account can ignore the power of "Chineseness" as a uniting force, in particular, when it is set against the alternative cultural traditions of the countries of the *nanyang*. Except for Thailand, which has maintained a strong Buddhist-based and royalty-centered cultural identity, and which has always retained its independence, the remaining host countries have universally suffered from the erosion of confidence and the denting of national pride which tend to go with being colonized. To exaggerate the point, it is a national form of being raped, and leads to damaging after-effects.

The clear and strong kind of cultural affinity and identity which one can observe in, say, French, English, or Japanese people is normally based upon centuries of what they perceive as a particularly successful form of civilization. They view the rest of the world in the light of it, if politely, nevertheless still often disdainfully. So too do the Chinese, and their disdain, though rarely voiced, could justifiably be in proportion to the antiquity and achievements of Chinese civilization [4].

Journeying to the south with this kind of psychological baggage, the Chinese found themselves more often than not in a country without its own unified form of civilization. In Indonesia, a Dutch superstructure overlay a set of feudal and hardly united princedoms, using an imported Islamic religion over a deep layer of animism, and containing four hundred language groups, largely mutually incomprehensible. Rich and varied it certainly was, but not a monolithic united civilization comparable to that of China.

In the Malay peninsula, the same applied, but with a British overlay. In the Philippines, the overlays were Spanish or American and Catholic, but the base society was again fragmented and relatively primitive. For the first half of this century, Taiwan, Hong Kong, and Singapore were all colonies.

In these circumstances, it is not surprising that China and its philosophies of living should remain a basic reference point. Nor is it surprising that, in the turmoils and uncertainties of the past century, the traditions of an earlier Chinese civilization should continue to be magnetic.

Such traditions, let it be remembered, were forged over centuries of almost entirely rural existence. Most Chinese values find their origin in village life, and more specifically family farm life, and virtually all emigrants from 1850 to 1940 were peasants from the rural areas of the south (Hamilton 1977: 377). For most of Chinese history, and for most of the people, existence was at little more than the subsistence level, and in the background was the constant threat of falling below that into various levels of deprivation. The sources of such threats could be pressure from landlords or tax gatherers, the natural events which can regularly afflict farming, and the subtle but wide-ranging effects of a population increase which saw numbers mushrooming throughout the nineteenth century.

Life was hard for the average Chinese peasant, and there were few guarantees of security. In such an economy based as it was on muscle-power, three crucial sets of values crystallized out in the service of survival (Ryan 1961). These will be examined in more detail later but may be introduced in simple terms here. Firstly, the central pivot of life was the family. Its capacity to provide welfare was in proportion to the loyalties and contributions it could command from members. The state religion of Confucianism served to reinforce acceptance by all that the basic building block of society (and mini welfare state) was the family.

Secondly, work itself was, of necessity, accorded high value. Subsistence farming, especially by manual labor, very obviously demands it and very obviously exposes the person who does not pull his or her own weight [5]. The ideological base for such a work ethic lies in the deep sense of obligation to family, and the supporting social control mechanisms which reinforce it operate through the process of maintaining "face." To be considered lazy and selfish, to have made no contribution, produces not only practical sanctions in the non-availability of benefits but also severe psychological sanctions of a kind the majority of people would wish to avoid. This is not to argue that Chinese people are somehow "naturally" more hard-working than others, but simply to say that their social conditioning is such that, as long as the obligations are felt, the dedication of effort is straightforward and seemingly unconscious. It has been an important contribution to the success of the Overseas Chinese that they have maintained the social fabric which perpetuates that conditioning.

Thirdly, and finally as a centripetal value under conditions of insecurity, is the role of wealth and its day-to-day manifestation in the lavishing of attention on the question of money.

It is a frequent object of bemused curiosity among Westerners in Hong Kong to find Cantonese people so completely ingenuous over the topic of money. To be asked at a cocktail party how much you paid for your suit, or what you are paying the caterers, is for them perfectly normal and not something to be whispered out of earshot. It is as if many other cultures felt the need to cover the very basic fact of their personal wealth with a veil of symbols, leaving the inquisitive to interpret their meaning. Enhanced by the sensitivity to face, this technique is also embraced by the Chinese, especially the affluent, and especially via brand names with a cachet, but at the same time they show no embarrassment in probing down to the basics of what, in cash terms, will indicate your worth.

This frankness suggests that the money itself has become for them an especially potent symbol, around which much meaning circulates. We shall examine in the next chapter the social origins of this complex, and simply here note it as an important contributor, alongside familism and the work ethic, to the psychological armoury with which Chinese people have for so long battled against uncertainty and insecurity.

Footnotes

[1] The *comprador*, a respected role throughout the Far East, was the native agent, or general factotum, who would be responsible for blending the indigenous services into the foreign, usually colonial, organization. He would employ his own staff to provide the necessary services such as selling to locals, buying from them, record-keeping, warehousing, local transport, etc. He worked for a commission, and many *compradors* prospered to become important community figures. The system has lasted well into the twentieth century, and remnants of it remain in large corporations today. It was still visible, for instance, in the Hongkong and Shanghai Bank into the 1950's when the system was dismantled on account of the problems of a Cantonese *comprador* dealing with an increasingly significant and newly arrived Shanghainese business elite.

[2] These official barriers were based on making it very expensive, applying language criteria, and age barriers, for instance a minimum application age of 21, once-only applications, etc. The "practical" solution could be very costly.

[3] The author remembers a copy of *Newsweek* delivered to his Jakarta hotel room, in which photographs of a parade in Taiwan and some regional hotel advertisements had been partially blacked out to obliterate Chinese script.

[4] There is, of course, a degree of romanticism necessary for this to work, and a need to look more kindly than is perhaps justified on the past four centuries of Chinese history, but the Chinese are highly emotional on this subject, and thus inclined to the romantic view, as are most patriots.

[5] John K. Fairbank produces an interesting and important qualification about the contribution of women in his observations on footbinding, the significance and extent of which he sees as having been underestimated. Even in a farming context, the majority of women sacrificed their mobility and the strength of their legs, as well as much else, to this strangely perverse custom. The contribution of women was thus artifically handicapped. "A bride without small feet in the old China was like a new house in today's America without utilities—who would want it? Consequently in the 1930's and 1940's one still saw women on farms stumping about on their heels as they worked, victims of this old custom," (Fairbank, 1987: 71.)

Chapter 3
The Psycho-Social Legacy of China

The previous two chapters have suggested that the Overseas Chinese carry with them a heritage, and that this contributes to their capacity to organize themselves so effectively in the sphere of business. As this book proceeds we shall delve more deeply into the way that heritage affects their behavior, but before doing so, it is necessary now to present an outline of the main constituents of Chinese culture. This is therefore an introduction to where they "come from" psychologically and sociologically. It will be followed by two chapters in which Overseas Chinese express in their own words how that cultural inheritance maintains itself. Having then examined the sources of individual and relational behavior, the analysis will then move up in later chapters to the level of organizations and society.

It is difficult at a practical level for Westerners to comprehend the way in which the power of Chinese tradition still permeates everyday life among the Overseas Chinese; to perceive the extent to which this is still a very "old-fashioned" people. As so much of their life is conducted in a dialect of Chinese, and as so many of their emotions are concealed from public view, they are less transparent than many other cultures.

The tradition is thus conveyed in attitudes more often than in declarations, in nuances of behavior and in eventual courses of action rather than in open discussions of the rights or wrongs of an issue. It is only when one observes a present-day high-tech office full of well-qualified and highly efficient operatives of modern office equipment going through a *feng-shui* ritual to appease the spirits which control the fortune of the location, that one is suddenly jerked back to a pre-scientific but still highly relevant mental world.

This will be a necessarily brief and exploratory journey into the world of Chinese tradition, and only an introductory survey of the principal values which define Chinese culture. Also the focus remains the modern Overseas Chinese business person, and it is thus necessary to refine out values of particular relevance to current organizational life. In doing so, it will be necessary to consider the origins of the values, in order to understand their apparent tenacity. Hence this chapter will be set against the social history of China, and the analysis of a culture which, although treated historically, is nevertheless very much alive today, not just among the Overseas Chinese but beneath the communist veneer of the People's Republic. [1]

It may be salutary to remember the issues always in the background and they may be boiled down to three questions:

(1) Why did capitalistic bureaucracies, and a managerial class, not develop in China?
(2) Why has capitalism flourished so spectacularly among the Overseas Chinese?
(3) Is there some special form of capitalism and organization which the Overseas Chinese use?

For this to be less of a mystery tour, it may be helpful to indicate the destination by previewing the conclusions. These, simply put are:

(1) There is much in Chinese history, social, economic, and political, to explain why China was barren ground for the development of a modern capitalist economy based on rational bureaucratic organizations. These forces are still present. This is not to deny that historically it had an alternative economic system which worked.
(2) The business environments of the Overseas Chinese proved fertile grounds for the encouragement of a special form of capitalist enterprise, based on family ownership and control.
(3) This latter form of organization is special in (a) the consistency with which it finds expression, and (b) its resistance to many of the rationalizing processes found in other economic cultures.

Before we understand, however, the nature of organizing in Chinese society, we must first understand the basic unit of organization—the Chinese person. Such an understanding can only come from seeing the cultural matrix in which he or she is embedded. In the Chinese case, this must begin with the religions and belief systems, within which Confucianism is dominant. From an analysis at the level of religions, it will then be useful to proceed to three separate areas of analysis which move in closer towards day-to-day behavior. The first of these will be the basic social structures, of family, class, social networks, and ethnicity; secondly, the rules which govern the main relationships (a) vertically within the social units, (b) horizontally within the social units, and (c) towards those outside. Thirdly, we shall examine some of the main rules which guide action, particularly those which might have a bearing on life in the business context; namely, the work ethic, money-mindedness and frugality, and pragmatism. Lastly, special note will be taken of a deeper layer of culture suggested by some of the above but still lying below their surface, namely the form of Chinese cognition.

Presented diagrammatically, the shape of the analysis in this chapter is as follows:

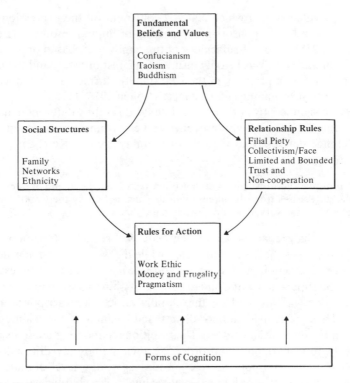

Figure 3.1: Cultural determinants of individual Chinese values

Fundamental Beliefs and Values

Confucianism

In order to understand the functioning within society of the main traditional Chinese religions, it is necessary to make clear some important East–West differences in the way society is organized.

In the case of China—"a civilization that represents one of mankind's great efforts to build, rationalize, and adorn the good society" (Wright 1962: 3), the prevailing ideology for most of its recorded history has been a set of ideas which go under the convenient label Confucianism.

To understand Confucianism, however, it is better to begin by examining its function in society and the way it has provided a particularly Chinese form of order linking the individual and the state.

China has always been an agrarian state and one in which subsistence level living has been the lot of most people. In these circumstances, there is much to be said for a value system which places a constraint on the expression of individual desires and also sponsors group sharing of limited resources (Bond and Hwang 1986: 215). The self-sufficiency of the family unit, based on its ability to manage its affairs well, was its only insurance against disaster, and the common budgets and common property of the *chia* (family) formed a rational collective response to the surrounding circumstances (Cohen 1976: 11).

Even more significantly perhaps, the state itself is subtly different in nature, or at least in the way it is thought of by its members, from its western equivalents. This difference derives from the role of morality, and as Ketcham (1987: 93) points out,

The most profound and revealing difference between East Asian and Western conceptions of the state arises from the intense infusion, insisted on by the Confucian way, of moral precept into the very idea of polity and nationhood.

What this means is that the Confucian state was seen by its members as an enormous, but nevertheless united *group*, while the western version is doctrinally at least an abstraction, a universal or absolute *idea*. Thus the Chinese state is in essence the super-family of Chinese people. Within this structure, the maintenance of order was founded on the morally enriched prescriptions for relationships. Thus the individual finds dignity and meaning in the maintenance of harmony in his own social context. The traditional ennobling qualities of righteousness, beauty, harmony, and order are then supposedly diffused into the surrounding family and political relationshlps up to the level of state government, where the emperor or his equivalent is finally also charged with exemplifying precisely the same virtues.

The society is constructed of morally binding relationships connecting all. In this the self is not an enclosed world of private thoughts (Tu 1984: 5). The individual is instead a connection, and the "totalness" of society is passed down from one binding relationship to the next, rather than by the Western mode of uniting loosely coupled and "free" individuals by their separate espousal of coordinating ideas and principles. For the Chinese, fulfilment comes from the very structure and dynamics of the relationships and emphasis on belonging (Ketcham 1987: 111).

Given the infusion of morality into social structures, it may be possible to comprehend the way in which a society so obsessed with hierarchy contains defences against the worst excesses and exploitations of authority. It should be said at the outset that it does not always succeed and that China's great handicap is its inability to maintain this balancing act in the political arena. As Nivison has pointed out, the neo-Confucian revival of ideals in the Sung was gradually distorted by succeeding emperors and literati to a point where by the eighteenth century "Chinese despotism had become as perfect as human things become . . . and the fate of the Confucian utopia was the fate that history so often metes out to bright illusions" (Nivison 1959: 24).

Exploitation continues and the Tienanmen Square massacres of 1989 were part of a long tradition. As a major review of our understanding of the East Asian transformation concludes, "Historians have hardly begun to get behind the official myths of imperial Confucianism and appraise the autocracy and elitism by which state and society controlled the individual" (Fairbank, Reischauer, and Craig 1965: 884).

The authoritarian state nevertheless contains enough cooperation within it, especially at lower levels, to hobble along as a functioning entity, and this capacity still rests heavily on the Confucian rules for relationships. In particular, the abuse of power is constrained by the morality of compassion and righteousness, espousal and practice of which is the main source of legitimacy for effective leadership (Bond and Hwang 1986: 216, Silin 1976: 128). The vertical relationship, especially where people come into contact with each other, is conducted via the adoption of roles, expressing mutual dependence, and we must now pause to consider the import of the notion of role and its significance in distinguishing Western and Confucian societies. Hamilton has provided a valuable distinction between Western and Confucian societies in saying that the Western system emerged via the institutionalizing of power, and thus of jurisdictions. The traditional Roman *patria potestas* defined a field within which the head of the family could exercise personal discretion and control (Hamilton 1984: 411). From this developed systems of jurisdiction which attempt to place boundaries around individual freedom without prescribing individual behavior. The person is thus left with much discretion and initiative and in practice encouraged to exercise them. The stability and order of Western society rests, obviously with variations, on the acceptance of the boundary constraints, and the principles they rest on, by more or less independent individuals.

In China, the state has not traditionally maintained order by jurisdiction. The ruling elite was small in number and scattered over a vast land (Wright 1962: 11). Civil law was not developed (Wu 1967: 344). Instead, a system grew up in which "the social order could operate by itself, with the minimum of assistance from the formal political structure" (Yang 1959: 164). For this to work required two crucial components: getting people to understand their prescribed roles; and ensuring, largely by the fear of punishment, that the prescribed role behavior was maintained. The former was achieved by the Confucian teaching deeply embedded in the school system and the processes of family socialization (Wilson 1970). The latter was achieved by severe and widely promoted punishment for deviation. The Draconian rigor with which authorities could treat breaches of role performance is frighteningly illustrated by Hsu (1970: quoted in Hamilton 1984: 417), in the grim story of the Cheng family.

In October 1865, Cheng Han-cheng's wife had the insolence to beat her mother-in-law. This was regarded as such a heinous crime that the following punishment was meted out. Cheng and his wife were both skinned alive, in front of the mother, their skin was displayed at city gates in various towns and their bones burned to ashes. Cheng's granduncle, the eldest of his close relatives, was beheaded; his uncle and two brothers, and the head of the Cheng clan, were hanged. The wife's mother, her face tatooed with the words "neglecting the daughter's education," was paraded through seven provinces. Her father was beaten 80 strokes and banished to a distance of 3000 li. The heads of family in the houses to the right and the left of the Cheng's were beaten 80 strokes and banished to Heilung-kiang. The educational officer in town was beaten 60 strokes and banished to a distance of 1000 li. Cheng's nine-month-old boy was given a new name and put in the county magistrate's care. Cheng's land was to be left in waste "forever." All this was recorded on a stone stele and rubbings of the inscriptions were distributed throughout the empire.

Such an example is of course extreme, and by contrast the principles of compromise and persuasion are often cited as essential to the legal process in China to the present day (Creel 1987: 133, Lubman 1983). The fact can never be escaped, however, that without a codified civil law the average Chinese person seen by Western eyes has never been other than a more or less passive victim of a system in which any notion of his rights was not so much excluded but simply not comprehended as relevant, in that universe of ideas. It was role compliance which protected him, not the law.

In such circumstances, the family is the first and last resort, and for most the only resort. This is in itself a consequence of the Confucian state ideology designed to leave welfare as primarily a family issue, and to concentrate people's loyalties on the family as a means of stabilizing the state. An inevitable consequence of this is the rivalry of families as they seek to control and accumulate scarce resources in competition with each other. Individual achievement becomes an aspect of family achievement (Wilson and Pusey 1982: 199), and the spirit of family enrichment at the expense of other families becomes a primary force described as "magnified selfishness" (Lin 1977: 164), and opposed to a wider sense of community and societal responsibility.

An introductory outline of Confucianism will inevitably be too condensed to do justice to the complexity, range, and adaptability of such a complex social philosophy. It is only feasible to discuss it at a general level, but it should be noted that Confucianism contains many interpretations within it, and that it is a live set of ideas which has developed and changed over time. Its complexity was a perhaps inevitable result of the impossibility of its task. The Confucian order "was in the final analysis more fundamentally moral than it was rational" (de Bary 1959: 41), and as such could never extend true humaneness effectively and reliably outside the family. The harsh realities of power eventually deny a totalitarian utopia (Nivison 1959: 24), but the attempt continued for centuries. Each time a new interpretation emerged it owed its inspiration to a return to the original pure well-springs (de Bary 1959: 47) until it finally exhausted itself in the upheavals of nineteenth-century Chinese history and retreated below the surface of society or went abroad.

The paradoxes with which Confucianism has always had to deal have been described by Schwartz (1959) in terms of three polarities in thinking. Firstly, there is the tension between self-cultivation and the ordering and harmonizing of the world. Secondly, there is the related choice of concentrating on the inner realm or the outer realm of social order. Thirdly, there is the choice between knowledge and action. Confucian thinking has roamed over all three continua at different times in different ways, and, although in the process, the ideology did not ossify (Hamilton 1984: 418), nor did it retain much recognizable simplicity.

In terms of its manifest workings, there are three differences separating Confucianism from many other religions. Firstly, it contains no deity but is based instead on rules of conduct. Secondly, it is not promoted in such a way as to compete with other religions, living as it does in the minds of many alongside Buddhism, Taoism and even Christianity. Thirdly, it has no large-scale institutional "church," with priests, ceremonial and laity. [2]

Its dominance came about because it provided the philosophical basis for the filial piety which supported the family structures and in turn the state itself. It was the basis of a gentleman's education, a prerequisite for a career in government, and the eventual source of control for society at large. It was the main contributor to the making of a highly integrated society in which the elite and the peasantry shared the same world-view via a common literary culture. This latter was aided for over a thousand years by higher levels of literacy than, for instance, in Europe, and by the publishing of books six hundred years before Gutenberg.

Its dominance did not, however, give it a monopoly, and an understanding of Chinese religious influences cannot ignore the parallel forces of Taoism and Buddhism, each of which was able to appeal to more individual and inspirational sentiments. The endless rules and guidelines of the Confucian order left many people still hungry for something closer to nature, something which could allow for magic and the idea of guardian spirits.

The average peasant, assimilating the Confucian doctrines via the basic guidelines for family life, and not spending years of study on the Analects, would still turn to a variety of alternative shrines and temples to pray for success, safe conduct, a good marriage. Living so close to nature tended to rule out secularism as an option, and a live religion of one form or another is still very much a part of the Overseas Chinese mental make-up. The forces of nature, perhaps interpreted now more in the context of markets and prices than in that of storms and harvests, are still pressing from "out there," and help is still needed to accommodate to them.

The lack of an institutional structure and of an identifiable laity means, of course, that to profess oneself a Confucian is, although not empty of meaning, nevertheless not as clearly committing a statement as professing Islam or Christianity. Confucianism, like capitalism, is a matter of what you do. In consequence, the Asian region is full of people who behave according to Confucian precepts but who would not think of themselves as members of a Confucian sect. Its power is thus widespread but extremely difficult to delineate.

The way in which it still penetrates society is via a combination of school and family teachings. Parents are constantly instilling notions of discipline and order and, above all else, of identity within the family. While children below the age of five or so are indulged and usually provided with a very secure emotional foundation visible later in at least public self-confidence and stability, this same indulgence tends to create high levels of dependence which can later serve to ensure compliance. The withdrawal of affection, or the threat of withdrawal, can act as a severe sanction for the dependent personality. From the age of five onwards, the tendency in child-rearing is for discipline to be added to the indulgence, and observations by Westerners of Chinese home life commonly refer to the strictness with which older children are controlled. This is especially visible in the context of education and learning where exacting demands are made and normally complied with.

Although specifically Confucian education is not universal for Overseas Chinese, especially given the powerful inroads made by Christianity via schools, it is nevertheless still a major force in Hong Kong, a dominant one in Taiwan, and an officially sponsored one in Singapore. It is commonly reinforced in Indonesia, Malaysia, and the Philippines by the social systems used to perpetuate Chinese ethnic solidarity. In Thailand, perhaps more than elsewhere, it has given way in favor of the Buddhism which so permeates Thai life, but its golden rules are still acted on in family life.

In the school context, Confucianism is taught by the study of the main writings and the discussion of their implications. The child is encouraged to memorize the classics and to build relationships based on the Confucian principles. In the school, this means learning to develop the social finesse which so clearly delineates the Chinese person. In this endeavor, the principal sanction is loss of face, and for this to operate requires the inculcation of a strong potential for feeling shame. Creating this capacity for behaving according to the Chinese rules for civilized conduct requires much attention to the sense of belonging to social groups outside the family. Such classmate groups have remarkable longevity and relevance.

The Confucian philosophy is an attempt to find a form of order for people which will be in accord with the order of the natural world. By the cultivation of interior goodness and by coupling it to exterior grace through the encouragement of social decorum, society at large would come to exhibit the kind of balance, reasonableness, and considerateness typical of the best human beings. This notion of balance and reasonableness is contained in the idea of The Way whereby progress may be made between such alternatives as submissiveness and independence, punctiliousness and irregularity. Negotiating such a Way requires an understanding of the correct protocols, the cultivation of a sense of when appropriately to apply them, and the self-discipline to carry them out. The son, pursuing a career in medicine in Canada, but called back by the father to Hong Kong in order to take over the responsibilities of the family business which has run into problems, must understand the duty imposed on him by the protocols of filial piety, must follow that duty without complaint, and must discipline himself to a new life-style. Chinese social philosophy in its Confucian version is made up of myriads of such examples, coupled with their eventual justifications in the traditional scripts, and extending over the full range of questions posed by day-to-day existence.

The basic building block of the stable Confucian order is the family, and within that, the crucial stabilizing feature is filial piety. If that is established, other relationships begin to fall naturally into their important but secondary places, for instance that of husband and wife, that between brothers, between master and servant, etc. It was always in the family context that the cardinal lessons were learned, and where the sense of gentlemanly conduct was inculcated.

This conduct centered on two crucial virtues which lie at the heart of Chinese character building, *jen* and *li*. *Jen*, often translated as "human-heartedness," has been described informatively by Carmody and Carmody in the following terms:

The ideogram for *jen* represented a human being: *jen* is humaneness—what makes us human. We are not fully human simply by receiving life in a human form. Rather, our humanity depends upon community, human reciprocity. *Jen* pointed in that direction. It connected with the Confucian golden rule of not doing to others what you would not want them to do to you. Against individualism, it implied that people have to live together hopefully, even lovingly. People have to cultivate their instinctive benevolence, their instinctive ability to put themselves in another's shoes. That cultivation was the primary educational task of Confucius and Mencius (Carmody and Carmody 1983: 135).

Li is what in English would be called good manners, or gentlemanly conduct. In a sense, it turns *jen* into action. Less a set of rituals than a cultivating of a sensitivity to what is appropriate at any time, it provides the lubrication necessary to reduce social friction and it fosters the sublimating of self-indulgence in daily interaction. A Western equivalent at the simplest level is the English gentleman's being defined by his consideration for the feelings of others. The difference between the Chinese and Western systems is not one of principle, as there is much overlap, but simply one of the centrality given to appropriate behavior. It has, for Confucian Chinese, moved to the core of life.

Confucius lived between 551 and 479 B.C., and his ideas were adopted as state orthodoxy in the Han dynasty which lasted from 206 B.C. to 220 A.D. For the next thousand years, they contributed to the stability of the state and to the flourishing of a very advanced civilization, clearly pre-eminent in world terms by the Sung period. During this same period however, alternative philosophies flourished, most notably Taoism and Buddhism. The thirteenth century brought a period of intellectual consolidation which attempted to fuse the essentially social philosophy of Confucianism with the more nature-related Taoism and more spiritual Buddhism. This synthesis became known as neo-Confucianism, and having developed the original ideas from an ethical code to a full philosophy, it has lasted until the present day.

Taoism

The incorporating of Taoism added the link with nature, and allowed the admission of an idea long fascinating to the Chinese, that of the tension of fundamental dualities—hot and cold, light and dark, male and female, *yin* and *yang*. This duality is relevant because of the need to comprehend how the apparently dominant can be effectively counteracted by the power of passivity, of yielding, of non-activity. As much power in nature is subtle and not reliant on obvious force, a society might benefit from the principle of *wu-wei*, or active not-doing which lies at the center of the Taoist paradigm. The remarkable success of the Hong Kong government's official policy of "positive non-intervention" practiced over the last two decades might well serve as a symbol, echoing ancient Chinese understandings of the workings of influence.

The second main tenet of Taoism is the notion of underlying natural order, the metaphor for which is the grain in a piece of wood, and the social implication being to search for the grain and work with it, not against it. There is, of course, much else in Taoism: a search for communion with nature which might often border on the naive; an obscurantism which could lead to mysticism and the flirtation with magic; the advocacy of a docile, and by implication ignorant, populace. It was in the realm of aesthetics that it made perhaps its greatest obvious contribution, fostering as it did great artistic depth by its advocacy of ultimate truth in nature.

Buddhism

The incorporating of Buddhism into neo-Confucianism was made easier by the fact that, like Taoism, it offered a wider philosophy of man's relation to the natural world which was complementary to the practical ethics of daily life so typical of the original Confucian thinking.

Buddhist teachers may have arrived in China from India as early as the first century B.C., but they had not spread their influence significantly until three hundred years later. By that time, and continually from then on, a process of sinification took place as texts were translated and as indigenous Chinese notions found their way into the thinking through the Buddhist borrowing of Taoist terminology.

Buddhism, like Taoism, is about man's place in nature. It differs from it, however, in its focus on a faultless and god-like being, a perfect example like Christ or Mohammed. This makes it perhaps more accessible to the average person, searching for an authority figure, but it is still not a religion with a god. Buddha never claimed the existence of one. Instead, he took the position of being a human who had found the key to living well. This had been achieved through a process of enlightenment during which he had encountered and come to terms with some fundamental reality. Attempts to explain this "reality" are usually given in terms of what it is not, as it is sufficiently unworldly to defy description in worldly terms, and this mysterious nothingness, or nirvana, at the center of things, seen nevertheless as a source of perfection and fulfilment, is the reason why Buddhism remains magnetic. It allows the individual room for interpretation, and at the same time focusses concern on ultimate issues rather than more obviously pressing ones. It also provides a philosophy wherein all nature is one and nirvana is present everywhere.

It was this ability to present a philosophy about the harmony of all nature's elements which attracted the Chinese to Buddhism. Although Taoism set the individual in among the rhythms of nature, the meditative techniques of Buddhism were better developed for moving people toward an understanding of the oneness of things. As Carmody and Carmody point out,

> Chinese . . . could satisfy their native hunger to be at one with nature by following the new wisdom's way. More profoundly and intensely than with their native religious systems, they could enjoy the beauty of emptiness, of fullness, and of Buddha-nature's endlessly creative overflow into trees, mountains, streams, and people (Carmody and Carmody 1983: 101).

The Chinese interpretation of Buddhism led in turn to its amalgamation with native magic and the world of spirits, and although it has declined since its peak of influence in the thirteenth century in China and been partially absorbed in neo-Confucianism, nevertheless it remains evident in philosophy, funeral rites, and art.

Religion and Social Order

The society which developed was strongly hierarchical. Not only was the individual part of nature, but also part of a natural human order which took much of its meaning from a ruler who had a mandate to conduct to earth the governing power of heaven. The imperial role became a cult and forms of deference and ritual extended the cult through all ranks representing it down to the base of society. At that base lay the family, and much effort went into ensuring that the family itself could serve as a stable basic building block by incorporating into it the disciplines of hierarchy. The social results of this intense focus on family will be examined in more detail shortly.

A further significant feature of the Confucian social order was veneration of the past, and its extension, veneration of the old as the sources of wisdom and guidance. It can still be startling to a Westerner in an office in Hong Kong to be confronted by a clerk quoting with perfect seriousness a thousand-year old text as an authoritative guideline to a modern business problem, like a Victorian preacher with his pat biblical quotations.

A number of themes may now be drawn together to allow consideration of one of the most important effects of Confucianism, and one of the principal determinants of social and economic behavior. This is the passivity induced by a system which places the individual in a powerfully maintained family order, itself inside a powerfully maintained state order, itself seen as part of a natural cosmic order, and all dedicated to the maintenance of the status quo. When the only true authority is tradition, and when deviant behavior meets heavy sanctions from an early age, when deference to elders is automatic, and when dependence on those same elders is non-negotiable, then all the ingredients are present for producing a social system characterized on the one hand by an impressive stability and on the other hand by a debilitating incapacity to adapt, innovate, and change.

In his study of the connections between Asian religions and economic progress, Bellah (1965: 193) noted two especially unfavorable conditions. If on the one hand there was "too close a fusion between religious symbolism and the actual world," then the religion would perpetually sanctify the status quo and provide no leverage for change. Without a complex theoretical structure, based largely on social conformity, paying little attention to a transcendent goal, Confucianism with its central cult of family, displays its archaism and its ultra-conservatism.

On the other hand, a religion, such as Taoism or Buddhism in its purer forms, both of which stress "The utter disjunction between what is religiously valuable and the actualities of this world," may equally retard social change and progress by discounting the practical world as a sphere for valid endeavor.

It would appear that China has succumbed to both handicaps in its religions, at least as far as material progress is concerned. The lack of creative tension between religious ideals and the real world has implications for the way economic activity comes to be organized. At this point, however, where we are concerned to depict the make-up of the typical individual, it is sufficient to note that compliance and conservatism are widespread characteristics to a degree where they might be taken as central parts of the ideal-type Chinese personality.

It is also worthy of note at this stage, and in the light of the larger theme of this book, that the more debilitating effects of Confucian traditionalism have either been shaken off, counteracted, or subtly amended, for most of the Overseas Chinese. There is no doubt that the traditionalism remains, but in new contexts, it has different effects. Again, it is worth reiterating that the complexities of explanation are such that simple direct links betwen religious norms and economic behavior are not part of our agenda.

Social Structures

Family

In a study of Hong Kong society, Lau (1982) characterized it in two significant ways, describing the social fabric as "minimally integrated" and suffused by "utilitarian familism." The extensions of these key particulars are that the families remain the basic survival units, that they are largely self-sufficient, that they do not fuse naturally into a general community, that they are fundamentally competitive, and that their members are largely motivated by the pragmatic exigencies of protecting and enhancing the family resources on which they in turn are highly dependent.

In order to understand why the family takes on this particular meaning, it is necessary to make some attempt to see it from the standpoint of a Chinese person. For this, an account is available from Margery Wolf's study of a Taiwanese village, and it will stand to represent much that motivates Chinese behavior and attitudes throughout all the Overseas Chinese societies. She describes the pivotal role of family in these terms:

> The interaction of the Taiwanese villager with his friends and neighbors is like the spice in his soup, savory, but of little sustenance. It is with his family, his parents and grandparents, his children and grandchildren, that he takes the measure of his life. His relations with his parents may be strained, with his wife distant, and with his children formal, but without these people he would be an object of pity and of no small amount of suspicion. He would be pitied because he had no parents to "help" him and no children to support him in his old age, pitied because he had no place in a group, because he didn't belong anywhere. For these same reasons he would be the object of suspicion. A man not thoroughly imbedded in a network of kinship cannot be completely trusted because he cannot be dealt with in the normal way. If he behaves improperly, one cannot discuss his behavior with his brother or seek redress from his parents. If one wants to approach him about a delicate matter, one cannot use his uncle as a go-between to prepare the way. Wealth cannot make up for this deficiency any more than it can make up for the loss of arms and legs. Money has no past, no future, and no obligations. Relatives do (Wolf 1968: 23).

One can see from this the way in which the person is perceived to exist only in terms of his immediate family network, and by extension that society is seen as comprising not individuals—who in themselves have no legitimate place—but families, around which life is formed. Moreover, the notion of what a family is extends beyond its members to encompass its property, its reputation, its internal traditions, its ancestors' spirits, and even its future unborn generations (Yang 1945: 45). The connection with property and location is subtly conveyed in the overlap of meaning between the ideograms for "home" and "family," viz. : home (家), family (家庭).

Inside the family, its regulation is based on a set of rules about deference. The five main ones, known as the *wu-lun*, specify an order of ranking, with the first-named given preference: father–son, husband–wife, elder brother–younger brother; ruler–subject (or boss–subordinate), and as well as these clearly hierarchical distinctions, there is a more general set of rules governing expectations of trust and reliability between friends.

Such hierarchical prescribing rests on a more fundamental idea which gives man a high place in the cosmic order. The *san kang* or trinity of the universe consists of man, heaven, and earth, with man himself infused with the same ethereal substance, *chi*, that went into the making of heaven and earth. The Way of Heaven (*tien tao*) and the Way of Man (*jen tao*) interpenetrate, and this creates the notion that man is perfectible and able to interpret what is required for civilized society to flourish (Yang 1961: 273).

In practice, male domination is normal, and in practice also control can often be heavy handed and strict, acknowledging as it does the security provided to the dependent member of the family circle. Also common is the set of tensions inevitable when people are forced into mutual dependence, often in conditions of scarcity. Tensions between the generations, between the sexes, between the hard-working and the lazy, between the different personalities, have also provided a challenge which the Confucian recipe of dignified restraint and human sympathy was designed to cope with. It must be acknowledged that the ethic has continued to this day to meet the demands made on it for social stability. The family boardroom may be the scene of the most bitter and vituperative quarreling but it would be unthinkable not to present a united front to the world outside. As well as being its own welfare state, the family polices its own domain. The placidity which characterizes most Chinese societies, even though it cannot remove any more than in any other society the tensions which are inevitable in human interaction, disguises them better than most.

In making the point that the family is largely what Chinese society is about, and following Lau's contention that, apart from inside those units, society is "minimally integrated," it is necessary now to consider those larger units, and to understand the weakness of what might be termed community. This will be seen later to have substantial ramifications for organization, as it throws light on the problem of trust which so limits the growth of the Chinese family business. For the moment, however, the level of analysis will stay with the individual and his relationships, and questions of organization as such will be examined in chapters 6 and 7.

Networks

The larger units of Chinese society of relevance to the individual, although they can be differentiated into endless detail for the purposes of anthropology, will be taken here more simply as the lineage, the village or neighborhood, and special interest associations. In addition is the clan, or collection of lineages sharing a surname.

The lineage is an extension of the family and is normally defined as the patrilineal descendents of a particular, identifiable ancestor. There is no rule for how many families can make up a lineage group but one of 500 people made up of 15 families would not be unusual. It is also easily possible for an even larger lineage group to develop in an area and to contain several sets within it. Such a group is described by Hugh Baker for his study of the Liao lineage group of Sheung Shui, Hong Kong. This has 3,400 members and traces its origin back 600 years. Significantly, it is also characterized by intense rivalry between the groups which go to make it (Baker 1979: ch. 3).

Such rivalries are likely to be fought out between the smaller groups which subdivide a lineage group and which are known as *fang*. The *fang* is usually defined as a five-generation family group, and it provides a network within which the individual can still be known to all.

The reason why lineage identity is maintained has largely to do with the assistance such a collectivity is able to provide to the individual. His or her loyalty to it, constantly reinforced in the rituals of births, marriages, funerals (especially the latter, which test obligations and remind members of ancestral descent), is an indication of the person's dependence and the lack of alternative sources of support.

This latter point is evident from descriptions of Chinese village life in its traditional form, for instance that of Strauch (1981), and an especially pointed account is provided by Yang (1945). In this he argues that in the first place the purposes of village organization were negative. The duty of the village elders was to preserve tradition, and to prevent any new ideas from threatening the old ways. Although there would normally have been an organized system of defence against crop theft, there was almost never any positive approach to recreation, socializing, cleaning, improving water supplies, or community welfare. Secondly, the village in many parts of China, and in the south especially, was less a focus for associations than would be the case in other cultures such as Japan. Instead, associations would tend to be based on special interests, locality, kinship, or religion. Because of the internal cohesion and potential rivalry of these alternative groupings, joint action between them and across the village community was regularly thwarted.

Thirdly is the question of clan interest, which dominates in all village affairs and interposes a further set of rivalries to prevent community cooperation. Clearly the Chinese village is not a "community" in the sense normally meant in the West. It is the geographical location where rival families and lineage groups come to accommodate to each other. It has utility for defence, for exchange, for shared facilities, for fostering communication, but compared to its equivalent in many other countries, it would appear to lack the "sense of community" which can offer to the individual a viable and not necessarily contradictory alternative identity to that of family membership. The surface bonhomie of much social interaction conceals a wary distancing from close involvement with others. It typifies the social contexts which for many Overseas Chinese remain "minimally integrated," and which are seen as concentric circles—family, lineage group, no-man's land.

But a no-man's land has still to be traversed, its dangers minimized, and for this venture an individual's or family's resources may be inadequate. It is here that other social networks beyond the family or clan come into play. These have been especially significant for the Chinese outside China, and more so when they are part of a host nation and in need of cooperation among themselves.

The most common response to such needs has been the Chinese voluntary association, and a study of these forms in Singapore by Hsieh reveals patterns which show, as he notes, "some basic and essential organizing principles which are derived from patterns indigenous to China herself and which underlie the superficially different characteristics of various Chinese communities abroad" (Hsieh 1978).

The plethora of associations which Hsieh reports in Singapore, and which are commonly described elsewhere (e.g. Crissman 1967, Lee 1988, Mackie 1976, Skinner 1957, Willmott 1960), are organized along four main lines: firstly are those based on kinship and identified by a surname; secondly, many are defined by area of origin in China; thirdly are those which perpetuate a dialect; fourthly, there are those based on occupation or craft reminiscent of the guilds of tradi-tional China. It is also naturally possible to combine criteria and to have, for instance, the Foochow Barbers' Association. In addition to these main classifica-tions, there are also ones based on forms of commerce such as the rice traders' group, cultural and recreational groups, and religious and charity associations.

It is clear, as has been pointed out by Mak (1988) that there are two organiz-ing principles at work in this process of associating. Firstly is the place of origin, defined variously in terms ranging from specific village up to province. This would tend to divide the society up, as it were, vertically, into competing blocs. But running across these blocs, as it were horizontally, are connections based on religion, or surname, or clan, which serve to counteract the divisiveness. "These integrative organizations then put the structurally segmented people under one roof, yielding the unintended effect of neutralizing any ill-feeling resultant from structural segmentation" (Mak 1988: 237).

The origins of such networks in urban China, and their value in providing the regulation of transactions in the absence of state institutions for that purpose, have been commented on by Hamilton (1977: 339), as has also the wide variety of social positioning of the Overseas Chinese in Southeast Asia, and consequent differences in the types of association which become prevalent. But however the precise form, the function is constant and largely pragmatic. As Mak (1988: 236) has observed, "they aligned themselves according to almost any social criterion that was to their advantage." Just, one is tempted to add, like most people in their position would, but perhaps more so. This vast network of social connections then serves a number of important purposes for the Chinese individual and reveals an important operating principle about the workings of selective cooperation, a question to which we shall turn more specifically when considering in the next section the relationship rules.

Before that, however, it is necessary to add one further element to the analysis of social structures. This is the factor of ethnicity, and it is particularly salient for the Overseas Chinese.

Ethnicity

The assimilation of the Overseas Chinese into the host cultures of Malaysia, Indonesia, and the Philippines is noteworthy for its slowness. Reporting, for instance, on the Chinese community of Iloilo in the Philippines, Omohundro (1981), describing a history of four hundred years of settlement, concluded that assimilation is still a matter for the future. This group, of Fukienese origin, still retained their Chinese dialect and much else in the way of Chinese conservatism. Their norms included the retention of racial purity and may be symbolized by the attempt by one family head to re-establish the face he had lost when his daughter insisted on marrying outside the Chinese ethnic circle. To conceal the chagrin and regain respect, he gave the grandest party ever.

Accounts of such retention of ethnic separateness are common, and the feature would appear to have a long-standing and consistent history. Although it inevitably results from many forces, there are three principal causes which come to mind as determinants: firstly, the Chinese are resented for their success and band together defensively; secondly, they perceive that Chinese culture is superior to its alternatives; thirdly, it may simply be more humanly comfortable, at a very basic level, to associate with one's own kind.

We have already noted the economic success of the Overseas Chinese as being out of all proportion to their numbers in the ASEAN countries. Omohundro's micro study reinforces this with the finding that the Iloilo Chinese make up only 2% of the city population but pay 35% of its business taxes. This kind of performance, repeated in country after country, is inevitably going to produce if not local resentment, then at least local guardedness and suspicion. Reciprocally, the Chinese themselves must inevitably derive quiet satisfaction from the results of such labors, and they would not be human if they did not take pride in at least one indicator of a particular form of superiority.

They would not be Chinese if they did not, at the same time, understand with full sensitivity, the effects of their success on people in the host culture, and the kind of resentment which might ensue. In consequence, a wary and defensive insistence on the maintenance of their own group solidarity is entirely predictable.

A logical extension of such success is to point to the source as Chinese civilization itself. If seen retrospectively, and the traditionalist perspective tends to ensure this, and if seen romantically (not difficult at a long remove from the events), then Chinese civilization has massive authority based on its achievements. It is not surprisingly still a guiding beacon, and in consequence a shared focus, universally understood and strongly cohesive in its workings.

The retention of ethnic identity by staying with one's own people on grounds of simple human comfort is a common enough social phenomenon worldwide, and requires no explication as to motives. It should, however, be added that in the case of the Chinese an extra incentive exists to dissuade incursions of outsiders or the venturing out of insiders. This is the awesome barrier of the Chinese language, fluency in which only comes at a very high price. For a Chinese to give this up is a major sacrifice; for a foreigner to learn it is a major challenge. As long as the language is retained, Chinese separateness will be sustained in host countries, and elsewhere Chinese ethnicity will be daily demonstrated and reinforced (Ho 1976).

The social matrix in which the Overseas Chinese individual is embedded is thus conceivable as a set of concentric circles, an image first proposed in Fei's classic study of rural China (Fei 1939, transl. 1987). At the core is the family, a unit with such potent appeal that other sources of identity pale into relative insignificance. Surrounding this is the lineage group, or extension of the family, serving to provide more general support than the family itself and source of a more general feeling of identity commonly associated with place and with ancestors. Further, a set of specific interest groups serve to foster information exchange, contact making, and general socializing. Ultimately, being Chinese is itself important, and significant for much interaction and attitude taking. The perception of these concentric circles forms the basis for the rules which govern relationships, and we now turn to those rules to see how the individual manages the various roles demanded of him.

Relationship Rules

In order to be civilized, an individual must fit into and conform with the basic social order of his surrounding world. This requires mastery of both vertical and horizontal relationships. The Chinese have developed clear and well-understood rules for these linkages, and their workings make for a quite distinct version of human order.

The most immediately understandable aspects of social structure are the rules governing vertical relationships. For the Chinese, these are conveyed in the notion of *hsiao*, or filial piety, seen commonly as the foundation stone of Chinese society.

Filial Piety

That this should be so dominant a theme derives from the nature of what Weber saw as the "patrimonial" state, the distinguishing feature of which is that the ultimate power which rests with the head of state is personal and is dispensed and dispersed by representatives who also interpret it personally. For this system to remain stable requires a form of authority seen as legitimate by those subjected to it, the Chinese solution to this challenge being strict role compliance by both parties. If roles are strictly followed, power is not abused, and Confucian doctrine aims to produce just such acceptable leaders, respected for their wisdom, humanity, and propriety. Nevertheless, the concentration on conformity *per se* is intense. To be without filial piety is the only "sin" in a society otherwise devoid of such a transcendental concept (Weber 1951: 228).

In the family setting, a feature which enhances the power of the father-figure is the common ownership of family belongings. Possessions are normally seen as belonging to the group, and although individuals may have stewardship of certain of them, the right to call them in (and the reciprocal obligation to return them to the pool) is sufficient to prevent the emergence of the kind of psychological separateness which allows the central authority to be challenged. Without clearly independent resources, the individual remains bound and to some degree disenfranchised. Naturally, this is a source of substantial tension in many families, and naturally there are people who succeed in breaking away, but the norm is conformity, and acceptance that the price of protection is loyalty.

The workings of these pressures are conveyed graphically in Margery Wolf's description of events in a traditional Chinese village, when a strong minded son broke away from the authority of too inconsiderate a father. Her account begins by describing the son:

As a child he feared his father's punishment; as a youth he resented it; as a young man, he looked outside his home and found that there he too could be respected, feared and obeyed. He and his father were seen in conflict over his outside activities. The more his father attempted to restrain him, the more satisfying (he) found life outside his family. He became a leader among the young men . . . At the age of nineteen (he) left the family home and severed his relations with his father.

To the Westerner accustomed to adolescent revolt and the approval of independence in young men, this may seem like an entirely reasonable and justifiable action. In the social context of (the Chinese village) it was an act of extreme moral violence. A Chinese son's first duty is to obey, respect and support his father. Children exist for the sake of their parents. When a Chinese son dies before his father and is thus unable to take care of him in his old age, the father is expected to ritually beat the coffin at the funeral, "to punish the child for being so unfilial as to leave his father alone in his old age" . . . His neighbors condemned the boy as unfilial, but for (the father) this held little solace. It only increased his humiliation. Rather than accepting the exoneration of his neighbors, he recognized the failure for what it was. With his remaining children he struggled, with some success, to soften the harshness of his character (Wolf 1968: 46).

Power Distance Index (PDI)

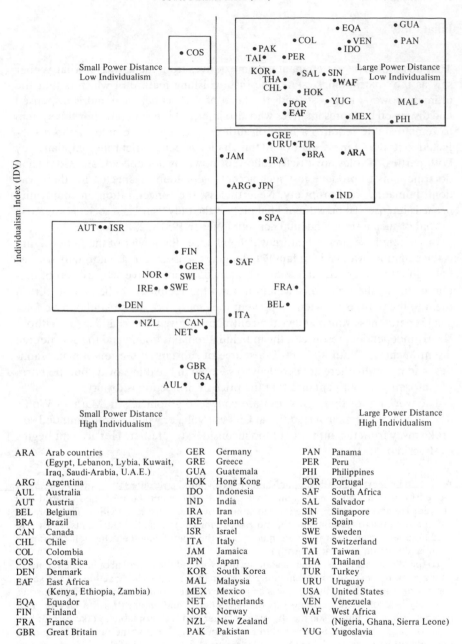

Figure 3.2: The core values of power distance and individualism/collectivism in different societies

Source: Hofstede 1984

The Chinese person emerges from up to twenty years of disciplined paternalism in the family, having had his or her sense of vertical order reinforced in the school context, where teachers represent the learning on which authority in China was traditionally allocated (Ho and Lee 1974). The sum of these individual perceptions makes what Hofstede, in a major international study of values, terms a "high power distance" culture (Hofstede 1980). Figure 3.2 illustrates the position of a large number of countries on this dimension, and also on the dimension of collectivism to be discussed shortly.

A high power distance culture is one in which people express, in their behavior and attitudes, a strong sense of vertical order. They understand that they fit naturally below some people, and, just as significantly, above others. Living on a form of ladder is not a cause for resentment as that is how their social world has always been designed, and, in any case, a superior position carries obligations. Abuse of these responsibilities will undermine the authority and destroy the allegiances of those below. The core of that responsibility is the paternalist concern for the subordinates' general welfare, something for which much conformity is offered in return. Although at first glance, and particularly to the Westerner brought up in a more egalitarian world, this verticality might appear stifling, and the acquiescence implied in it debilitating, it is important to acknowledge certain advantages in its operation.

The principle one of these, and one of particular relevance to life in organizations, is that the individual has a built-in sense of the legitimacy of the superior–subordinate relationship. Whereas in the Western case, considerable effort goes into ways of justifying the authority structure, and an equal amount to challenging it from below, for the Chinese, it is an extension of a natural order. The open challenge of formal authority is rare. This is not to say that compliance is mute and unthinking, as there are endless possibilities for subtle resistance and for disguising the unwillingness to conform, but the general tone of vertical relationships is that there is not an issue of principle at stake about rights and duties.

From this flow the ensuing advantages that decision-making rights are not normally disputed. Leadership is looked for and more or less followed. Also loyalty, and its extension in diligence, are, under normal circumstances, offered from below as part of the exchange.

The cultivation of filial piety which lies at the heart of family design, and which in turn sets the tone for the larger social structures which have traditionally extended that basic design to the total state, thus creates a vertical order which, although not unique in world terms, is nevertheless derived from distinct causes. It cannot help but seep into the modal Chinese personality.

Collectivism and Face

Turning now from vertical relationships to horizontal ones, it is necessary to begin by observing the seemingly inevitable linkages between them. A society constructed with such powerful vertical bonds can be expected to look at horizontal bonds from a special perspective. In short, if vertical family allegiances dominate, then the horizontal ties will be secondary, and possibly subservient. As is evident from Figure 3.2, those cultures with high power distance also exhibit high levels of collectivism, those with low power distance are characterized normally by individualism. Human society finds a balance between the two forces, and arguably the combination of elements which make for this balance adjusts as forces of social change, and especially the freedoms associated with economic wealth cause a rise in individualism and a consequent decline in the power of hierarchy.

Whatever the determinants, it is clear that the Overseas Chinese as represented in the scores for Hong Kong, Singapore, and Taiwan are consistently collectivist as societies. They are not so to the most extreme degree but they are clearly so in a way which separates them from virtually all Western cultures.

To understand the implications of a collectivist society for the nurturing of a particular kind of individual, it will be useful to consider firstly the ground rules under which a person perceives his or her place alongside others, and secondly the effects on behavior of those networks of influence. In the Chinese case, this takes us into questions of socialization, of "face," and of social control. It will also allow us to examine more closely the context in which cooperation is or is not exercised.

Weber makes the point that, in the Chinese ethical system, the ultimate judgment about how to behave is not based on any distant religious ideal conceived in abstract terms, but instead on family piety, something immediately accessible, but moreover something which is largely acted out in terms of relationship rules. Sensitized to the feelings of others, the person guides him or herself through life as if in a web, the vibrations from which act to assist in navigating the essentially social world.

The lack of an ultimate authority, such as a supra-mundane God, leaves the individual without grounds for supporting as a separate person a sacred "cause" or a universally applicable principle, such as Christian charity, and replaces them with piety towards specific people, especially those in close related proximity. At the most fundamental level of fitting into the world, the person is tied closely to the sources of understanding what is good and bad, right and wrong, and the meaning of most behavior. For the Chinese, this is a social rather than an intellectual set of influences.

One of the outcomes of this process of living, as it were, in a web is that the web becomes part of the person. The self is embedded in relationships, inextricable from them, and not thought of as independent of such attachments. People need this "placement" and, to function smoothly, society needs to be able to "place" people.

The resulting phenomenon of what might be termed the "networked self" is sponsored not only by the social activities of daily life, but also by the society's most fundamental beliefs. The Confucian ideal is that family, clan, and head of state take precedence over the individual. In Taoism, your body is lent to you by the universe in which you should lose yourself "as fish lose themselves in water." In Buddhism, the ego is seen as an illusion, and the aim is to transcend it to the unborn pure being. The dignity of the person as an end in itself is not part of the most fundamental Chinese ideals.

Empirical evidence for the downplaying of self and the upgrading of relationships by Chinese people in the organizational context is available from a survey of perceived need importance, the results of which are given in Figure 3.3. The respondents, who were middle managers, display in the Chinese case a concern for the importance of social needs which is fairly close to the salience attached to autonomy and self-actualization. For the large sample of Western managers, the gap between the two levels is wide and the importance of the self is clearly dominant. This also corroborates the differences in collectivism—individualism scores shown in Hofstede's data in Figure 3.2.

The way in which the person becomes sensitive to such surrounding vibrations is depicted in Wilson's description of the socialization of children in Taiwan, a system of child-rearing which he argues to be common to Chinese everywhere. In this process, great emphasis is placed on techniques of shaming, and on inculcating a sensitivity to "face." He moreover points out that "There seems to be an intimate relationship between face and values that support a predominantly vertical group structure" (Wilson 1970: XI).

The child, under a combined and apparently concerted set of experiences at home and in school, is taught to suppress aggressive behavior. Although physical punishment can occasionally be rigorous in the home, disorder at school is eliminated by non-corporal means of punishment which rely heavily on moral education, on the promotion of examples to follow, and on the value of group membership. Such groups, which in the school context just as at home are graded hierarchically inside, afford the psychological benefits of membership in exchange for work and achievement. The person "invests" in the group, and the investment which he then cannot afford to lose becomes his "face."

Although face is a human universal, and most societies civilize their members by raising their sensitivity to the views others hold of them, the importance of it for the Chinese is quite simply that much greater. Given the lack of alternative forms of control, such as the call of some more abstract morality, this is not perhaps surprising. The result for Chinese is that loss of face, as Hsu points out, becomes "a real dread affecting the nervous system . . . more strongly than physical fear" (Hsu 1971).

A significant element of the workings of face is that it relates to a particular set

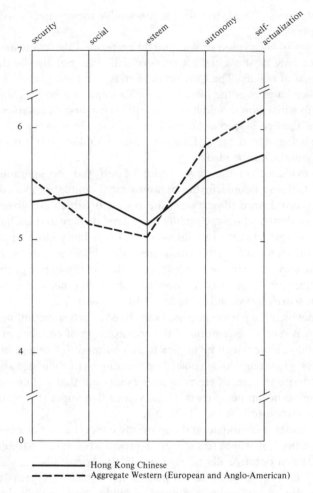

Figure 3.3: Comparative perceptions of need importance, Chinese and Western
Source: Redding 1980

of people, and not nearly so powerfully to society at large. The power of its
effects on the individual varies from situation to situation. A person will have
invested very heavily in it with his family, with his classmates, with his social
reference group, and with his work group. With other people, however, he may
feel less constrained by its pressures on him. The workings of moral suasion are
thus highly contingent, and a powerful and important element of flexibility enters into the ethical system. This becomes an important determinant of the structures of cooperation used in the economy, as will be argued later.

In day-to-day interaction, the workings of face are immensely subtle and difficult for a Westerner to disentangle, as they often involve third parties who are not members of the immediate interaction. Consider, as illustration, these two incidents taken from a study of the workings of face in the context of Hong Kong business (Redding and Ng 1982).

The Shipping Seminar

I work in a company dealing in spare parts for a world-famous marine engine. Each year, the engine manufacturer sends a senior engineer to Hong Kong to give seminars introducing their new models and explaining modifications to existing ones. As I am in charge of that department, I have to organize the seminars.

I usually send out invitation cards to superintendents, captains, and ship owners to ask them to come. For those not so important shipping companies, I telephone them to ask them to give me face by attending the seminar. We Chinese usually say, "please give me face and honor us with your presence." But for the more important shipping companies, I will take the invitation cards to them in person to show that they are our highly esteemed customers, and thus hope that in return for my giving them face by inviting them personally, they will also give me face and come to the seminar. I also arrange the front seats for the more important companies' representatives as a gesture of giving them more face than others.

For a time this method worked well, but after a few occasions the smaller companies noticed that I had *sent* them invitations and arranged their seats in a lower order of importance. Some of the more face-conscious ones began to complain and even challenged me. "We are a small company, so our attendance is not so important as that of the big companies!" Usually such shipping companies in Hong Kong are run by Shanghainese people, who are known to be the most face-conscious among Chinese people.

So I have now fallen into the trouble of trying to fill the seminar and losing face when most of the seats are empty. Somehow I have to find a way of overcoming the difficulty. But if I do the same to all the shipping companies, the larger ones might begin to think that I am not giving them enough face if I do not treat them a little differently from the smaller ones. I have to show that I esteem them more and this, of course, they think they deserve.

The New Assistant Manager

This incident begins with the appointment of a new assistant manager in an engineering company, who was being too "bossy" with the mechanics. It came to a head when they downed tools on the arrival of an important job requiring overtime work. He turned for help to an older manager who narrates the story:

The poor chap, having lost all face, came to me for help because I am a good friend of his father. So, because of the face of his father, I took him to meet the mechanics and told them that he was my good friend's son, and wished to apologize for the misunderstanding (although it was not really a misunderstanding). At first the mechanics would not give way. In fact, I was afraid that if they did not give me face because they were so angry with him, then it would be my turn to lose face in that I failed to help. Fortunately some of the older mechanics knew me well and finally gave me face, convincing the others to cooperate. However, the unfortunate young man still had to do the face-losing work of telling the client that the job would be finished later than promised.

The first incident shows how business networks, which become reference groups for a particular individual, behave hierarchically, and how sensitivity to displays of respect and deference become the coinage of social interaction. In this instance, face stands partly for the smoothing activities which console such sensitivities, partly for the self-esteem which the unfortunate individual in the middle sees defined so much in terms of what others think, and partly also as a bargaining chip with clear value. The second incident, as well as showing an initial failure in negotiating face with a subordinate group, and thus the capacity of face to work up and down as well as sideways, also introduces the element of face owed to a third party, in this case the father. Again such considerations are obviously not solely the preserve of the Chinese, and all collectivist societies display central values which promote high levels of interpersonal sensitivity. [3] It is, however, significant that the feature is such an open concern, and one taken seriously as a determinant of action.

What has been said so far about the effect for an individual of a collectivist society, has been concerned with the influences of family and of circles of acquaintanceship. The person's relationship with society at large, and particularly with people he does not know, now needs to be described and accounted for, as it is significant for much that occurs in the realm of economic organization.

Limited and Bounded Trust

Lin Yutang put the matter succinctly when he stated that nowhere in Chinese ethics is there a notion like that of the good Samaritan, adding piously "and great and catastrophic was the omission." (Lin 1977: 172). Weber, equally succinctly, noted that "The Confucian gentleman, striving simply for dignified bearing, distrusted others as generally as he believed others distrusted him" (Weber 1951: 244). Softening the issue to a more neutral question of non-trust rather than active distrust, Silin, in the only detailed monograph extant in English on the workings of an Overseas Chinese factory, pays considerable attention to the negative expectations about cooperation in Chinese society and points out the inevitable conflict between *hsiao*, or filial piety, and *chung*, or loyalty to the emperor figure (Silin 1976), there being interestingly no term native to the Chinese language expressing loyalty to the society in general. [4]

The key feature would appear to be that you trust your family absolutely, your friends and acquaintances to the degree that mutual dependence has been established and face invested in them. With everybody else you make no assumptions about their goodwill. You have the right to expect their politeness and their following of the social proprieties, but beyond that you must anticipate that, just as you are, they are looking primarily to their own, i.e. their family's, best interests. To know your own motives well is, for the Chinese more than most, a warning about everybody else's.

People thus conduct their lives if not quite from the safety of walled encampments then at least with some wariness and in order to interact in a wider sense, make "treaties" with neighbors. To the extent that these connections are essential for survival, they become strongly bonded, and so the networks grow. There is a process of establishing and maintaining them which explains a great deal of daily behavior and much of the clearly visible public socializing and hospitality, but a number of key features distinguish the Chinese network form of society from many others.

Chinese networking, synonymous in China with the ubiquitous term *guanxi*, begins with the problem of growing and protecting family resources. For reasons which will be examined in chapter 6, the family's position *vis-à-vis* the state is defensive, and it must look to its own survival on the assumption that no other organ in society will take responsibility for the welfare of individuals. Sharpened in the experience of Chinese social history, this attitude has remained resilient with the Overseas Chinese. A corollary of this is that all families are subject to the same regime and none have any choice but to see their milieu as fundamentally competitive.

Two forces are able to counteract the anarchy which would result if this were all that inspired behavior. In the first place, open conflict and overt self-interest are seen in Chinese ethics as deeply improper, and in effect ruled out from the range of acceptable behavior. Aggressive desires, and emotions generally, are normally sublimated, and the society lacks any clear guidelines for the management of conflict situations (which, as a result, in practice may either run quickly out of hand, or be quietly shuffled around while the issue festers or becomes more marginal). [5]

As well as this tendency to avoid confrontation, there is the positive feature that it is essential to make linkages if one's own purposes are to be served. The creation of wealth in one family unit cannot be managed in isolation; it must buy and sell, exchange information, borrow money, seek advice. To do so, it establishes a network of the necessary connections, and to make such networks operate reliably, Chinese society has come to attach central importance to the notion of trust. What is Chinese about this trust, however, is that it is very specifically circumscribed. It is limited to the partners in the bond. It works on the basis of personal obligations, the maintenance of reputation and face, and not on any assumption that a society's shared faith makes all who share it equally righteous regardless of whether you know them or not.

A description of its workings, this time derived from a study of ethnic Chinese businessmen in Vietnam by Barton (1983: 50), uses the phrase *sun yung* to describe this crucial component of character:

In a community almost totally oriented toward business transactions, *sun yung* was the most important aspect of a person's character and not merely a quality to be considered in economic affairs.

Sun yung referred not only to credit, in the sense of goods or services lent without immediate return against the promise of a future repayment or to "credit rating," which is an assessment made by a lender of the risks involved in extending credit to a specific individual; it further carried the connotation of a person's total reputation for trustworthiness and in this sense was a statement of a person's social and psychological characteristics as well as strictly economic reliability.

This heightened sensitivity to the importance of trust serves to make the networks strong, as individuals fear to infringe such a powerful norm. It does however also point up the inability to connect easily into areas of society where the network does not penetrate, and where work is needed to establish it. The Chinese find it very difficult to come to terms with neutral, objective relationships, where they cannot "read" trustworthiness, and tend instead to work at creating trust beforehand. This may well be done via the use of intermediary connections known to both, or by assessing the other's position in a reputable clan.

Such processes account for much effort, but they also yield substantial savings in the control of risk. They also reveal a society in which the writ of universal law does not yet penetrate all the crevices, and litigation is not yet a first resort.

The end product of these forces, as far as cooperation is concerned, is a society which contains three principal components. The families into which the society is atomized, and which are basic units around which life is conducted and security derived, display inside themselves intense loyalty among members, and an equivalent level of cooperation. The second component consists of the networks, each family with its own, and each bond usually initiated first out of a pragmatic need and then cemented fast by obligation, trust, and friendship. Outside these is the third component, that of society at large, with which are maintained polite but guarded and somewhat distant relations, stopping well short of involvement in other peoples' lives, and at times capable of being expressed in displays of indifference which can verge on the callous. [6]

The individual in such a matrix will carry with him a subconscious sense of whom to trust, with whom to cooperate, and for what ultimate purposes. These questions will be seen in terms of concentric circles of obligation and will make his responses vary. As we will later note, this introduces certain strengths to the economic system, but also raises some severe limitations on what organizational options are possible, as cooperation itself becomes highly contingent.

Rules for Action

This assessment of the roots of Chinese behavior must now turn from the social structures surrounding the person, and how he or she connects with them, to the more focussed and pragmatic guidelines which are likely to influence economic behavior. Because of this focus, we may leave out of the account many areas of

Chinese values and instead attempt to concentrate. Given that it is not possible to be exhaustive, much flavor may still be conveyed by an analysis of the following: the work ethic and the notion of perseverance, money and frugality, and pragmatism. It will be suggested that the way in which such values emerge owes much to the culture and social history of China, and the subsequent experience by Overseas Chinese of much environmental uncertainty.

The Work Ethic

The dedication to working hard is not inherited in the genes of a culture. Factory owners in Hong Kong who have the opportunity to employ (a) local Chinese, (b) Vietnamese refugees, (c) refugees from China, employ them in that order of preference on the grounds of their attitude to working. As many of the Vietnamese are ethnically Chinese, it is clear that the social experiences of three groups of the same people have contributed to three different outcomes. It is also an assumption that newcomers to Hong Kong will absorb its frenetic atmosphere and learn how to work hard.

The question of work ethic is thus one of circumstances as much as of people. In that event, the study of it becomes frustratingly complex and, in the end, perhaps more effectively analysed in terms of its manifestations in performance rather than the intricacies of building a model of how the performance came about. In this, some comfort may be derived from the fact that motivation theory, even in cultures subject to massive research effort, remains still somewhat nebulous.

That the Chinese were traditionally seen as hard-working people is evident from many historical accounts. Sir Thomas Herbert's "infinitely industrious Chyneses" were seen, especially in the subsequent colonial period, as ideal laborers, and reliable intermediaries. Records of their work on plantations attest to their superior industry, and although they were prone to drive a hard bargain, insisting for instance on piece-work, they would produce more than other ethnic groups in the same circumstances. They would also take on heavier and more difficult tasks (Purcell 1965: 342).

One of the components of this trait is what Herman Kahn (1979), in attempting to explain the success of the "post-Confucian" cultures of East Asia, called "seriousness about tasks." He attributed this to a sense of responsibility which reaches unusually high levels, ultimately based on the onus of duty which turns filial piety into practice. In a society where each family is dependent on its own resources for its survival, and where each individual is in turn dependent on family support for so much in life, the person who is not working as hard as he or she might for the common good will come under intense social pressure. With sensitivity to social influence running so high, the only relief will come when prosperity has been guaranteed for the future, a state which few families will concede. It is doubtless this component of duty, which so sharpens the perception of the link between work and reward when dealing with a third party outside the family circle such as an employer.

A further somewhat unusual element of the well-motivated Chinese person's behavior in work is the difficult to define, but nevertheless significant, feature of "perseverance." It is not possible to find research attesting to this, as it appears to have escaped attention as such, but the word captures much that is commonly observed in factories and offices employing Chinese people. There may be something in the idea that the daunting task of learning the Chinese language, with the need to memorize thousands of characters, combined as it is with an unusually disciplined and restraining upbringing, leads the person to a rare tolerance of repetition and boredom, and a dedication to completion of a piece of work.

In Hong Kong, the crane drivers loading containers onto ships operate at substantially higher rates of speed and productivity than those in Western ports. The welders sent to England for training on the complexities of building the very high-tech new Hong Kong Bank headquarters requested to come back after only half the training time allotted and achieved welding quality standards clearly ahead of the rest of the world. Children perspire into the night to achieve examination successes which separate them from other ethnic groups in North America (and lead them into the safe haven of the professions). Factory workers outpace those in South America and Africa, and are renowned for their manual dexterity and speed of absorbing training (Morawetz 1980). The work ethic permeates Overseas Chinese life and, no matter its origins, be they family duty, acceptance of discipline, fear of insecurity, bred tolerance of repetition, or highly tuned pragmatism, its universality is sufficient to make it an expectation of those dealing with them.

Money, Frugality, and Pragmatism

The idea of pragmatism might be explored in conjunction with the question of money, and we may take as a guideline Osgood's comments from his detailed three-volume study of a local community in Hong Kong, that "It is easy to gain the impression . . . that nothing interests the adult population as much as money" and "The delight taken in eating is spoken of perhaps only less often than the desirability of making money" (Osgood 1975: 1061 and 1108). This key essence of life was remarked upon also by Ryan in one of the few detailed studies of Overseas Chinese values, this time in the context of Indonesia (Ryan 1961), but note should perhaps be taken that money-mindedness has commonly in Chinese culture been attributed to southerners, and been seen as part of their somewhat outlandish and uncultured deviance from the central civilization. That most Overseas Chinese come from the peasant and artisan classes of such groups has already been noted (Hamilton 1977: 337), and due allowance should be made for their possibly heightened pragmatism in this regard.

Osgood describes how the child is taught early to value money, to bargain, and not to be easily deprived of it. Those familiar with Hong Kong society will know the naturalness with which it enters conversation and may well have cause to contrast that with Western inhibitions over the subject.

The sophistication which can result is the subject of a classic note by Freedman. In this he attributes the financial skills to three characteristics of traditional Chinese society: "The respectability of the pursuit of riches, the relative immunity of surplus wealth from confiscation by political superiors, and the legitimacy of careful and interested financial dealings between neighbors and even close kinsmen." These latter dealings are commonly described for the Overseas Chinese and in particular the credit associations where ten or so people will join together under a promoter to enter a complex process of mutual help over funding. That these should proliferate, and that a perpetual state of borrowing and lending should be normal, may well owe much historically to the official financial superstructure in which a peasant would have great difficulty borrowing at less than 5% per month. Freedman's conclusion is that such experience must have taught "entrepreneurial, managerial, and financial skills of considerable importance" (Freedman 1979: 26), a point to which we shall later return in discussing business behavior.

The inseparable twin of money-mindedness is frugality, again so commonly found in descriptions of Overseas Chinese norms as to be proverbial. Care must be taken, however, to avoid seeing this in Western terms, within which frugality is often overlapped by meanness. Chinese standards of hospitality, and of sensitivity to the perceptions of others, are such that scrooge-like meanness appears to be extremely rare, and the frugality in question is more a matter of self-denial (and perhaps strictures within the family) than of an unashamed parsimony. It would for instance be almost inconceivable for a Chinese to emulate J. Paul Getty in providing guests with a pay phone.

The frugality owes much to living for so long at the subsistence level, something which has been a feature of Chinese life, since the population explosion of the nineteenth century put most people at or near the breadline (Fairbank 1987). Although prosperity has since attended the efforts of so many of the Overseas Chinese, old habits die hard and wealth cannot be guaranteed to last. In any case, as Clammer (1978) points out, there are still large numbers of Chinese in the region who are struggling to cope with poverty.

Money-mindedness and frugality may be seen as subsets of pragmatism, a Chinese value with broad application but one which resists precise description. It will be argued shortly that (a) Chinese perception is especially "immediate" and sense-based, (b) that Chinese morality is contingent rather than being based on absolutes, and it has already been contended that (c) social control comes principally from one's immediate circle, and (d) dedication to family survival is a

dominating motive for behavior. In these circumstances, the taking of decisions
on what appear as practical grounds is to be expected. The machine operator
who has been expensively trained in a shirt factory may move to a semiconduc-
tor factory down the road for a few more dollars a month because those few
dollars are seen as significant in family terms, and obligation to the shirt factory
is not an issue. The "using" of people for the contacts they can provide,
although it may be cause for Western cynicism, is less so for the Chinese when
everyone understands the rules and reciprocity can be calculated and, in effect,
traded. The network society is designed for mutual exploitation.

Forms of Cognition

No discussion of a culture, even an introductory one such as this, should ignore
the deepest and possibly the most significant layer to which it permeates. This is
the invisible construction of reality which takes place in people's minds and
which almost imperceptibly operates with thought processes which are themselves culturally conditioned. Given the radically different nature of the Chinese
language (and its Japanese derivative) from those of the West, and given the
isolation in which China's cosmology emerged as well as the all pervasive impact
of such a paradigm on Chinese life, it should come as no surprise that Chinese
people "see the world" differently from others. Nor should it be surprising that
the understanding of such a difference presents a formidable challenge. To get
outside one's own world-view sufficiently unencumbered to be able to empathize
with, let alone understand, someone else's is a feat of mental agility beyond
most of us. When the Chinese language is part of the barrier, then the problem is
formidable indeed. All that one can realistically ask for is a suspension of disbe-
lief and a willingness to accept the possibility that certain fundamental processes
of the mind vary by culture. That these differences are significant for behavior,
rather than simply intriguing in their own right, and that they have an impact on
the perception of and eventually the constructing of organizations, are propositions which cannot easily be tested empirically. The idea of such differences is
nevertheless offered to allow an exploration into a contentious and largely un-
charted area, and one which Chinese themselves commonly find difficult to discuss, in unacknowledged, unjustified, and unconscious awe as many of them are
at Western intellectual tradition and science.

    Clifford Geertz, in reviewing developments in anthropology, proposed that it
must be incorrect to see the mental dispositions of man as prior to culture.
"Pure" human nature could not work without the addition of tools, hunting,
families, art, religion, and later, science, and these become ingredients of human thought. Thus "human thinking is primarily an overt act conducted in terms
of the objective materials of the common culture, and only secondarily a private

matter" (Geertz 1973: 83). What constitutes reality for a person is constructed by the social experience which forms his mind (Berger and Luckmann 1966).

Given that is the case, and given in any event that culture is itself now normally defined (inevitably in slightly different ways and contentiously) as lying in the realm of "knowledge" or "constructed reality" (D'Andrade 1984), what follows will illuminate Chinese culture perhaps more significantly than might first be supposed. It is proposed to explore briefly an element which arguably underlies most thought processes and their results in action: the question of how things are understood and the notion of explanation.

Although there is a clear difference between what goes on in a scientific laboratory and the mental world of the man in the street, there is nevertheless some overlap. The "scientific method" and the use of rational logical patterns of thought in Western culture percolate through the education system, and the various levels of literature and communication, to ensure that certain fundamental components of thinking, such as "having reasons," "looking for an explanation," "predicting the consequences," become normal. They are practiced at different levels of sophistication but the main components are retained. In looking at the contrasts between Western and Chinese forms of explanation at the scientific level, therefore, an assumption is made that a more widespread societal phenomenon is being reflected.

How things were traditionally "understood" in China began with the idea of a cosmic order. But whereas the parallel search for a cosmic order in the West, perhaps best exemplified in Newtonian physics, proceeded via the empirical refinement of laws of causation, and the use of the "scientific method," building understanding as it were from the ground up, that in China sought to comprehend the order of nature by fitting everything into a great man-made scheme. This great scheme, exemplified in the Book of Changes, allowed for things and events to be "placed" and notionally understood. The scheme could take account of time, space, and motion, and was founded on the idea of things as groups of relations, and causation as part of the tension between opposites in nature (Needham 1956: 324).

The tenacity of this ancient scheme had in many ways a profoundly inhibiting effect on Chinese science, and Needham's summary of its impact is unambiguous. Although he acknowledges that seeing events in terms of force-fields was fruitful for science, the pre-ordained classification system was not:

The elaborated symbolic system of the Book of Changes was almost from the start a mischievous handicap. It tempted those who were interested in Nature to rest in explanations which were not explanations at all. The Book of Changes was a system for *pigeonholing novelty* and then doing nothing more about it. Its universal system of symbolism constituted a stupendous *filing system*. It led to a stylisation of concepts almost analogous to the stylisations which have in some ages occurred in art forms, and which finally prevented painters from looking at Nature at all (Needham 1956: 336, original author's italics).

And yet it persisted, this cosmic metaphor, and to explain its longevity and its salience, Needham proposes that in a society where "conservancy-dictated bureaucratism" and a passion for the classification of everything were always there, then needs would always exist for a bureaucratic and highly organized cosmology. By using it, humanity and the natural world could be blended. "Both human society and the picture of Nature involved a system of coordinates, a tabulation-framework, a stratified matrix in which everything had its position, connected by the 'proper channels' with everything else" (Needham 1956: 338).

To bring the story up to date, and bring the classificationist theme to life, the reader will perhaps forgive a long quotation from Colin Thubron's recent account of Chinese explanation. It displays eloquently how the quest for understanding can be sent up a *cul-de-sac*.

Labelling: the old necessity. Things should be correctly named, said Confucius, "so the human spirit is not beset by misunderstanding." The imperial Chinese categorised and numbered everything from the Five Colours and Five Tastes to the five varieties of creature (scaly, feathered, naked, hairy, crustacean). Under Communism the prefabricated class labels—Rightist, Leftist, Bad Element (twelve categories), Capitalist Roader, Revisionist—have become cruel substitutes for thought; and the power of the Chinese concepts is perhaps heightened by their embodiment not in a fluid alphabet but in immutable ideograms. Political life is riddled by such definitions and figurework. It is hard for anyone to keep abreast. As early as 1951 the Three Antis campaign (anticorruption, anti-waste, anti-bureaucracy) melted into a Five Antis onslaught on bourgeois businessmen, to be echoed long after by an Eight Antis crusade against intellectuals. Then there were the Four-Pests—rats, flies, mosquitoes, sparrows (later elevated to five by the addition of Rightists)—the Three Loyalties and the Four Infinities, the shining Four Bigs, the pernicious Four Olds, the Three Prominences and the struggle to erase the Three Differences. Schoolchildren embraced the Five Loves and liberals welcomed the Four Great Freedoms until they were expunged from the Constitution in 1980. Others had to cope with "one-struggle two-criticism three-reform" or the "one point two plans tactic." Recently newspapers had advocated the Four Beauties and the Five Stresses—a campaign for hygiene and morality—and everybody was now concentrating on the Four Modernisations (Thubron 1987: 199).

As I write, the press has just announced the pursuit of the Six Evils, and a stark fact about China's capacity to "understand" continues to lie in the background. It is perhaps best described in the words of Joseph Needham who has devoted decades of monumental scholarship to the question.

I regarded the essential problem as that of why modern science had not developed in Chinese civilization but only in Europe? As the years went by, and as I began to find out something at last about Chinese science and society, I came to realize that there is a second question at least equally important, namely, why, between the first century B.C. and the fifteenth century A.D., Chinese civilization was much *more* efficient than occidental in applying human natural knowledge to practical human needs. The answer to all such questions lies, I now believe, primarily in the social, intellectual, and economic structures of the different civilizations (Needham 1969: 190).

In exploring now the intellectual component of that trio of forces, it is necessary to see in perspective the accidental nature of what Graham called the West's "discovery of how to discover" (Graham 1971). The Western scientific method has emerged as the search for a deductive nomological explanation, argued with the utmost logical rigor, supported by empirical data, and constantly reverberating between an abstract and theoretical level and the tangible evidence of the real world. In a delightfully cryptic letter by Albert Einstein, quoted by Needham, the luck involved in making that method normal is noted (Needham 1969: 43):

Dear Sir
Development of Western Science is based on two great achievements, the invention of the formal logical system (in Euclidean geometry) by the Greek philosophers, and the discovery of the possibility of finding out causal relationships by systematic experiment (Renaissance). In my opinion one need not be astonished that the Chinese sages have not made these steps. The astonishing thing is that these discoveries were made at all.
Sincerely yours
Albert Einstein

The West thus had the benefit of this accident, and used it to establish massive technical dominance based on science. We have noted the pervasiveness of the highly classified grand scheme of man and nature used by the Chinese for explaining things, but for further illumination we must also take account of the nature of the Chinese language.

Like Egyptian hieroglyphics which developed at roughly the same time, Chinese script is ideographic. It is a series of pictures, most of them transformed over time but many of them still showing the original depiction of, say, a man, a horse, a field. The total number which a fully literate person might master could reach over 30,000, but for normal literacy a person might be expected to know around 6000. [7]

A language which is essentially graphic may be contrasted with a phonetic language in one particularly important aspect. The graphic language relies for the creation of its components on the medium of the senses. To draw a picture of something requires that it has some tangibility, that it can be "seen." The emergence of purely abstract and non-tangible notions is thus hindered. In the case of a phonetic language, the direct link with the "real" world is broken by the interposing of a shorthand for sound, i.e. the alphabet, from which selections are made and taken, as it were, to a higher level for use in expression. Although this does not in itself foster abstraction, it does not handicap it in any way.

The relative lack of abstracts in Chinese was noted many years ago by Granet in a study of classical Chinese literature (Granet 1920). Nakamura (1964) extended this by noting the lack of "universals" whereby a notion could be transferred as it were to a different level of thinking—the move, for instance, from "sincere" to "sincerity." It would, however, appear to have wider implications than the limitations it might place on abstract theorizing, and to enter everyday conversation as an intriguing sign of the sense-dependent immediacy of Chinese thought processes. Consider this comment by Bloom (1981: 22) on the world beyond the senses:

Chinese and English both have precise means for expressing descriptive statements such as "John went to the library and saw Mary" and for expressing straightforward implicational statements such as "If John went to the library he saw Mary." But Chinese, unlike English and the other Indo-European languages, does not have a distinct means for expressing counter-factual statements such as "If John had gone to the library, he would have seen Mary" as distinct from their descriptive and straightforward implicational alternatives. Chinese, in other words, has no way to mark distinctly that mood which, in English and other Indo-European languages, invites the reader or listener explicitly to shunt aside reality considerations and to portray a state of affairs known to be false for the express purpose of drawing implications as to what might be or might have been the case if that state of affairs were in fact true.

Further to this, and possibly reinforced by a view of the world perceived essentially through the senses, the Chinese notion of reality tends to be one in which situations are perceived as a whole, in all their sometimes paradoxical untidiness, and without the urge to see abstract patterns within them. This "holism" has been remarked on by a number of scholars, as having certain likely effects.

Northrop (1946: 375) described the world perceived through Chinese eyes as an "undifferentiated aesthetic continuum" in which "methods of intuition and contemplation become the sole trustworthy modes of enquiry." Nakamura (1964), in his survey of "ways of thinking," concluded that Chinese thinking displayed five characteristics.

(1) Emphasis on the perception of the concrete.
(2) Non-development of abstract thought.
(3) Emphasis on the particular, rather than universals.
(4) Practicality as a central focus.
(5) Concern for reconciliation, harmony, balance.

Needham concluded that in the Chinese view cause was never thought of as mechanical, as it is for instance in Newtonian mechanics—still so dominant a paradigm in the everyday application of Western science. Instead, cause for the Chinese is a matter of "connectedness," of understanding the mutual, reciprocal interplays between a large array of forces.

An attractive compliment can also be paid here to the Chinese scientific method, and may serve to counterbalance the negative sense of much that has preceded. This is that the world of modern science, and especially branches such as nuclear physics and the bio-chemical study of organisms, have needed a "tao" in which to work. They have found that the Chinese have already been there (Capra 1975, Zukar 1979). Classical Newtonian natural science has had to develop by the incorporation of much more organic ideas, more complex models of causation. As Needham observes:

The gigantic historical paradox remains that although Chinese civilization could not spontaneously produce "modern" natural science, natural science could not perfect itself without the characteristic philosophy of Chinese civilization (Needham 1956: 340).

As Einstein implied, you cannot be critical of a culture for missing out on a miracle, and the inappropriateness of the Chinese approach to understanding for creating an industrial revolution should not, in the world context, be seen too critically. For that reason, it will be salutary to take note of certain strengths in the Chinese approach to explanation, which may otherwise be obscured by the apparent glory of Western science. We need at the same time to return to the mundane.

As Lin Yutang points out, although there is no Cartesian rationality in Chinese science, and although Chinese thinking is holistic, there is nevertheless great value in being able to think about problems as deeply embedded in a context. To be able to assess an entire situation and to learn how to accommodate the nuances of influence of many forces, is often far superior to the naive extraction of supposedly key variables and the attempt to link them causally especially in the social world. For the Chinese, "reasonableness" is superior to "reason" (Lin 1977: 86). A nice example occurs in the context of business planning. Western-type corporate planning has been notoriously unsuccessful the more it has attempted to be scientifically rational (Ansoff 1976). Economics generally suffers the same fate from being unable, or unwilling, to include enough factors in the equations it lives by. The Chinese businessman, thinking in Chinese, does not look for simple explanations torn out of context. Denying the usefulness of formal planning, he prefers to absorb information and to use his intuition to process it. There is evidence from their business success to suggest that this allows for a better match with the complexities of this world.

Footnotes

[1] The author was struck by a comment made to him very confidentially by an elderly professor at the reflective conclusion of a dinner party in Canton: "The thing you must remember about China is that for the past thirty years we have all been acting."

[2] This latter point is no longer valid in parts of Indonesia where Confucian church ceremonies are now being held with prayers, hymns, congregations, preacher, and sermons in a replication of Protestant Christianity (correspondence from Charles Coppel). This feature is interesting for its deviant nature.

[3] In Asia, one might note the following core values: the importance of *omoiyari* in Japan; *kibun* in Korea; *pakikisama* in the Philippines; *krengchai* in Thailand. All represent the capacity to empathize with others, and reflect the delicacy with which immediate social interaction should be handled. They explain much Asian behavior often puzzling to the more direct Westerner.

[4] I am indebted to Gary Hamilton for this observation.

[5] For a discussion of East-West differences in conflict handling, see S.F.Y. Tang and P.S. Kirkbride (1986).

[6] *Prima facie* evidence for this callous indifference to the social world outside, and its extension in a lack of community consciousness, is available in the gargantuan efforts required to prevent litter. Dramatic instances of litter blindness are the uncaring ejection from high balconies of unwanted refuse, including the recent fatal ejection of a bicycle in Singapore, and in Hong Kong of a luckily non-lethal six-foot sofa, and a refrigerator, in all cases from a height of around a hundred feet onto public areas.

[7] It is possible to extract the key meaning from a newspaper article with about 600 characters. Although literacy was by no means universal, and is still not, the script itself penetrated to all areas of the Chinese empire and still acts as a powerful unifying symbol. In particular, it over-rode dialect, and the pronunciation of it varies sufficiently as to make many of the dialects mutually incomprehensible; for instance, five is pronounced *ng* in Cantonese and *wu* in Mandarin.

Chapter 4
Seeing Oneself

Earlier chapters have outlined the facts of Chinese penetration and economic dominance in the region to the south. Also the notion of a coherent economic culture based on Chinese values has been suggested as a contributor to the obvious success. The previous chapter has presented an outline of those constituents of that culture capable of influencing the Chinese self and relationships.

The questions now are: how do those influences manifest themselves in the present-day mentality and behavior of Overseas Chinese chief executives; what kinds of organization result; what kind of society emerges? The remainder of this book addresses those questions.

The explanation is designed to work at two levels. At the first level there are the building blocks, namely the "typical" person including his or her way of relating to others. This level is the subject of this chapter and the next, devoted as they are to self and relationships respectively. They are intended to illuminate the outcomes of the cultural inheritance just outlined in chapter 3.

Following that, more explanation will then be offered about Chinese cultural origins, but this time in terms of societal structures and business traditions. This in turn will serve to illuminate later descriptions of the typical present-day organization, the family business, and the views of society held by businessmen.

Diagrammatically, the framework of analysis and the structure of the core of the book may be seen as in Fig 4.1.

Nature of the Data

The reader is invited to the anthropological experience of entering a village in a culture which may be new to him or her. A few background briefings have preceded the visit, and the skeleton framework of how it works has been explained, but not its moving spirit. We now move among the inhabitants and listen to them explaining their behavior. We hear them talking partly to the outsider, but also discussing things among themselves. The spirit of Chinese capitalism is that set of beliefs and values which lies behind the behavior of Chinese businessmen, and this is an attempt to tease it out and depict it, and in doing so to explain it in terms of the forces which may be argued to have formed it. In later chapters, its implications will be considered.

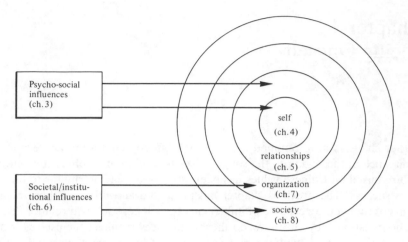

Figure 4.1: Sequence of the analysis and chapter framework

In such a venture, which is neither a straight survey nor a piece of concentrated ethnographic fieldwork, but rather a hybrid of the two, a number of issues connected with the research process itself need to be addressed. They will be considered briefly here to provide, for business practitioners and lay readers, some grounds upon which they may believe what is reported to be genuine and representative. For those with more epistemological concerns, an Appendix provides amplification on the research method *per se*.

There are great problems in researching people's beliefs and values, especially when the topic in question, in this case the managing of organizations, is the subject of a vast store of doctrine and a set of orthodoxies. There is the simple structural dilemma of whether to look at one organization really deeply and then to face the question, "Is it representative?," or to survey many companies, inevitably superficially, and then face the question, "Do we have here the truth?" The underlying issue is that of getting at representative truth. Compounding that problem in this instance is the fact that businessmen do not normally philosophize about their beliefs, and would be likely to find some of the probing puzzling, even unwelcome, something against which to erect barriers in the form of safe but platitudinous statements.

It was necessary to find a method which would allow probing without raising defensiveness and which would be reasonably representative. Above all, it should sponsor discussion of topics which were delicate, rarely articulated, and possibly in some cases not consciously analyzed previously. If culture is the collective programming of the mind, much of that programming may create predispositions which are not perceived until triggered.

The eventual format used for most of the research was unusual. Its intention was the capturing of long conversations. Certain topics would be covered but not in the form of a straight questionnaire. It was what Merton once called an "objectifying interview" (Sjoberg and Nett 1968), i.e. one in which interviewer and respondent(s) would come together as equals to discuss matters of mutual interest which lay somehow "between" them, in this case the Overseas Chinese managing of organizations. The format allowed for the pursuit of ideas and the expansion of topics. Above all, the process was relaxed and unpressured and conducive to rumination, to thinking aloud, to reflection, and, in many instances, to debate.

The majority of these conversations took place over a dinner table, in a private room in a hotel, with three or four people present. Most were tape recorded, and the reporting of them is thus verbatim. These were evening occasions and would normally last $3\frac{1}{2}$ hours: the last 2 hours being recorded, and the first $1\frac{1}{2}$ dedicated to scene setting and social chemistry.

What such research does *not* provide is a neatly arranged set of statistics. It is not intended to. There are ample enough data of that kind already visible in the journal literature, and given in the bibliography of this book. Such surveys do not appear to have taken us much further than repetitive and simple descriptions of professed attitudes. What was being attempted here was an advance beyond that into the realm of reasons. These are much more interesting but much harder to categorize neatly. The precise methods whereby hundreds of hours of conversation were compressed into these four chapters is given in the Appendix, but for those not concerned with methodology, it is perhaps enough to say that (a) all tapes were combed for key statements and reduced to 136 pages of notes, (b) these statements were categorized by subject, (c) the subjects were collected together under four main themes, each making a separate chapter. The guiding principle was to let the businessmen's own responses determine the shape of the findings, rather than a preconceived theory. Having started with very open-ended questions, and then probed and pushed people to roam more widely, a very wide spectrum of ideas was covered. A reconstruction of these in terms especially of the frequency with which they occurred, yields a glimpse of what moves this set of executives to behave as they do.

A hidden feature of such a research method, with its sponsorship of open-ended discussion, is that it also reveals what is *not* referred to. These omissions are often as intriguing as the commitments, and although not analyzable in themselves, will nevertheless provide grounds for reflection during the succeeding account.

In considering the nature of such data, some note must also be taken of what kind of "truth" is being revealed. Even in a relaxed setting, with congenial colleagues, and many barriers down, there will inevitably be wishful thinking, a degree of posturing, the expression of hope rather than reality. As far as possible, steps were taken to find what people really thought: they were challenged;

arguments took place; examples were asked for; statements were probed; amplification was requested; bluff was called; not just by the interviewer but by others at the same table. By this means some excesses were filtered out. Even so, although we have here views which have been stated and defended, we nevertheless have views which do not necessarily guarantee logically consequent behavior. Nor should that be expected.

What we have is "espoused theory." This is distinct, as for example Argyris (1976) has pointed out, from "theory in use." The connections between the values and beliefs of managers, and the kinds of organization they construct, can only be demonstrated in the consistent patterns of those organizations. We will in fact be demonstrating this later and claiming close connections between values and behavior, but by way of scientific concern must point out that (a) what people believe and what they actually do may not always coincide, and (b) there are many other influences on the behavior of organizations than the values of their chief executives.

Before beginning to look at the detail, it will be useful at this point to provide an overview, and for that purpose figure 4.2 outlines a schema for the presentation of all the findings about values. It is important to note here that these combinations of ideas flowed out of the interviews and were not derived independently of them. Classifications of statements fell into these categories, and the connections were suggested by the main arguments made to explain things. This is thus an attempt to reconstruct the mental world of the Overseas Chinese owner-manager, staying as close as feasible to the original expression of it.

In working through the data analysis, a theme kept repeating itself and it serves to unify the overall model. It suggested that there is a state of tension between, on the one hand, (a) the ideals of civilized conduct, paternalism, hierarchy, and familism which the Confucian order inculcates, and (b) the insecurity generated in a society accustomed to despotism and autocracy. This tension is released through the working of personalism, which serves to define an arena for the expression of the higher ideals of behavior and, at the same time, a refuge from the endemic problem of mistrust.

This mechanism for releasing some of the paradoxes inherent in designing a stable society is evident at all levels. At the level of the self, the Confucian stress on role compliance is capable of producing high levels of self-confidence and a subsequent urge to control one's fate, a drive which is reinforced by and able to counteract surrounding insecurity. At the level of relationships, family coalitions counteract the problem of mistrust by the use of extensive networking. At the level of the organization, the patrimonial atmosphere is used to counteract problems of employee loyalty and bonding, by creating personalistic obligation ties. For the society as a whole, mechanisms for the limited but adequate maintenance of horizontal cooperation serve to defuse the tension between the strong vertical order and the divisiveness and suspicion which is permanently latent and in part due to such order.

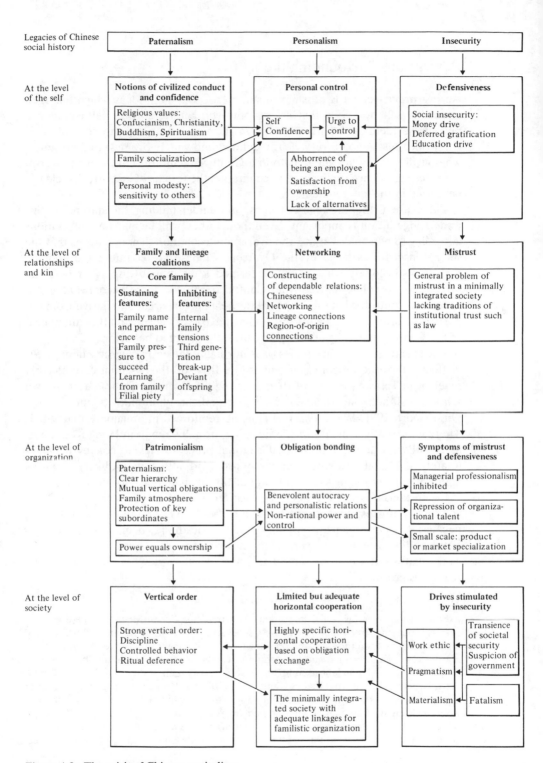

Legacies of Chinese social history	Paternalism	Personalism	Insecurity

At the level of the self

Notions of civilized conduct and confidence

Religious values: Confucianism, Christianity, Buddhism, Spiritualism

Family socialization

Personal modesty: sensitivity to others

Personal control

Self Confidence → Urge to control

Abhorrence of being an employee

Satisfaction from ownership

Lack of alternatives

Defensiveness

Social insecurity: Money drive Deferred gratification Education drive

At the level of relationships and kin

Family and lineage coalitions

Core family

Sustaining features:	Inhibiting features:
Family name and permanence Family pressure to succeed Learning from family Filial piety	Internal family tensions Third generation break-up Deviant offspring

Networking

Constructing of dependable relations: Chineseness Networking Lineage connections Region-of-origin connections

Mistrust

General problem of mistrust in a minimally integrated society lacking traditions of institutional trust such as law

At the level of organization

Patrimonialism

Paternalism: Clear hierarchy Mutual vertical obligations Family atmosphere Protection of key subordinates

Power equals ownership

Obligation bonding

Benevolent autocracy and personalistic relations Non-rational power and control

Symptoms of mistrust and defensiveness

Managerial professionalism inhibited

Repression of organizational talent

Small scale: product or market specialization

At the level of society

Vertical order

Strong vertical order: Discipline Controlled behavior Ritual deference

Limited but adequate horizontal cooperation

Highly specific horizontal cooperation based on obligation exchange

The minimally integrated society with adequate linkages for familistic organization

Drives stimulated by insecurity

Work ethic

Pragmatism

Materialism

Transience of societal security Suspicion of government

Fatalism

Figure 4.2: The spirit of Chinese capitalism

Perceptions Surrounding the Self

As just previewed, it is possible to summarize the main ideas which emerged about the self by saying that a very powerful central core of self-confidence becomes evident, and particularly so in the form of an urge to control. This confidence rests upon a very clearly defined and widely promulgated notion of what civilized conduct amounts to in a Confucian culture. Given this powerful base, the confidence can be used to counteract the threats of insecurity so clearly perceived in the environment.

There are many subsidiary themes, but understanding the nature of this underlying tension is important. Even though there will be many manifestations according to personality traits, the overarching common denominator is that the special insecurities faced by the Overseas Chinese are counteracted and the threats resolved, by what might be termed a disciplined display of personal force. The discipline derives from Confucianism, the force becomes almost a passion to control. That this is special to them may be argued to derive from the particular forms of societal insecurity they have experienced and the uniqueness of the Confucian heritage in shaping culturally accepted behavior.

The teaching of Confucian ideas was normal in the early days of schooling for virtually all of the executives in this study. It is still the essential core of early teaching in Taiwan (Wilson 1970) and among the Overseas Chinese at their own schools in Indonesia, Malaysia, Thailand, and the Philippines (Coppell 1983, Omohundro 1981, Wang 1981). It is being reinforced in Singapore (Tu 1984). There is currently some decline in its being formally taught in Hong Kong, but, as elsewhere where the normal educational process is felt to convey it inadequately, the family itself picks up the burden and, although not likely to put its children to memorizing the books, will instill the main behavior principles.

Confucianism is not a religion as such. It is a set of guidelines to civilized conduct. Many respondents noted that it is "so deep I don't think about it," and because it is not organized with any kind of priesthood, being Confucian does not preclude turning to other religions at the same time, especially Christianity, as we shall shortly note. A typical summary of many views is given by a Hong Kong businessman. [1]

Hse:
I think Confucianism is rather important—it sets a moral code for the Chinese people. Frankly speaking, even though we don't consciously know that we are following Confucianism, in fact traditionally we do follow that . . . and you can observe this by comparing the Hong Kong people and the people in China. Now the people in China because they broke down Confucianism completely—that is why their mentality, their moral standard, is quite different from that in Hong Kong. So far as I am concerned, sooner or later China will bring this back—this moral code—to the Chinese people—although they wouldn't bring it completely. I am now going back to the olden days—trying to find some wisdom in Taoism and Buddhism, looking through these books like *I Ching*. As far as I am concerned, this is a sad thing if it breaks down or disappears completely. Of course,

there are some elements which are out of date, but it at least set a moral standard for the people to follow.

What the moral code is about is behavior, much of it interpersonal or at least that exercised within a limited circle of acquaintances. It is about reasonableness, tolerance, and especially respect for the hierarchy of age. It is also about discipline. Later we shall note other dimensions, and particularly trust.

Hap:
My style under a microscope is basically Confucian. I always take the middle of the road. I have never been known for extremes. Never rock the boat.

Hsiang:
In the Chinese family, they all have to respect their parents and elders—including the uncles and all this—anybody older than you, you know. And we have some traditions—respect for the eldest; to be friendly with people who are the same age; and also help to bring the youngsters up by setting up a model for the young.

Hsiung:
You must be gentle, be honest, and so on. These are the basic things which Confucianism teaches you—to be honest, to be loyal, and be—like—decent. We were taught. We had to memorize the whole book section by section.

Har:
There used to be on my grandfather's desk a Chinese sign—"tolerance." I have this on my desk now. . . . Chinese say "if you can be tolerant a hundred times you will become gold." Now I have done so; this company earned 36 million dollars last year (US $ 4.6 m.).

Among this group of executives, something like 60% clearly espoused Confucianism, and the bulk of the remainder could be said to be acting it out in blending with the rest of society. There was, however, a large and partly overlapping group, of the order of 40%, who were Christian. Much of this derived from being educated at Christian schools, predominantly Catholic, but what is perhaps surprising is the extent to which a religious commitment should be present among a random selection of business leaders in societies which at first glance can appear especially materialistic.

In discussing Christianity, however, few of the executives related it to behavior, except one obviously devout Singaporean chief executive whose dedication to good human relations was clearly more than pragmatic. There was in fact some reticence about Catholicism especially.

Hung:
Religion (Catholicism) is more of a hindrance than a help in business. There are a lot of things we cannot do. There is a lot of struggle inside.

The essential pragmatist was a Taiwanese company president:

Tsang:
I don't have a religion but I try to contact any religion to see if any element can be applied to business management. I feel that Christian songs are helpful for relieving employees' tiredness and exhaustion.

Many were happy to be "mongrels," and the oriental capacity to see blends rather than paradoxes is evident in this description of a mixed Catholic, Confucian, Taoist, and Buddhist heritage.

Ho:
I was born a Catholic. My family was one of the first to get baptised in Shanghai, and for four or five generations had Christian names. My father is very Western. My mother became a Catholic when she married my father. Before that—her family was Buddhist. So I find my mother very strange. She is one of the most devoted Catholics I think. She goes to church on Sundays, makes confession on Fridays, communion—everything. But I find her practice—when I was young—I found it funny. At Chinese New Year saying, "You can't do this, you don't do that. You have to keep together" . . . so for us, when we were young we thought it superstitious, because in the school they would say it was superstitious, so you say, "Mother, you're a Catholic, how come you are still practicing this?" But you find out that it is not superstitious—the culture is part of the Chinese way of living. As long as she doesn't worship any other gods, then it's ok.

Tsai:
My religion is Buddhism, which is really a folk-belief, and I will worship in any temple wherever I see one. It doesn't have a direct influence on the work situation but I apply some of the Buddhist concepts to work, such as the middle way, kindness, optimism.

Of the ten people who claimed Buddhism as their religion, most indicated that their wives had another religion. It became clear that tolerance about belief systems, elasticity about membership, and an eclectic capacity to combine them, are all normal characteristics. About a quarter of respondents professed no particular religion, but of those a significant number referred to a spiritual base which might be identified as Taoist insofar as it dealt with balance, harmony, and reasonableness. "It's important to be spiritual—you tend to care more for people" (*Shen*).

The belief most strongly expressed as a guide to behavior, and one with clearly Confucian underpinnings, was that of sensitivity to other people. Over two-thirds of respondents expanded spontaneously on this, and it is obviously a crucial and central value. It contains two dimensions. Firstly is the belief in humaneness, in understanding the other person's point of view; secondly is the more pragmatic need to be able to "read" other people and to search out their trustworthiness.

The humaneness is evident in principles of child rearing:

Shek:
I would wish my children to be exposed to all sorts of people—to learn humanity . . . I don't want them to be materialistic or mercenary.

and is reinforced by the overwhelming commitment by virtually every respondent that choice of career was up to the children—that it is wrong to dictate to them.

Confrontation is seen as uncivilized, what matters is "empathy—putting yourself in their shoes" (*Shum*), being "like a big ultrasonic machine—bouncing out beams and getting feedback" (*Hap*). Slavedriving will destroy your influence. Small acts of consideration count: "I always drive myself home so the chauffeur can go home early and I drive myself in the evening" (*Hwee*). The first principle in Chinese behavior is tolerance: "Cultivate your temperament, be tolerant—it creates less worries. Try to put the lawyers out of business" (*Shum*).

More pragmatically, you have to learn to read people, another aspect of a society based primarily on relationships.

Shang:
I always use intuition in judging people. Selling to or buying from somebody is a people-to-people thing. In selling, you sell yourself first.

Shum:
I will never do a large deal with someone I haven't met in person, and I will figure out his character using phrenology.

The cultural rules are clear, as are the costs of not understanding them.

Sit:
We went into a joint venture with the Japanese because their approach was more human. Western multinationals are too rational. All they wanted to know was "What is your track record?" "How many engineers do you have?" etc.

In considering humanism of this kind, it would be an error to mistake it for softness, and it does not obviate toughness and discipline where necessary. In an atmosphere of such finely tuned sensitivities, however, the messages conveying tension may well be so subtle that they would be operating at a plane below the range of Western sensitivies, tuned as they are to more overt expressions. Restraint for the Chinese is reinforced by two parallel forces: a moral strain which controls self-indulgence; and the cultivation of a modesty which could in earlier days be taken to elaborately ritualistic lengths in disclaiming personal interest, but which still resides in the notion today of gentlemanly behavior.

Hsin:
I can talk tough, and I can tolerate harsh manners, as long as it is not for self-interest.

The dislike of personal promotion and of showing-off was remarkable for its consistency. Nobody had a Rolls Royce (although there was one solitary respondent with a dramatically more expensive vehicle). Most people drove modest cars themselves, although there might be a company Mercedes.

Hsien:
I have four cars, but not a Benz or a Rolls Royce.

Hwa:
The person I admire has built a very successful empire here and overseas, but in very low profile; as he grows older he'll probably become even more like a Chinese scholar—I mean I don't mind to be like him some day.

Ting:
I drive a Renault, but I may change to a new car if the board decides. In fact, I would rather save the money to allow employees to go to Japan for internship training.

Shum:
I am an ordinary man, with an ordinary life. [Note: founder and builder of a huge commercial empire in Singapore.] Last year I went back to China to pay respect to my ancestors. In my village, the road to the cemetery was a dirt road. The officials there were apologetic and promised me that they would rebuild it. I refused and rejected the idea. I don't want the village of my people to get special treatment because of me.

Reference to modesty should not deceive one into thinking that it accords with a retiring personality. There was naturally a very wide range of characters among the seventy-two respondents, but although some could be said to be of a relatively shy disposition, and some were particularly opinionated and extrovert, in terms of their underlying dispositions, there was one universal drive which united them. It was the most commonly referred to theme in the entire set of conversations. It was the urge to control, to take charge of events, to be master of the situation, and to achieve this by carving out an area of life in which such control could be exercised. Modest behavior is thus a matter of interpersonal style. The underlying predisposition displays a deep-seated self-confidence, over which gentlemanly conduct lays a protective and attractive gloss.

The sources of this urge to control are complex and partly bound up with societal questions to be considered in later chapters, such as mistrust, transience, a sense of threat, perpetuation of the family name. For the moment, it is proposed to consider the statements which convey the remarkable intensity of feeling about being your own boss, about not working for other people. It should also be remembered that the reaction against working under others must be seen in the light of the autocratic and centralized style of decision making typical in most Chinese organizations. In a sense the system, by being hostile to strong minded talent, may force it out, but we precede ourselves and will return to that point.

The search for control was held by a number of people to be a basic instinct, somehow a natural part of being Chinese.

Hu:
I think the Chinese are rather obsessed with power, personal power, and the Chinese managers and owners are very afraid to let go and lose control.

Hoi:
I think it has something to do with the family tradition. In the Western world, family is not a coherent factor, so companies are not handed down; for various reasons, conglomeration takes place much easier. But then, particularly for southern Chinese, the independent spirit of owning a company is somehow very strong.
Question:
Why does conglomeration not take place?
Hoi:
Because somebody will have to give. Give up control.

Shang:
It was my father's influence—to be your own boss. Determining your own fate is important.

Huang:
My grandfather had a saying which he used to tell my father, "The word 'worker' means you can't expect a lot of achievement working for somebody else." There's no good being an employee. [The respondent then went on to draw the ideograph showing a horizontal line which is taken to signify a barrier to upward progress].

Hu:
When my father retired, he handed over the family business to my brother. I worked for him for four years, and it seemed very natural for me to be my own boss, so I branched out . . . I was very young when I started my own business. I was only twenty-three . . . I never thought of working for anybody else but myself or my father. I didn't even want to work with my elder brother. And that happened to me in the case of my younger brother when he came back from Canada. He wanted to work for me; now after two years he's gone on his own. So it is something which is inherent I think.

Hsiang:
I was teaching in a private school . . . I came from a big family, six sisters and six brothers. Each of them owned a business. I am the one without working any business, so I want to run my own business also, so I started.

The reasons offered during these discussions for such independent control tended to fall into four categories: freedom to do what you want; perpetuation of the nuclear family's achievement; search for status; search for wealth. It was common for all four to run together, but they may be inspected separately.

In a number of cases freedom *per se* was an aim in itself.

Huang:
I don't like to work for others, be controlled by others . . . It's the freedom that attracts me, not making more money.

Ha:
I thought if I could do it myself I could successfully run the company, then I would be free to really develop what I wanted to develop. When I was working for somebody, in a way because I was employed by somebody, your ideas didn't get accepted. You have to do instructions you are given.

Hon:
[in answer to a question on why run your own company rather than return to work in a multinational] One of the reasons is the upside potential for financial reward, and I stick to that. The other thing is being your own boss—the freedom of doing your own thing. And there's a certain satisfaction out of achievement that you feel directly.

Heng:
I built up the company over fourteen years and was getting ready to hand it over to somebody, and ran into a problem. I wanted the company run *my* way and wasn't willing to do it any other way. When time ran out I had gone through three professional managers.

Har:
I think to be your own boss is the highest self-respect. I don't see any other position as being superior to being your own boss. The organization I want is an organization that serves my own purpose. More or less an extension of myself.

Another version of the extension of the self is the son and heir, even when, as in this case, there is not one yet present.

Hsia:
I have this idea of building a large corporation and to hand it over to my child. I just cannot accept the idea of having a professional man to take care of the company which I have started. I don't know why. I may even think of getting a son just for this purpose.

A parallel admission came somewhat poignantly from *Hap*, now in doubt as to whether he will have a son, when he confessed to the impossibility of maintaining his present intense dedication without a successor. As we shall note later when considering family—the family name is an important symbol. In many cases, where families had been impoverished by the massive social upheavals so common to the Overseas Chinese, it would be a matter of repairing the family's reputation. "There is always this drive to have my own business—to rebuild the family name" (*Huan*). In other cases, the expression is more pragmatic, and gives evidence of the minimal level of integration in this entirely familistic society.

Hui:
Chinese philosophy is the family, the unit, and the propagation of the family name. They don't like the good things to go to other people, and they would like to have it remain in the family.

The drive for wealth will be examined in greater detail later, but before doing so, its naturalness as a reason for ownership may be noted.

Tsui:
Since childhood, because of my family's economic condition being so poor, I made up my mind to become a businessmen.

Huen:
If you've lived in Hong Kong long enough and talked to people often enough, you get the feeling that it is better to be your own boss. If you're earning a salary, there is only a certain limit you can go, but being a boss the sky's the limit.

Hioe:
When you work for a big company, it's somebody else's company. You are just one of the staff, one of the tools. I would say to myself, "I work hard for this company, and the majority of it goes to the company, so the ultimate benefit to myself is very little. If I have my own company, most of the profit will go into my own pocket."

In a small number of cases, respondents would reveal that the naturalness of their choice of a business career was less a matter of burning desire, and more a matter of "What else do you do?" Many see it as the only option. If you're not professionally qualified and have your eyes set on wealth, then you are, in a sense, backed into it. This is not only revealing of a mistrust in routes to success in large companies, but also, given the normally disadvantaged starting point, of substantial self-confidence and ambition.

Huan:
My grandparents were businessmen, and a lot of their property was confiscated. As a result, we had a period of economic decline for the family. The burden falls on the oldest

son and it fell on my shoulders to rebuild the company name—the family name—again. My father was not able, because of the Japanese war and the communist revolution. If you do not have a degree what can you do? Be a government clerk or a bank clerk? The only option is I have to go into business.

Heng:
I wanted to teach. I like literature. But the revenue limitations were not acceptable. My parents swear that they did not put this into my head, but to prove to myself that I was successful I had to make a lot of money. So there weren't too many fields open to me besides business—so it was the obvious choice.

It has been argued that the Overseas Chinese owner/manager develops as an individual within a field of forces which see confidence, based on deep societal discipline about behavior, pitted against insecurity. The confidence is manifest in a fierce desire for independent control. We now turn to consider the way in which the insecurity is manifest in an extreme form of materialism about wealth, and in a parallel and related fixation on education of the most pragmatic kind. Firstly, let us consider the basis for the insecurity.

As we shall explain later, China's benevolence towards its people was always limited by the constraints of maintaining central domination, and the tradition of a government which could often be more rapacious than responsible is remembered.

Hai:
China has been plundered for centuries by invaders, but they are plundered even more by their own government. The kings and emperors, the republics, the rulers, the warlords, whoever takes charge, the poor folks haven't got a chance. So they mistrust their governments. They don't like their emperors. They are heavily taxed, dominated, ruled. They haven't got a say in running the country or anything. So because of this mistrust they rather look at themselves—do things for themselves—for their own family, for their own future. This is my observation. And that becomes a very selfish motive. This is very apparent even in Hong Kong. Even though it's a British government, they have a certain mistrust . . . They take no pride in citizenship, in public life, no pride. If they are benevolent and philanthropic towards other people, it's because for their own good . . . The Chinese become so self-centered. They rally round their family, their own people, and say "at least I'm doing something for myself."

This outburst was rare in that it shows a Chinese person denigrating the heritage which is normally seen so romantically. There is no doubt that criticism of China (as opposed to criticism of communism) is a matter for inhibition. The more normal response is not to think about such matters; they may be taken to lie below the surface. But as we shall note, the pathos of many family histories brings them to people's minds with some tangibility.

Question:
[in a discussion of the short time horizon for many investment decisions in Hong Kong] Is it a matter of insecurity?
Hon:
Oh, you can say that.

Hong:
It may be, but being ourselves we don't want to analyze ourselves.

The majority of the Overseas Chinese have left China because of either poverty or oppression or both. One of the Hong Kong executives told of visiting the village of Toi San, one hundred kilometers away in China, where he was told by the mayor that although there were nine-hundred inhabitants, their overseas relatives numbered 1,100. Many are the stories which lie behind an exodus of this kind, their settings normally being one of the southern provinces of China, or post World War II Shanghai.

Hoi:
Our fathers' prime years were spent in turmoil—a lot of wars. And they understood the volatility of business, and they want their children to have something they can hang onto, when there's another war. Hong Kong is a transient place. People come here only to escape the turmoil of other places.

Hsieh:
Chinese society is still old-fashioned. We grew up from a poverty situation where the society is very poor, and the family. Life can get away from you, and things bad can happen to your society, and so we don't demand much from society. We are on our own. We work hard, obey—even though we didn't want to—so we could get a living. We don't have dignity. We don't have the rights, to start with. So we suffer a lot.

Hai:
The selfishness of people—I don't think it's entirely their fault. We are on the run all the time. It's ridiculous.

In circumstances such as these, it should come as no surprise that what Lau Siu Kai called "utilitarian familism" should come to typify the social fabric (Lau 1982). Each family is pitted against all the rest in the quest for maximum security, and wealth is the surrogate for that security.

Hai:
Materially in Hong Kong, there is no guarantee, so we all try to grab as much as we can.

Hung:
This is a very mean society in a sense. No protection.

The transience has a further contribution to make to the insecurity. It prevents the development of alternative and non-materialist cultural focuses, thus perpetuating the materialism beyond the point where it might in other situations begin to tail off.

Heng:
You get taken care of in Hong Kong. Fifty percent of the population is in government housing of six-hundred bucks a month (US $ 77). I think Hong Kong people have more residual income than the average American. The drive for material goods is because there is nothing else. The Swiss like the Swiss countryside, the Americans go for politics or a couple of other things. In Hong Kong, you go for a Rolex watch.

Hoi:
[continuing same conversation] But that is not confined to Hong Kong alone. Taiwan, Southeast Asia, in every community it's that way. Overseas Chinese in all these communities are excluded from political power—and the only measurement is how you fare vis-à-vis your compatriots. Their aim is to make money.

This last point, that of being so commonly a guest in a host country, calls forth another feature of defensiveness.

Shum:
As an Overseas Chinese you should not run into trouble with government or with tax authorities.

Materialism will be examined in more detail later, as a societal phenomenon. Concluding this look at insecurity and its effects on the person requires that some attention be now paid to the security surrogates of money and education.

That money is the hub around which most action circulates is a common cliche about the Overseas Chinese. That they understand it with finesse and sophistication is commonly remarked upon. But the literature is silent as to why this should be so, and the somewhat cryptic reflections which now follow from successful practitioners of the art of money making must provide us with notions which are not fully understandable until all pieces of this cultural jigsaw are in place, several chapters hence.

Hoi:
Getting rich is the only yardstick in Hong Kong. People come and go. Nobody thinks of Hong Kong as home. So how do they show that they have made a successful sojourn in Hong Kong? The yardstick is how much they brought in and how much they brought out eventually.

Huang:
Money is the only determinant of your dignity.

Hsieh:
Money is the source of status. I don't like it but that's the way it is.

Huan:
I have a Ford Laser DT548. Literally that means there is no chance to become rich. But my wife says there is another interpretation—you can be rich for five generations. We simply cannot escape from the idea of getting rich.

Heung:
My elder brother has a listed company and is very successful. I learned a lot from him. He used to tell me if you go into business and are successful, one year earning money can equal your whole life earnings working for other people, and that's why you have to start a business yourself.

In an environment where such status is attached to monetary success, and where conversations, media, entertaining socially, relationships, are all regularly reflections of the same drive, the process itself can become intoxicating.

Hong:
In my case, I would say wealth is definitely, initially, the top first priority. That's the driving force, and later on—maybe—will be enjoying the process of making money. You know, the process, because you're already accustomed to the way, to the action, to everything that you see, you do, everyday. You enjoy it.

Approximately three quarters of respondents acknowledged money as a significant motive, even when not always happy to confess it as their own, then certainly for the surrounding society. A milder fixation, but a fixation nonetheless, was on gaining as high an education as possible, but with a condition. It had to lead to a practical profession such as medicine, engineering, law, business. There was a clear bias towards science over arts, not only in their own backgrounds, many of which were distinguished (seven had doctorates), but also in the way they spoke of their children's education. "I don't care what he does as long as he goes to MIT" (*Hoi*).

The typical case which will stand for the rest is a Singaporean industrialist.

Shang:
My father put very high stress on education, especially science and engineering. I have two brothers, one is a computer scientist, the other a surgeon, and I did electrical engineering at Stanford. I have four sisters, three with engineering degrees and one a dietician.

Very often higher degrees are able to provide a fallback position, another option in case of need. Members of the sample included a medical doctor, a university teacher, a veterinary scientist, a lawyer, the holder of a masters degree in Fine Arts, all of whom preferred the world of business. Even so, for many, perhaps less ambitious financially, or perhaps not so burdened with the responsibility of being the eldest son, the professions are the preferred refuge, the ultimate solution to the problem of security, if not for them personally, then for their children.

Footnote

[1] The data are presented as verbatim quotes straight from the tape, usually as single statements, but occasionally also as conversational exchange. No informants are identified by name, but instead a system of alias names is used in order to preserve some threads of connection between the statements of a particular individual about different topics. Another form of coding conveys the country where the respondent lives and works: all names beginning with H are from Hong Kong; with T from Taiwan, with S from Singapore, and with I from Indonesia. For more details see Appendix.

Chapter 5
Life in a Networked Society

Life in a collectivist and group-dominated society means that the Chinese self is not isolated in the same sense as the Western one. Other people are bound up into the identity of any single Chinese person, and the relationships are carried round as part of the person. He or she is inextricable from that network and not really understandable in isolation. One of the early problems in the development of mainland tourism recently was the Chinese inability to understand the notion of single rooms—why would anyone want to be so alone?

At the root of this need for a network are two primary, and connected, forces. Firstly is the insecurity which emerges in a society living traditionally close to the subsistence level, and where officialdom's behavior is unpredictable and not always benevolent. This tends to heighten the importance of knowing people who can be trusted, and of course greatly strengthens the centripetal pull of family.

Secondly, the forces of modernization which tend to introduce institutions, such as law, bureaucracy, contract, and other means of resort when trust fails or is unavailable, have not yet moved to a point where the old-fashioned means of coping can be abandoned. Certainly this is still the case in China; and emerging from that culture, the Overseas Chinese have carried with them the appropriate instincts to make life workable, but it is also still true for many Overseas Chinese contexts. Less so than in China, but governments are still perceived as interfering, lawyers and contracts are not natural parts of Chinese business behavior, and institutions are not yet depersonalized. It is a form of society which remains "old-fashioned," consciously so, and in many instances with good reason.

The heart of the matter is trust and dependability. For this to run smoothly requires either a supportive network of emotional ties based on long-standing, complex obligations, such as are found in a family setting; or a stable system of identifying more distant others in a context where psychological pressure is on them to behave honorably. Typical would be a lineage network where membership is valuable to individuals, and being an outcast thus a severe sanction. The Overseas Chinese use both these means to generate dependability.

For executive behavior, it is very difficult to establish which of the two—family or external network—is more important. References to them are about equal, and this would suggest that, at least in the context of business, they both have a significant impact on the thought processes of the Chinese owner-manager.

It should not be taken that such connections are entirely beneficial. Although clearly the access to people who are trustworthy will in general bring benefits to the organization, there are many hazards in the way of the smooth functioning of such processes. Tensions inside families can lead to much behavior which is against the organization's best interests. The use of networks based on regional or extended family loyalties will inevitably create cliques, and factionalism will undermine cooperation in all sorts of ways, most of which are invisible, often frustratingly so.

We begin this account by considering the question of trust, as discussed by the seventy-two executives, before analyzing their perceptions of the two major responses adopted in pursuit of it, the use of family, and the building of networks.

There is a fundamental notion in traditional Chinese culture which says that honesty is an essential part of the righteousness which permits a person to claim the status of a gentleman or lady. This position of respect may be attained by anyone regardless of social status. The gaining of face is more through decency of behavior than through mercenary achievements. As such, the inculcating of righteous behavior is a proper and natural concern in childrearing and in the building of norms via popular culture.

Shek:
I came from a broken home. My father had many wives. My mother was a seamstress, and kept seven children that way. We were poor and I even shoplifted once at the age of thirteen. Then I learned how to talk to myself. . . I got my philosophy of life from Cantonese movies and dramas; they are all about honesty, righteousness, and things like that. . . You have to be honest. Recently, one of my staff members told a small lie to a client to get our company out of an embarrassing situation. I immediately rang the company to tell the truth which was that things had gone wrong because my company had forgotten to pay a bill.

Hsu:
I cherish the idea of fairness, and this is very much my father's influence.

Hu:
I think for all children—all Chinese children—you mustn't tell lies. It's a big crime. You know we try never to tell a lie. I think this is the first thing that we have to learn.

Such notions are of course reasonably universal in all cultures, but it is interesting to see that, in the Chinese case, a thriving popular culture, in the form of the Cantonese drama and the prolific output of the Overseas Chinese film industry, is still focussed on these very straight messages about rectitude, probity, and honor and regrettably also, vengeance. The traditionally clothed heroes, heroines, and villains who so populate the television and cinema screens of the region, using a dramatic style which reminds Westerners of the caricature-like posturing of pantomime, the medieval mystery play, or Victorian melodrama, are in fact promulgating the Confucian interpretation of honor. More interesting than that fact itself is the high level of sustained dedication of Overseas Chinese people to the absorbing of such messages. The stability and discipline of their societies suggest in turn that the messages do not go unheeded.

The ideal of gentlemanly behavior, in the Chinese case, traces its origins to a period which contained central ideals of chivalry, and of duty. Unlike the chivalry of mediaeval Europe, however, the duty is more likely to be directed toward some specific part of the social fabric rather than towards some abstract noble cause or vocation. This is reflected in the comments of an executive about the respect a boss might expect to receive from subordinates.

The conversation was in regard to business relationships which operated along networks of friendship.

Hwa:
The owner might do foolish things, but if he betrays a friend, then he would lose respect. If he is loyal to a friend, then he keeps the respect of the workers. But if he goes to girlie bars every evening, he is still respected, as long as his company is doing well. [Note: i.e. as long as his behavior is not wasting money and threatening workers' livelihoods, a point similarly made about gambling.]

This latter comment on sexual morality is not a universal reaction, and although prudishness was never evident among respondents, there was nevertheless an impression among several that active behavior on the nightclub circuit would not gain you any face among the true arbiters. In a situation revealing of the persistence of old values, one respondent (acting this time in the role of academic accompanying a group of businessmen) had been seen in the company of one of the more adventurous executives and a number of nightclub hostesses. It was made clear to him subsequently that such behavior could be just about tolerated in a businessman but not in a professor. The fact that he had preserved his innocence was of no account. Appearances matter.

The ideals of trustworthiness and reliability, or integrity, of behaving in an honorable manner, are reinforced by an essential and very common element in collectivist societies such as this, namely reciprocity. Throughout the Far East, the making of a civilized person is a matter of making sure that person understands obligations and is sensitive to the subtle balancing of forces which maintains social life. This is strengthened further when such maintenance may well prove to be a determinant of survival (at least in the earlier conditions in which the values formed). This raises the criticality of interpersonal sensitivity—the invisible antennae—and is commonly the central theme used to explain Oriental cultures to Westerners. In the Chinese case, this is conveyed in the notion of face; in the Japanese, *omoiyari* most simply translated as empathy; in the Philippines, *pakikisama*; in Korea, *kibun*; in Thailand, *krengchai*. In all instances, the properly acculturated and thereby civilized person, the one who can set an example to others, is above all else able to read and to emit the signals which govern the interchange of one obligation for another. This is what makes the networks purr, and it is the subject matter for much of Chinese ethics.

One Hong Kong respondent (*Hsui*), prefacing his discussion of this with the comment that "I lay more emphasis on ethics than anything else," went on to describe how he had begun in Hong Kong in 1949, after escaping from Shanghai, and started a small factory in a two-tenement flat. An export business had been built using Hong Kong export agents to manage the marketing process. Now production volume is such that it would be economically much more rational to sell direct to large distributors in the USA, from whom such requests come in a regular stream. Although this would yield higher profits to his company, each request is refused and he continues to market through the export agents who helped him get started about forty years earlier. For him, this is an ethical issue.

Such anecdotes are common, and are regularly attached to the heroes of the Overseas Chinese business world. Li Ka Shing, now the pre-eminent Chinese businessman in Hong Kong, is renowned for such loyalties. A knowledgeable commentator in Singapore (*Shum*) noted that "it's credibility that matters. Robert Kuok of Malaysia, Liem Sioe Liong in Indonesia—they have integrity. With a good reputation, people will trust you, and the business will grow."

A fine distinction in such matters was made by another hugely successful Singaporean chief executive (*Sit*) when he noted that "What matters is credibility for a trader, business ethics as a manufacturer." What is meant here is that a commercial trader depends more on the reliability of himself (as opposed to his products). As *Hsu* pointed out, "If I lose my reputation, then I lose all the capital that I have." Money is commonly borrowed from friends on trust, and transactions often of great size are also dealt with by common understanding and a small note jotted in the diary.

For manufacturers, ethical questions more normally surround different issues—product quality, a usually restricted set of buying and selling relations, and of course, employment issues. The tone of responses is conveyed in *Hsing*'s comment on honor with suppliers, indicating as it does also a concerted response by a trade network:

At one time, the Hong Kong spinners bought cotton from East Africa. Suddenly the prices collapsed but the spinners honored every contract. We honor what we do. In manufacturing, others might fail but there are very few dissatisfied people who buy from Hong Kong.

In employee relations, fairness for many executives was obviously an ethical issue, and underlay much of the paternalist welfare which will be evident in chapter 7. The ethical point was the denial of selfishness, as *Hsing* pointed out. "None of my staff have grudges against me. I have never tried to maneuver deliberately against anyone for selfish benefit."

An inevitable outcome of processes of this nature is the division of the people with whom one might deal into two categories, an in-group of the trustworthy and an out-group of those with whom trust has not been established. This latter might further be subdivided into those with whom trust *could* be established, given time and opportunities for reciprocity to build, and those with whom trust under the normal Chinese rules is unlikely to develop. In this latter category are the bureaucrats of the more rationalistic, usually foreign, banks, many foreigners in multinational corporations ignorant of Chinese cultural norms and also probably transient government officers constrained to be impersonal, and perhaps also, far different reasons, members of Chinese sub-groups, clans, or competing families whose loyalties are not negotiable with any degree of reliability.

This is most obviously evident when it comes to sharing power in the boardroom. When considering who really has a stake in the company, *Hai* observed:

It is often more a matter of trust than of contribution. Who can you trust? An outsider can betray you, so certain powers cannot be given to an outsider.

Similarly, as *Hwa* noted, "It's very much an insider game for the Chinese when they have this family sort of business, right?" The issue is very basic and very simple:

Hou:
I know a lot of Chinese companies that put relatives into key positions because—if you're my brother, you can't run away with my money.

The boardroom will inevitably be the last bastion of the war of attrition as modernization and economic development gradually rationalize and depersonalize the business world. Although, in the Chinese case, the course of this war may not run similarly to that elsewhere, and although it may take much longer to have an effect, nevertheless changes are evident.

Hsian:
[discussing investment to support the company] In my father's days, he asked friends— basically people from the same vicinity. In my generation, if the company is in need of money, most probably we would go to a bank first, rather than a relative. In previous generations, most Chinese were afraid of banks, and afraid of getting into debt with banks, because they cannot be trusted. They are outsiders. Because banks mean strictly business—there is no emotion involved. If they want to foreclose, they have the law behind them, whereas if you go to a relative or a corporation that is friendly to you, they won't see you sink. They'll give you a real hand.

Before seeing this as a sign that capital raising has now moved to a Western model for the Overseas Chinese, two features of their business would need to be acknowledged. Firstly is the tendency of many Chinese banks to lend on the basis of trust rather than hard statistics, and banking is thus not as coldly rational as it might first appear. Secondly is the commonly espoused insistence by many Chinese companies to fund themselves and to use banks simply as somewhere to place money.

Given that trust and dependability based on social obligations rather than contractual relations are central to the understanding of Overseas Chinese business, we now turn to an examination of the two mechanisms used to exercise this necessary process, namely the family and the networks. In considering the family, it will be looked at, following the way it was discussed by the respondents, firstly in terms of the forces which maintain its importance, then in terms of its workings. Its workings are seen in terms of those features which tend to sustain familism in business and those which tend by contrast to inhibit it. These latter are the explanation for the constant bubbling up of new families in the economy and the difficulties of sustaining a dynasty for more than the notorious third generation.

There is clearly an element of "face" attached to the family name for many Chinese entrepreneurs, such as to provide a substantial motivation towards its enhancement. The matter was discussed openly by about a third of the respondents.

Har:
I think for Chinese we normally worship the grandfather, or the father. We cannot argue with our parents ever. Everything they tell us we just got to follow, we can't answer back . . . it's a kind of admiration. That's why whenever I do a thing, I've got to think "I cannot ruin my family's name." I've got to do honorable things. I've got to do good things. It has a good impact for me.

Chinese philosophy being "the propagation of the family name" (*Hui*), there is the inevitable attempt to create dynasties. *Hsien* in discussing his son noted that he had written to his grandmother saying he supposed sometime in the future he would join the firm; *Hai* then commented, to *Hsien*'s agreement, that it was probably the grandfather who wanted the child to run the business, not for the sake of being a businessman, but to keep the family name. *Huan* has a clear mission to "rebuild the family name" after the confiscation of its property in China, and was full of admiration for a young Jewish entrepreneur he had worked for, who "was twenty-four and had rebuilt his family name by expanding his father's company." According to *Hsien*, an executive's loyalty is "first to the company name," for as *Hou* pointed out, having observed from the inside a dramatic and very public corporate collapse, "The reputation of the family name is critical. Even though financially they're in trouble, the reputation of the old man is still there."

A dramatic instance of how such reputations are protected was visible in Hong Kong when the Chao family in 1986 sold its collection of antique porcelain, the passion of its founder and a collection taking decades to build. This was because the collapse of the shipping industry had brought the family to its knees financially, and it insisted on dealing honorably with the debt. The contribution of the sale to solving the problem was quite insignificant, but as a gesture towards maintaining the honor of the family name, it made a deep impression on the business community. Not all those financially troubled take the next plane to Taipei or Vancouver.

One of the side effects of this impressive hauteur is that the criteria for judging contribution to the company may displace normal rationality somewhat:

Hai:
You see there is no sin worse than betrayal in a Chinese family. A son is expected to be loyal. If he is a lazy bum, if he doesn't perform, that's fine, as long as he doesn't betray the interests of the family.

This potentially debilitating tolerance finds its intriguing opposite in the dynamism visible in *Hsia's* make-up, starting as he did with parents who were "just workers," achieving a doctorate, now building his fortune, and explaining that "I had no family name to take care of. I could do anything I liked."

The permanence of family is a concern which clearly reflects the perception of its role as a mini welfare state, and with that the need to transmit security to future generations. "Wealth is a foundation for the next generation" (*Sit*), and the reasoning is as follows:

Hai:
For thousands of years we have had a system where a person could never retire without fear of death or starvation, or the children uncared for. So everybody has to accumulate some wealth to guard old age. That is universal for all mankind. But the Chinese believe in a certain permanence for their family, for their name, so that if there is a business, it can be carried out like a dynasty.

Without this motivation, as *Hap* pointed out,

If I stop trying to have kids, my goal will be different. I will be more relaxed because I have nobody to give it to. Once I have a kid, no amount of security will be enough.

Sung remarked on the emotional pride he felt in the link between family lineage and corporate identity, and this was also expressed by *Shing* as a reason for property development: "What we build will remain there for years to come." The search for permanence is often expressed in the drive towards ownership of property and the subsidiary enjoyment of the founder's name on the building— not an entirely Chinese obsession admittedly but one exercised with a noteable lack of inhibition. In a more immediate and more tangible sense, however, the permanence of family is perhaps best represented in *Sit's* description of the way every Sunday all members of the family gather at his home for lunch and dinner. This set of sons, daughters, grandchildren, brothers-in-law, nieces, nephews would normally make a group of thirty to forty, week after week, year after year, generation after generation, for as long as their highly cultivated social skills, and deeply embedded social mores, can sustain it.

The sustaining of family, and particularly the sustaining of its overlapping counterpart in the economic world, the family business, is a matter for the playing out of a battle between the opposing forces of construction and destruction. On the constructive side are the three forces of (a) filial piety, (b) pressure to live up to family expectations, and (c) family training. On the destructive side are (d) family tensions which eventually emerge with new generations, and (e) the dysfunctions of nepotism which reveal themselves, according to common folklore, in the third generation.

The somewhat old-fashioned phrase "filial piety" is the subject of comment by about half the respondents, and there is universal agreement as to its nature and its significance. It contains two focusses of obligation, the first and most obvious being to the father. The second is to the family at large.

The view of the father, already somewhat worshipful in the classic Confucian manner, is added to by a sense that there is a burden of work to be taken up.

Hsien:
If you don't take over, your parents—or people in the previous generation—have to slave away. Then the filial piety aspect of it comes into play.

Sung:
I took over when my father had a stroke. I'm the eldest son. I had to.

Im:
I'm not an employee of someone else because of an obligation to all the family to keep the firm running.

To:
I came back to Taiwan [from the US] because of my father's health . . . I had a chance to be with my parents again and there was some satisfaction in that, but my wife had to give up a very good job in the US and that was something I feel sorry about. I also made a financial sacrifice, as I could make more money doing my own business in the US.

Children feel this pressure at an early age, although there is an overpowering sense, in the responses, that children should not have such a choice forced on them.

Tin:
As the fourth generation in this business, I felt great pressure to work in it, but I don't wish to bring that kind of pressure on my own children.

This is clearly a paradox of some magnitude and suggests that the obligation is left to penetrate by innuendo, or example, rather than being made explicit.

Hse:
You don't tell them exactly what to do. The priority is for them to have sufficient education that they then choose. My son feels—inwardly—that he has the responsibility to take up my business—eventually . . . He always feels that he's got the pressure that he should pass examinations, and do my business . . . He's the only one (son), so he's got this kind of natural feeling.

Similarly with *Hu*, whose son was ten at the time.

It's happening with our son already. Because my wife is also a director of the company, so we discuss business every hour of the day. When we are in the car we discuss business, and one day after a very involved discussion we didn't realize that he was standing behind us in the car, with his two small hands on both sides, and he was listening very intensely; then he was already offering suggestions to company problems, he was making observations.

But he has been doing that since he was seven . . . He feels that he has the responsibility to take over the company from me, but sometimes when he has got other attractions, maybe after a movie and he has seen some pilots, he will ask, "Is it really necessary that I take over the company?"

The problem of the nonconforming son will be considered later, but he is less typical than his conformist counterpart who is aware in many cases of parental sacrifices made on his behalf, of parental pride, and of the wide net of obligations. Much of *Huan*'s motivation was that "My parents had suffered quite a bit in financing me in that period" (of education). *Sung* wanted to "make the company something my parents would be proud of." *Hon* explained his obligations:

My thinking was that I always wanted to conserve some wealth so I could look after other members within the family net. There are my brothers, three in China, and my parents. My wife has seven brothers and sisters, all in Hong Kong. That is all within the family.

Once the individual is committed to the family business, and regardless of whether he is the chief executive or in another role, the tendency is for behavior to be loyal and dedicated. For the chief executive, his performance creates or denies him face with his family. Because of the ownership structure, it is not the anonymous market which judges him, but the people whose personal money he is using. Success itself brings a tightening of obligations, as he becomes an example to others within the circle.

Hon:
I am not allowed to do anything wrong. There are so many relatives who point me out to their children and say, "Look at him."

For the more junior family members joining the firm below the level of the chief executive, obligations are also understood.

Hsing:
There are some advantages in employing a family member, because perhaps the member can devote all his time and effort, be willing to work overtime, help you.

A subtle means whereby the idea of commitment to the family can be enhanced is the training of family members by other family members. In this case, not only is the mind shaped to think along certain lines but also Chinese deference to the teachers would equally cement the bonds of obligation. This process is informal and unstructured. It is also long lasting and can begin early. It takes place in two main locations, the workplace and the family dinner table.

Hap started to go to his father's factory at the age of 12. *Huan* "spent most of my time when I was young moving around the factory and got used to the idea of manufacturing. I was doing that kind of work when I was six or seven." *Hon* described his learning as follows:

My father and grandfather were both in business. It's in your blood. I was very young when conversation began. My father was in manufacturing, and the treat we had on Sunday was going out to the factories. At nine or ten years old I was being baptized in the business environment. My father came home and he talked to people on the phone—it's on business. You can't get away from it. Most of the time we go out for dinner with friends—my father would be talking business . . . That influences you directly. You over-hear conversations about making deals, profits, losses. My father was hit very badly one year because of a bank crisis—1964—and for weeks on end I see my father with a long face—bankers calling him up.

The family dining table is in many cases almost a permanently running business seminar. *Hsing*'s father kept on lecturing him and "always philosophized at the dinner table" about business matters. *Hsieh* who was the youngest of five brothers "mostly learned about business from the dining table—my brothers and my father would talk about the office—they would always talk business." *Hsien* reported that his wife "is sometimes very angry with me" for perpetuating his own family tradition and talking about business over the family dinner table, the place at which he says he was "subconsciously educated."

In all this, it is naturally the father who is the principal mentor. *Shen* was brought up by her father to be familiar with business functions, meeting people, travel. *Hu*'s father "taught me very little apart from business as far as I can remember." But often the lessons are more subtle and indirect. The rather aloof ideal of fatherhood in the Confucian culture could lead to a combination, as reported by *Sung*, of "respect and love from a distance," and "striving to think and behave like him."

Obligations to family are thus reinforced by societal messages about filial duty, by peer group pressure, and by training within the family. Such under-standings about obligation, however, are not always enough to guarantee the long-term survival of the company, and the Chinese family business remains, in historical perspective, a somewhat impermanent structure. Company histories go back decades rather than centuries, and even in the context of China, where economic change has been slower in pace, the longevity of companies pre-war was commented on more for its rarity than its presence.

Searching for the sources of this weakness, at least those attributable to socio-cultural determinants which come to rest in the institution itself, it is possible to isolate two, namely (a) internal tensions, and (b) the inefficiencies of nepotism. Both were widely acknowledged among respondents.

In understanding the internal tensions which exist within many Chinese family businesses, it is necessary to begin with the wider perspective. Despite feuds between members, when it comes to dealing with the outside world, a united front must be presented. Inside the boardroom, the debates may be vicious, voices raised, much anger and exasperation displayed, but on walking out into the public domain, there has to be a display of camaraderie, of bonhomie, of mutual respect, of order.

Hsien:
The family may apparently be feuding but when it comes to the crunch, it's "the family has to fight against the foreign invasion" type of mentality.

The sources of tension lie in the generation gap, and secondly in the eventual rivalry of siblings after the initial, usually strongly dominant founder has left the scene. References to a too conservative earlier generation are less common than to sibling rivalry, but this may be partly attributable to the traditional reticence about criticizing the usually revered old. Indications of it, however, are visible in the occasional rueful confession that all is not entirely harmonious between father and sons. Given the autocratic tradition from which many fathers emerged, and given the exposure of many sons to more liberal notions of freedom and self-expression (often gained in long years of Western education abroad), it is not surprising that some are not always willing to conform, or to accept years of subjugation. *Hsui*'s eldest son was an artist, as was also *Shum*'s—discussed regretfully for having insisted on pursuing his own artistic career elsewhere.

He hated whatever I'm doing. It's tragic. Of course, I would like him to come to Singapore and get involved in business, but if I force him, he may ruin my business. So I have to let go. What choice do I have?

Hon in discussing the son of one of Hong Kong's most successful entrepreneurs observed that he had refused to come into the business, had also qualified in an artistic field, and gone to live in Canada where he now runs a very successful business of his own, started from scratch.

The intriguing link in stories of deviant sons is that they tend to deviate into the arts—symbolizing perhaps the desire to be as far away as possible from the father's world of business. It is perhaps some indication of the intensity of generational conflict which can arise given a loosening of the traditional pressures to conform.

But even when conformity is achieved, the younger generation is unlikely to be entirely subdued in the face of the elderly cliques which may retain power and retain also their old-fashioned methods and attitudes. As *Im* in Indonesia reported,

I often buy new machines with my own money in order to prove to the old people that I can have better plans and strategies than them, even without their support.

Very often the transition of a company from father to son is indicative of the degree to which the heir's ideas have been bottled up and suppressed. Thrown out are the little hard seats with marble tops, the abacuses are replaced with calculators, the old typewriters with pc's, the brown timber grain walls are redecorated in pastels, and the company notepaper redesigned. The one feature which seems not to change is the crowding together of the desks of the clerks—a universal index of the sensitivity about costs and efficient use of space.

As well as tensions which run in a vertical direction between generations and thus between layers in the hierarchy, there are tensions which run horizontally between brothers, sisters, and later between cousins, and in-laws. These tensions proliferate as the coordinating dominance of a central figure begins to disintegrate, a process which can occur with time and over disputed blocs of power, but also with the increasing complexity of the organization, should it begin to expand into new products and markets. Such is, as *Hsieh* remarks, "The usual situation. The father dies and the children, when they are, say, forty-five to fifty-five—they have different ideas and they don't want their brothers to interfere. The second generation gets weaker and weaker."

The disunity begins to show as children begin to set up their own families, thus producing competing focusses of loyalty. One Singapore chief executive from a family of eight children, in which only the boys inherited shareholdings, complained bitterly of the time wasted in dealing with the incompetence and maneuvering of his brothers. Another similarly attributed the loss of his hair to "petty fights and canteen politics" within the family.

Although such tensions can often be contained, and although there are inevitably many cases where a succeeding chief executive is as skilled and dominant a coordinator as his father, there is nevertheless a tendency in the third generation for the sons of the original brothers to split the organization, or to start the whole sequence afresh on their own. It is a somewhat rare case when a large family remains united and tightly networked over five or six generations. This was remarked on with amusement by a member of one of the very few successful dynasties in Hong Kong, able to trace its power back over a hundred years. Discussing sources of funding he said,

Heng:
In my family it turns out that the whole family is into it—it's incredible. One of my uncles walked into one room one day for a business meeting and he was so disgusted—there were so many Hengs there, he walked out saying, "Sorry I must have walked into the wrong place."
Hoi:
[commenting] That's why it's grown into such a big business—but it's an exception.

The tensions which exist between rivals in organizations such as the Chinese family business might be argued to be constructive if they led to the rational and data-supported debates (albeit bitterly and no doubt politically fought) between professionals in a bureaucracy. In that case, something constructive might emerge, as is commonly the case when, say, the marketing director has expansive and expensive plans, the finance director won't agree the expense, and an accommodation is reached which moves the organization forward without destabilizing it. Regrettably it is more often the case in the more incestuous context of the family business that rational pursuit of organizational goals gives way to factionalism, emotion, jealousy, back-biting, and a displacement of organizational interest by sub-unit, i.e. sub-family, interests. Smooth coordination across any degree of complexity in the Chinese family organization appears to be unnatural, and growth is via diffraction, subdivision, and disintegration of the original framework into mini replicas of itself.

All such problems which arise from internal power struggles grounded in ownership rather than performance, come back to the issue of nepotism. This topic was understandably referred to with some diffidence by many respondents, nepotes themselves, although they would discuss other organizations than their own in those terms very readily. The typical case is that of the Singaporean industrialist with four sons and three daughters, all of them technically qualified, and all of them in the company. A revealing extra element in this case, however, is that he was keenly aware of the third-generation problem and had made a joint venture with the Japanese to ensure the maintenance of managerial quality. Speaking of the Japanese, he observed, "*They* will not fail. My grandchildren will be ok."

A less clearly focussed set of relationships, perhaps more typical of companies established longer, is visible in the manufacturing company in Indonesia, with five-hundred employees where the chief executive had two aunts as directors, an uncle as production manager, an uncle as finance manager, and a brother-in-law as marketing manager. The complexities surrounding his role are almost tangible, and he felt clearly the limits to his discretion.

The inhibiting effect of nepotism on the organization is due to the single fact that the person may not be the best person available to do the job. Underlying this is the problem that he or she may fall into the mental trap of thinking, perhaps subconsciously, that they do not have to try very hard. Evidence for this latter possibility is in fact scant, and pressure on people in Chinese society to meet their obligations is such that attitude problems of this kind seem exceptional. What is more likely to be the culprit is not attitude but ability—something which cannot be guaranteed by inheritance. It is perhaps the awareness of this which lies behind the universally espoused idea of letting children make their own choice of career, guiding them perhaps, but not dictating.

Hsui:
I have seen many failures in that respect. I have had friends who have had to sell their business because his children didn't like it.

The central dilemma of the rationality of professionalism versus the dedication of personalism is put by *Hai.*

You see when you have a family business that hires an outsider, you expect that outsider to not give his heart and soul. If it proves that he is doing very well, and being very loyal, then he may gradually be assimilated and become part of the family. It is very difficult for the outsider to prove himself. This is a dynastic mentality and it's ruining a lot of family businesses—because there is bound to be a bad generation.

So far in this chapter, we have considered the way in which questions of trust are dealt with by resort to family. It is now necessary to enlarge the boundaries to look at network systems in society at large. Clearly the intensities of obligation will begin to cause a separating of people into concentric circles of trustworthiness. It is necessary to understand the basis on which membership of these circles is maintained. Because the circles themselves will be different from individual to individual, some people being for instance more "clannish" than others, no clear universal pattern will appear. There are, however, certain widely held attitudes which are revealing, and to elicit them, it is proposed to examine the way in which two major sets of connections are viewed. Firstly are the clan or regional identities, second the personal obligation networks which are not based on shared region of origin but more on the accidents of meeting people at random and wishing to establish a connection with them. A third much more general category, of more significance in some countries than others, is the unifying force of Chineseness.

Regional identity may be understandable using the analogy of sub-groups in Western societies which have been built of emigrants. The sense of being Irish in Boston, Italian in Chicago, Spanish in Sydney, German in Milwaukee, Greek in Melbourne, begins with a shared language and much shared experience, particularly of upheaval, of deprivation, of striving, of needing to help one another. Eventually the identity becomes less fierce, less relevant, and likely to be maintained more out of nostalgia than necessity. It might still, however, make a new acquaintance easier to relate to, and more likely to be sustained.

In the case of the Chinese, their sub-groups also have different languages, mutually quite unintelligible, and, as is argued by many, different traditions of behavior. The Shanghainese and Cantonese see themselves as different, just as do the Germans and Italians. There are, however, two special features in the Chinese case which help to coordinate more of a common general identity than that found in Europe: the written form of the Chinese language which is universally understood; and the overpowering sense of being Chinese, a feature much stronger than any equivalent in the West, even for the most chauvinist Western countries. As *Hai* observed, "Chinese are probably the most racist and class-conscious people in the world."

Although the vagaries of their exodus out of China tended to keep people together in regional groupings, Hokkienese in Indonesia, Cantonese in Malaysia, for instance, the complexities of modern economies cause a great deal of mixing nowadays, and the maintenance of sub-group identity is not seen as especially necessary nor desirable. The reaction of most respondents was that it was a pleasant feature in the background, useful from time to time, but really they were above that kind of thing now and had gone beyond it. There may of course be an element of defensiveness in this position, if they think that such connections might be seen as somehow unbusinesslike, and one must search for its significance more in the workings of the system than in expressed attitudes about it.

The function of the clan is to act as an extension of the family in providing support to the individual, such support being needed in an insecure world where rivalry over resources is seriously threatening. In a discussion of why Chinese tend to be very secretive with people outside their circle, *Har* asked:

Would that be selfishness? I don't know. I've got a feeling that one explanation is also Chinese history, which has given the Chinese a great sense of insecurity . . . there are a lot of dynasties, wars, and some criticize the Chinese nature—they fight among themselves, but not unite and fight externally. That is one big criticism about the Chinese culture which is very sad. Chinese are like grains of sand—they never stick together. I think this may be a broad term but I think it's right—they are great at killing each other—just like in the cultural revolution, their worst enemy is their own people. Very sad for me to say that. It also gives the Chinese people insecurity, so they want as much as possible to control their own destiny. I think the Chiu Chow they stick together more, or even the Shanghai people they stick together more.

Mention here of Chiu Chow and Shanghainese as being particularly clannish was common throughout the discussions, and there may be here a distinct sub-cultural trait, albeit one varying by degree rather than being present in one group and absent in others. There was, for instance, also evidence of high cohesiveness among Hokkienese in Indonesia, also clear identity with area of origin among the Cantonese.

The fact that region-of-origin associations continue to thrive among the Overseas Chinese has been studied and commented on by many scholars (e.g. Armentrout-Ma 1988, Hamilton 1977, Jacobs 1982, Landa 1981, Mak 1988, Purcell 1965, See 1985, Wang 1981, Wu and Wu 1980). Dannhaeuser (1981), while acknowledging the practical usefulness of such networks in facilitating trust bonds, adds a further possible reason. In societies where public office through the political process is largely denied them, the search for status can be exercised through the clan societies. The owner of a possibly unglamorous manufacturing company making sumps or grommets might feel much better having been the annual president, or the vice president for international relations, or the chairman of the house committee, of the Chekiang and Kiangsu Association of Surabaya. There is, of course, a parallel phenomenon in the West which at least partly explains the proliferation of Lions, Rotarians, Masonic Lodges, and such like, but in the Western case, membership is less sub-culturally focussed. Nor do the Rotarians of the Far East, and their fellows, escape from the occasional disparagement of the high achiever in a status-conscious society, such as *Tseng:* "I don't have time to socialize with members of various middle-class organizations."

For a sub-culture to persist, it must have some common denominators which make it different, and Chinese perceptions of these, by both members and non-members, are thus of interest. They are of course impressionistic and prone to bias, but certain regularly stated themes emerged in the interviews which suggest that sub-cultural stereotypes are sufficiently real for many Chinese to influence relationships.

A large and economically very significant phalanx of Shanghainese came to Hong Kong in the late 1940's, as the communist government established its regime. Most of them had lost many possessions in the process, although much wealth had also been moved. It was this impetus of the arrival of experienced and skilled businessmen, aided later by the industrial demands of the Korean War, which led to the emergence of Hong Kong as an industrial center. In effect, the Shanghainese brought with them the textile industry, and they still largely control it (Wong 1988).

Compared with the Cantonese, they are seen as more subtle, more suave, more sober, or, depending on your standpoint, more devious. There is certainly a slight degree of wariness between them and the traditionally open and extrovert Cantonese. Consider the following discussion of them among Cantonese respondents:

Hse:
It's difficult for a Cantonese to work for a Shanghainese. Anyway there is a certain difference in mentality. Shanghainese are more diplomatic—they don't exactly tell you what they think. Their behavior is different. Like when they are not well off, they like to dress very nicely.

Hwang:
They may be living in one room, but when they dress up, you can see them like a general manager. This is not like the Cantonese. They are good businessmen. If you go to buy things in their shops, you are well treated. They would give you Coca-Cola, or even a bigger customer beer. So it makes that you don't feel very comfortable if you are not buying anything.

Hse:
In other words, they can hide their feelings better than the Cantonese. The Cantonese is more straightforward.

Similarly, *Hsu* observed that "The Shanghainese use a number of tricks. They pretend to be very generous to you—in reality they are so calculating."

What may be being reflected here is perhaps more of a class difference than a more fundamental contrast in nature. In discussing superstition, *Hsui* observed that the idea of lucky numbers was more of a Cantonese thing. "They've never heard of lucky numbers in Shanghai. Shanghai people don't go that way." This suggests perhaps the contrast between a Shanghainese urban elite, over time grown sophisticated (with all that the word implies about the use of deceptive subtleties), and a Cantonese populus much closer to its countryside origins among the farm people of the Canton delta.

An internal Shanghainese view claims some credit for a kind of civilized reticence, at least among the tight circle of the textile manufacturers.

Hsing:
Most spinners don't like public show. This is reflected in their style of living. Enough is enough. Show doesn't help the business. This is the Shanghainese view (although some shipowners are different). People who have just enough want to show it so people know. People who have plenty don't have to show it.

The significance of being Shanghainese lies in the networks which it defines. The club of the cotton spinners is entirely Shanghainese and very powerful within the larger Hong Kong textile industry, being capable of powerful lobbying of government when needed. Senior positions in their companies are normally in Shanghainese hands, although this may be more due to the promoting of trusted employees who happen to have moved with the industry than to any real policy of discrimination.

Hwang:
The Shanghai big families brought in the capital and the technicians. They made huge profits but gave much in benefits to the employees—they want to maintain the best workers. Their own people—their clansmen—would still occupy the big positions.

Huan:
One thing noticeable about a Shanghai textile factory is all the top layers are in Shanghainese hands.

Reinforced by the use of the Shanghai dialect (one chief executive, in Hong Kong for forty years, remarked that his Cantonese was still weak), the regional network may supplant the family in the funding support for a family business venture, and there was a clear consensus that whereas the Cantonese business model tends to be father and son for the Shanghainese a much wider spread of ownership among them is more common. This suggests a difference in their capacity to build cooperative systems, and it may thus be no accident that they are commonly associated with larger-scale, more complex organizations than are the Cantonese. [1] What is held to be true of the Shanghainese finds many echoes also in the case of the Chiu Chow, with comments regularly occurring about their language, their great closeness, and even their social discipline:

Hsui:
Only Chiu Chow people employ each other, and they're probably the closest grouping. They do look after each other. And when they get together, if the most senior starts to say something, the younger will just shut up, until he's asked to speak.
Hon:
I can believe that. I have Chiu Chow friends.

As was noted earlier, however, the influence of clan networks is not always benevolent, and it inevitably introduces a element of clan rivalry which can destroy the normal working of the market system. As *Shum* observed, "The worst thing in Chinese communities is factionalism. I refused to join the Shanghainese when I was a trader in Burma in the 1940's and 1950's. I always keep away from clans." Similarly, *Sit* tried not to have too many dealings with his Chiu Chow acquaintances, preferring for instance to use banks identified with other clans.

   Clan networks are thus a social device to be used with discretion. They are not, however, the only form of network available, and we turn now to consider the networks which a person builds for himself independent of his sub-cultural allegiances, networks which, in many cases, because of their strong personalistic contents, become very significant to the individual.

Personal networks are built in order to control uncertainty in three senses. Firstly is the gathering of information, and for this, contacts in an industry are crucial. Secondly is the stabilizing of sources of supply and markets. Thirdly is the cementing of certain key relationships in the organization. In all of these fields, personal networks based on mutual obligation and exchange may arise to supplement clan ties which may also be available. Another field in which networks may be developed is in starting up a company.

The use of networks for information gathering and exchange is illustrated in *Han*'s description of a major Hong Kong financial entrepreneur in relation to styles of decision making.

I don't think it's guesswork. They are well tuned to a network. Our late chairman could do this also. As far as I understand, there is a network whereby all the wealthy prominent Chinese businessmen are used to gathering every week or two, and they exchange all the information, and they are willing to share. A very close group. So when you talked to Mr. X, he would give you a very definite answer about what you should invest your money in and which currency. He's just well tuned.

Tsu:
I am a member of a dining group. These are nine owners from different retail sectors, but we are all similar in being chain-store oriented.

It is clear that for this mechanism to work, mutual benefits have to have accumulated sufficiently to loosen tongues, and this becomes one of the reasons for the retention of influence among the elderly whose connections are both wider and of longer standing. Each generation builds its own networks, and in such a hierarchial society membership across generations is not conducive to openness.

Tso:
We meet together and call ourselves the "dog" group. This is for friends, business related, but we were all born in the year of the dog.

Hsing noted that he obtained a great deal of advice from friends in the textile industry, about, for instance, foreign exchange, but that these contacts were of the same generation.

One of the most obvious ways for the generational network to establish itself is in the classroom. Being at school or university together creates special bonding in a context usually seen as significant by Chinese. As *Hung* observed, "With schoolmates, it is natural, pure friendship. Someone may be very rich, but it's not an issue then. You associate together, and you improve together as a group." It is as if the classmate group were extensions of the family core, almost honorary members in the Confucian tradition of specific limited friendship bonds. As *Hua* said, "I'm out of the regional clan system. I'm trying to build or connection with school mates. Chinese will tend to take care of themselves before they take care of others. It's a heritage. It's been the case a long time."

The establishing of stable supply and marketing networks based on ties of obligation will be considered later in the context of organization. Suffice it to say here that Chinese people will not do business with people they do not know, and network building for purposes of business deals has a high priority in their behavior. As Dannhaeuser (1981) noted in his study of Overseas Chinese channels of distribution, control of connections up and down the channel is one of the means of reducing uncertainty and of reducing transaction costs.

In the staffing of the organization, the paternalist response is to consolidate reliability by the use of vertical cliques. If you have given a person his first chance, trained him, and promoted him, then he owes you and will look after your interests. Given that subordinate expectations more often than not match this view, the creation of such cliques is a normal outcome in the Chinese company. Although usually invisible to the innocent observer, occasional glimpses of such coteries are possible when, say, a key marketing executive leaves a company and takes his team with him.

As far as the starting up of companies is concerned, it is very common indeed for friendship networks either to supplement or to supplant those of family. Such help is not always in straight finance. Many textile companies began with network help over the lending of raw material, and the pooling of spare parts. *Im*'s company began when his grandfather was given a second-hand candy-making machine by a friend. More commonly, however, the medium is financial investment. When *Hoi* went out on his own and raised funds, it was all from friends. *Sun*'s firm, although started with family money, is now fifty percent owned by his friends.

Looked at from the lender's side, another aspect emerges, which can also be a means of joining a network, especially if the borrower is prestigious.

Heng:
I've noted a lot of rich Hong Kong people like to take, say, a five percent share in all sorts of projects in order to be partners with many local businessmen.

Starting up provides one further means of adding to a network, and one very revealing of both pragmatism and open-mindedness. This is the seedbed phenomenon, whereby entrepreneurs keep springing out from companies but retain an identification with the original owner who employed them and allowed them a learning opportunity. This is remarkable for the lack of rancor with which it is discussed.

It is first of all seen as inevitable:

Hung:
If you don't treat the employees right, you will not have good workers. They will go out and start their own businesses.

If they do decide to leave, it may well bring advantages:

Ho:
There is a saying—if your staff leave, treat them nice, because they are the ones who will bring you more business, because they know the company best, they know the product best.

Hong:
You have some entrepreneurs, and if you don't take care of it, they will leave, and it's bad for the company. Cooperation would be fine, and then the family business can grow.

Sit:
I help them financially to start up, and eventually they become my subcontractors and dealers.

The degree of positive encouragement of such breaking-away is intriguing.

Han:
Some people say, "After a few years I may start my own business," and the boss actually congratulates you.

Hwa:
He's not seen as a rebel. He is now starting sort of his own family. What the junior would probably do beforehand is to ask the senior for his blessing before spinning off.

And the respect and civilized conduct is maintained:

Hsien:
It's part of the thinking of Orientals that they would like to keep the company like an extended family. We went to a Chinese wedding the other day, and an ex-employee who had gone out on his own and is now in competition with us—he came across and chatted and paid the greatest respect to my father
Hai:
Once a senior, he is always your senior.
Hsien:
Although you're in competition, you still talk to each other, you know?

This happy and benevolent picture is not, of course, the whole story. There are many instances where the moving-out of an executive, with not just a team of colleagues but also perhaps a book full of customers' orders or at least addresses, gives rise to extreme bitterness and tension. It is, however, a tribute to the Chinese genius for compromise and reason that in such a fiercely competitive context the prevailing tone is that of live and let live.

Footnote

[1] A new and intriguing explanation for this is provided by Hollows (1989) who argues that Shanghainese industrialists in the years from 1900 to 1940 were heavily influenced by Japanese methods of industrial organization which were very significant in Shanghai at that period.

Chapter 6
The Institutional Legacy of China

The business organizations of the Overseas Chinese are remarkably consistent in a number of key aspects, and this suggests that (a) they are successful adaptations to a common milieu, and/or (b) they carry some internal "programming," almost as it were genetically, which causes the type to reproduce itself, perhaps even regardless of milieu. This chapter will explain the original common milieu of the Chinese economy as a formative influence, seeing that environment as conducive to a particular response. A certain kind of organization was built for survival in those circumstances. Certain habits were formed which have served Chinese entrepreneurs well as they have moved into other countries and found circumstances in many ways similar to the ones they could cope with.

Later in this book, we must take on board the question of whether different, and perhaps more benevolent, external circumstances justify an alternative response, and whether the depth of penetration of the habits in fact produces inhibitions to adaptation. For the moment, however, it is the "embeddedness" (see Granovetter 1985) of the Chinese family business in the totalitarian state, in its various forms in China, which requires our attention.

There is a danger in such an analysis of looking at business from an entirely Western viewpoint. Such a perspective tends to lead to questions which imply frustration that the Chinese did not develop full-scale capitalism. Why did they not build a modern economy like Japan did? Why did they not develop a smoothly functioning banking system and a managed universal currency? Why did commercial law not develop to foster smooth and reliable economic transactions? In the end, this is rather like asking why were they not European or North American, and, when put in those terms, the naivete of that position is exposed. Japan is a very different case: it started from a very different social history (Jacobs 1958, Pelzel 1970), and its modern form, although it has borrowed heavily from the West, is still most decidedly not just a copy. It remains somehow true to itself. So has China remained true to its very different self, with all the good and bad things that that implies for that complex civilization.

The core question is then not about adaptation and survival in a comparatively unhelpful environment but about conditions which for the Chinese were entirely normal, and in which a perfectly normal response evolved. They were not trying to be anything else, and the state was not trying to prevent them from developing alternative business forms. What follows will occasionally appear critical of state policy, but it is an external view and based on hindsight. It is not intended to be a judgement of the individual actors themselves, or the policies of a very different time.

Details of the inner workings and structures of Chinese companies will be considered in the next chapter, but their character may be previewed by saying that they retain almost universally the characteristics of family business, even in the few cases which reach large scale. They would appear to be extensions of much of the patrimonialism with which Weber characterized Chinese society, suggesting as it does the retention of power invested in a patron-type role. The person in question, in the business milieu, is the chief executive, and the organization comes to revolve around him, and be dependent on him, to a degree unusual in the context of world business. In terms of boardroom mentality, the notion of the truly public company does not yet appear to have been absorbed except when public relations statements require its affirmation.

There are, of course, organizations in the West which come to rely heavily on their chief executives, but the extremes of personalism there tend to run into a number of resistances, not least from high quality organizational members who find it abhorrent, and from surrounding normal practices in other organizations, from consultancy, from the press, from textbooks and management education, all of which pinpoint its peculiarity. For the Overseas Chinese, the personalized organization, run paternalistically and with ownership overlapping normally onto one or two families, is still perfectly normal, and it is the neutral bureaucracy under public ownership and professional management which is the deviant and almost nonexistent case.

At a first level of analysis, our question is: "Why should this be so?" But behind that lies a qualified and even more intriguing question: "Why should this *still* be so?" Given, in other words, the openness to outside influence of most of the economies in which the Overseas Chinese flourish, why have organizational systems retained this deeply traditional form? Hong Kong has been, and will remain for a time, one of the world's most open economies. Taiwan has been influenced extensively by Japan and the United States, as has the Philippines. Indonesia and Malaysia have very long-standing, deep, and extensive connections into sources of European influence. Singapore has spent at least two decades deliberately courting Western technology via the multinationals. Chinese business for over a hundred years has been practised with the full knowledge of alternatives and with vast amounts of international cooperation. And yet its typical organization has retained its original basic character.

Assuming that this is partly a result of its working well, and partly a result of its "naturalness," the question to be addressed is, "How does it come to be so natural? Of what influences is it a product?"

The answer to this is seen to lie in the interplay of three main forces, all of which derive from Chinese culture and history, and which themselves are intertwined. These three elements reflect not only cultural factors, but also allow inclusion in the account of the political, economic, geographical, and institutional forces which have gone into their creation. In classifying them as a set of predispositions to behave in a certain way and shared by businessmen, an attempt is being made to build a bridge between attitudes and action. There is a degree of artificiality in subdividing any topic as complex as this, and each feature contains elements of the others. Their separation is thus an analytical convenience rather than a reflection of their independence.

In the first place is the factor of *insecurity* which derives from a historical combination of (a) the insecurity of wealth in a society without a fully reliable system of property rights, and (b) the general lack of trust outside delimited groups.

In the second place is the factor of *paternalism* which rests on a long Confucian tradition sponsoring familism and authoritarianism, and which creates norms of dependence and acceptance of hierarchy.

In the third place is *personalism* which denies the emergence of the kind of objectivity and neutrality in which truly rational and professional bureaucracy can flourish.

These three forces are carried in the cultural baggage of all Overseas Chinese societies and are apparently as resistant to change nowadays as they were when much earlier accounts of these societies were written (e.g. Vleming 1926, Wilhelm 1982 [1930]). This is not to say that change has halted, as the forces of modernization will inevitably eat into the old traditions. It is to say that modernization has not yet radically affected the most fundamental aspects of organizing. In parenthesis, one might add that, given their economic success, the validity of such forms is, if anything, being reinforced rather than reappraised. The form of organization also is such that it can, just like the Japanese, absorb and benefit from much in the modern technological world without undergoing a deep-seated change of character; a triumph, perhaps again, of the power of Taoist quiet accommodation.

To understand the resilience and the constancy of these core influences requires some examination of social and economic history in China, this time not from the point of view of the individual but now from that of the business organization. Such history will first be treated in a brief chronological review and then separately in terms of what it can contribute to the understanding of insecurity, paternalism, and personalism. By this means, some understanding may be achieved of those determinants of its present form which can be attributed to Chinese culture. Again a reminder may be due that culture itself is seen as only one contributor to the total explanation, but a significant one.

The Historical Progress of Chinese Business

The century beginning in 1400 marked a turning point in the history of business worldwide in that it saw the transition from what Braudel termed "an ancient parity" to the rapidly increasing growth of Western power (Braudel 1984: 535). The earlier parity was one of income per capita, and the ground in which Chinese business originally took root was one where the Far East, as the greatest of the internally balanced world economies, tended to dominate its counterparts in scale. Pliny the Elder noted that Rome had a deficit of 100 million sesterces in its trade with the Far East each year (a strikingly modern concern if one sees Washington as today's Rome equivalent).

This great Far Eastern economic bloc was maintained in balance by the internal tensions of its three main constituents, Islam, India, and China, with dominance shifting slowly between them.

China has for most of its history been diffident about territorial expansion, and although active in external trade, remained politically behind early versions of the bamboo curtain. This isolation prevented China from accumulating the network of connected states like those which provided such energy for Europe in the nineteenth century, and it did not thus evolve as a magnetic world economy in its own right.

By the nineteenth century, the disparity between East and West had grown to the point where Europe, with its large scale and particularly secure form of capitalism found that the Far East, "structured enough to be penetrated with relative ease, but not sufficiently structured to defend itself, was asking to be invaded" (Braudel 1984: 523). For China, the significant first step in this process was the reluctant conceding of Hong Kong, in 1841.

Inside China, for many centuries before then, there operated a vast free trade area whose population was greater than all of Europe. As Fairbank describes it:

Production of crops for comparative advantage was far advanced: the Lower Yangtse provinces specialized in rice production while the provinces just to the north produced cotton for exchange. Craftsmen in many centers produced specialties recognized all over the country: chinaware at Ching-te-chen, iron cooking pans in Canton, silk brocade from Hangchow and Soochow. Enormous fleets of Chinese sailing vessels plied the highway of the Yangtse River and its tributaries, while thousands of others sailed up and down the China coast, taking southern fruit, sugar, and artifacts to Manchuria and bringing back soybeans and furs. One early British observer was amazed to calculate that in the 1840's more tonnage passed through the port of Shanghai at the mouth of the Yangtse than through the port of London, which was already the hub of Western commerce (Fairbank 19: 49).

In this vast economy, the major part of the economic activities which kept it moving were the small-scale ones which made up the village and town markets, around which so much of Chinese life circulated and which have been estimated to number 63,000 at the beginning of the twentieth century (Skinner 1964: 24).

Agriculture, acknowledged as the core of life in the respectable status accorded the farmer, was based on small landholdings, often inconveniently separated. Techniques were labor intensive and, although in the early periods of Chinese history farming methods were advanced, they eventually fell behind those of much of the rest of the world. The trading of agricultural and other products was conducted via a vast commercial network but one characterized by large numbers of small organizations, linked through the market mechanism but not otherwise coordinated. Expansion in the total volume of commerce was steady and impressive for eight centuries, but "appears to have consisted mainly of more units of essentially the same activity" (Feuerwerker 1984: 323).

Elvin's description of this dense network of small organizations, in which "commerce substituted for management," based on an analysis of one of the most typical and important of industries—cotton, suggests its diffracted nature:

It would seem that an industry enormous in the aggregate was created not by expanding the size of the units of production but by linking a growing multitude of small producers through a market mechanism, with a minimum of direct functional integration between the various parts of the structure (Elvin 1973: 281).

The role of government tended to be that of providing infrastructure, such as the Grand Canal, the road systems, and the military maintenance of peace. Otherwise direct positive involvement by government in business was rare. Except for taxation it was not seen as necessary. For a thousand years from the Sung, China experienced what Feuerwerker saw as in world perspective a remarkable millenium of pre-modern economic growth but one must note the phrase "pre-modern." China had every reason for complacency. Until the disasters of the nineteenth century, living standards for all were normally adequate, there were no external wars or significant internal challenges. "The Chinese rulers already possessed 'all under heaven,' and they could hardly foresee how parochial that universal conceit would become" (Feuerwerker 1984: 323). Nor could they see the trap the economy was drifting into.

This "high level equilibrium trap" (Elvin 1973) occurred with the conflation of a number of forces: [1] the enormous supply of human muscle power made machinery unnecessary; the circular flow of small-scale production and consumption was in balance with primitive technology, and inhibited industrial investments; capital for investment could not accumulate enough to provide credit; the ruling group lived by tax gathering rather than wealth creation. The result of these forces was that productivity per person remained "trapped" at a low level, and, given the persistence of the causes, arguably has remained so.

During the nineteenth century, the impatient encroachment of the West put China under great pressure and coincided with a period of internal disorder which eventually saw the collapse of the Manchu empire. Throughout this period and since, the general tone adopted towards Western technology, both managerial and productive, has been to keep it if possible at arm's length, in an attempt to filter it into the Chinese system unobtrusively and in a controlled way.

The traditional filter mechanism was the *comprador*, and especially at the time of the treaty ports, he was a significant gatekeeper between the foreign enterprises bringing capital, and the world of the Chinese merchants who controlled the trade between the treaty ports and the interior. This internal trade proved largely impenetrable by Western interests and remained locked firmly in local hands, leaving the vast world of Chinese commerce quite deliberately protected against Western competition, and sealed against innovation. As Marie-Claire Bergere has noted, this "radical break between interior China (rural, bureaucratic, traditional) and coastal China (cosmopolitan, enterprising, open to innovation)" was one of the two major handicaps (the other being population pressure) bequeathed by the Imperial regime. These contradictions were only accentuated and worsened in the twentieth century (Bergere 1984: 335).

It is perhaps worthy of note, in passing, how the weakness and defensiveness of China in the face of modernization contrasts with the extremely proactive and positive stance taken by Japan over the same period. In the Japanese case, after the Meiji restoration saw the adoption of an official policy of modernization and industrialization, there followed an open-minded searching for new models of law, education, military structures, etc., all of which were carefully absorbed into a state which succeeded in remaining true to itself. In remaining true to its own self, China over the same period was only able to reveal the difficulties of strategy, coordination, and control involved in a state of such immense size, whose past glories served both to prolong traditionalism and by contrast to impair current pride and confidence; nebulous characteristics without doubt, but capable of subtle and powerful effect.

The Origins of Defensiveness and Insecurity

It was argued at the outset of this chapter that one of the prime determinants of the family-centeredness of Overseas Chinese business organizations is a deep-seated mistrust which causes them to be constructed with a view to defense. The centripetal force of family itself will be considered in the next section, and here concentration given to the external forces which contribute to such caution. Discussion of mistrust in chapter 3 has already set the scene for the businessman's stance towards his surrounding society, and the focus here will therefore be more on the role of officialdom in amplifying that problem. It may be taken from that earlier chapter that families would inevitably compete with each other; now we must consider how the state itself could act as predator rather than guardian.

The role of the state for most of Chinese history was to remain aloof from involvement in business and commerce. Although Braudel (1984: 523) argues that capitalism was quite deliberately and officially thwarted, a great deal of the dampening effect might have been simply an accidental outcome of the policy of national isolation and of Confucian disdain for the world of business. For most of the thousand years since the Sung, for instance, the great trade fairs so stimulating to the exchange of new ideas in business in the Middle East and Europe were restricted in China to a few on its outer perimeter and none in the center. It is not clear whether this was due to fear of their effects, or because China felt it could manage without them, but one can surmise that there was an element of both.

It would be exaggerating to describe the position of the businessman in traditional Chinese society as "besieged." The power of government was for practical reasons limited. As Feuerwerker (1984: 304) points out, all pre-modern societies suffer from a limitation on the growth of cities until rural productivity can be raised, and without such access points, control and direction from the center are hampered. [2]

Also the state, although it could become directly involved in commercial matters, as for instance in its attempted salt monopoly or its influence on the potteries of Ching-te-chen, was by and large unwilling to enter the vast world of private commerce. It had control over only a small percentage of the gross national product and this, "at the very least limited negative interference with the private sector where the most remarkable Ming–Ching achievements originated" (Feuerwerker 1984: 322). What was committed was a sin of omission, no doubt regrettable given hindsight, but certainly understandable given the brilliance of the earlier Chinese achievement.

What was the nature of this omission, and how did it leave the businessman protected so minimally (now in comparison with his Western counterparts) that he retained his cautious, personalistic, and family-based organization? Moreover, was it that he was forced into such a defensive structure, or, as now seems more likely, simply not tempted out of it? The background to such questions is the very radical transition required to move a society from a pre-modern economy to a modern one capable of releasing the power of technology to increase per capita productivity. In this context, an important caveat needs to be brought in, which is that the *successful* pre-modern form sows the seeds of its own destruction. As Feuerwerker (1984: 312) puts it, "The historical experience and institutional arrangements that might predispose to pre-modern growth may substantially impede later economic development of a different kind." If one of these "institutional arrangements" is an aloof and overcentralized government out of sympathy with the world of commerce, that is alone enough, if perpetuated, to prevent the transition from succeeding.

It is, however, in the practicalities that such aloofness manifests itself, and one might analyse the contents of the "sin of omission" by comparing the structures which other governments sponsored, in the West (and later in the Overseas Chinese region), with what did not happen in China.

What the businessman never had in China, and arguably what the government might have sponsored had it been so inclined, include the following:

(1) institutions for pooling capital (other than the partnerships, lineage common properties, and maritime trade joint ventures, none of which in any case were protected by legal codes or had rapid access to judicial procedures);
(2) legal, financial, commercial institutions (banks, security exchanges, insurance, brokerages, legal specialists), able to facilitate the shift of capital from commerce to industry, while protecting liquidity;
(3) a reliable currency;
(4) large-scale fairs in the interior of the country which would have facilitated the exchange of ideas.

Without these features to facilitate the more effective conduit of money into productive enterprise, it is not surprising, given the social values which the government in practice lived by, that capital would be misused, misinvested, and dissipated. It went into the purchase of degrees, titles, and offices, whereby it was converted into the daily running costs of administration. Or it went to worsen the already vast overinvestment in land.

The deep-seated nature of this issue is evident from the resistance to change met from the provincial bureaucracies whenever the central government attempted reforms in the nineteenth and early twentieth centuries. As Marie-Claire Bergere points out (1984: 334), blaming China's backwardness on the removal of capital by Western imperial powers is not in itself a convincing reason until you can prove that it would have been usefully invested otherwise.

The normal view of the businessman is made clear in an edict from the throne published in 1903, announcing the formation of a Ministry of Commerce. It begins, "Because by social convention. . . industry and commerce are thought of as matters of the last importance. . ." and goes on to advocate the removal of barriers between officials and merchants (Chan 1977: 19).

Two core values within the Confucian ethic contributed to this classical scorn for commerce: firstly, the virtue associated with agricultural work; secondly, the status attached to the "superior" man whose superiority is largely derived from education. Material possessions in themselves did not guarantee respect, although, as Godley (1981: 34) has pointed out, the disdain did not prevent many mandarins from taking a share in the profits.

The clear supremacy of the mandarin class of scholar-gentlemen-administrators, and the weight of their power, led inevitably to the need for sharing of wealth, and in turn to corruption at the point of exchange. This would vary over Chinese history from periods when a little "squeeze" to boost poor government salaries was seen as simply oiling the wheels, to periods of decline when rampant corruption went hand-in-hand with extensive spiritual decay (Sterba 1978).

The power of the mandarins, and their acolytes, was exercised through taxes, licensing fees, and travel and trade restrictions. In the absence of a codified commercial law, merchants were regularly at the mercy of the system. This called forth substantial skills in building defensive allegiances and contacts, and in learning to cope with the uncertainties of a political superstructure whose reactions could be benevolent or hostile but were never easily predictable until co-opted. The honing of such skills has contributed to the survival of many Overseas Chinese organizations in politically hostile environments and to their immense flourishing in benevolent ones. That they are still relevant in China today, where nothing deeply fundamental has changed, is evident from the constant references to the use of *guanxi* (personal connections) without which not much can be accomplished.

A parallel defense was to gain entry to the elite from which, by virtue of being merchants, they were excluded. This could only be achieved through education and the acquisition of office (which would in turn lead to the *real* opportunities to amass wealth), and there resulted a perpetual straining to escape from the limitations of their vulnerability. As Godley (1981: 36) puts it: "This basic desire to be somebody else, to gain respectability through education and bureaucratic service, characterized the commercial spirit of China."

Feuerwerker's (1984: 319) description of merchants in late Imperial China places them in three categories: firstly were those who continued to invest their profits in honorific titles and land; secondly, among the more wealthy, such as the leading salt merchants or the Shanxi bankers, were those who aspired to gentry status for themselves or their offspring; the third group were the entrepreneurs capable of finding new investment opportunities, but there appear to have been few in this last category.

An important outcome of this desire to escape from the merchant life was the constant dissolving of what might otherwise have become long-lived merchant dynasties, such as those found in Japan or Europe. Instead, profits would be diverted from the core business into the escape routes of land ownership or the attainment of rank, in either of which one was no longer at the mercy of the system but in control of it. It is reasonable to conjecture that this escapist tradition, formed over so many centuries, has remained as resilient in Chinese thinking as has, for the English, the notion of the gentleman with his country seat (Barnett 1986, Wiener 1981). [3] That this motivation has a long history in China is suggested in a twelfth-century manuscript quoted by Shiba (1970: 251). The writer is Li Hsiu, and he is discussing the rising price of land during the Southern Sung period. Of merchants, he writes:

They grasp their counting slips, their steelyards and their measures of capacity until they have amassed great gains, so that they may seek to own fields and houses, their principal wives be resplendent with hairpins and ear-rings, and their subsidiary wives pluck the strings of the zither. This is what merchants want.

And so it appears to have remained for a further thousand years. But why, one might ask, would they prefer to own fields and houses rather than plough back the profits into enlarging their businesses? What were they nervous about?

China was ruled for most of its history by a patrimonial bureaucracy which consisted of mandarins representing the personal power of the emperor. Thus the writ of the emperor, which was not subject to a clear system of law, penetrated all corners of the empire. Peace was maintained by intense socialization into the Confucian ethic and its being supported in interpretation and demonstration by the mandarins. To maintain the stability of this system, the power of the mandarinate, i.e. the emperor, had constantly to be reinforced, and this was done through the processes which maintained civil justice. At the same time, the emergence of any sources of alternate power needed to be curtailed. The rise of a rich and powerful bourgeoisie would have destabilized the system and was prevented. It still is.

Behind the government's behavior, then, lay the intention that the accumulation of specie, in any hands which were independent of the ruling authority, was to be prevented. The wealth of the country ultimately belonged to the emperor and to no one else. This interfering dominance was defended in ethical terms, but, more importantly, it was made easier by the fact that the law was not neutral. The merchant, if he were placed in a position where he had to defend himself, was severely handicapped. Firstly, the law was never codified and was based solely on the interpretation of general Confucian principles as they applied to a particular case. This interpretation was in the hands of a mandarin whose training in aloofness and austerity was only matched by the degree of potent but obscure superiority which his education allowed him to claim.

Secondly, it is of special significance that merchants were considered as non-Confucians, unable to oppose the Confucian ethic, and unable to call upon any alternative code to defend their interests (Jacobs 1958: 97).

Thirdly, there was no independent order of professional legal technicians who could act in guiding a defence, and create at least some semblance of fair play.

The position of the merchant then became increasingly vulnerable the more he prospered. He had no resort to a system of property rights, even when his prosperity had allowed him to buy land, as land ownership remained precarious and irrational and subject to the vagaries of fiscal policy, alternating as it did for 1500 years between arbitrary intervention and complete *laissez-faire* (Weber 1951: 80). The property which he held in his business was represented in cash and tangible assets rather than in shares, and was thus also subject to various forms of confiscation, operating commonly through the tax system.

Taxation was normally based on land ownership, itself subject to interference and rights of retraction of sale: tax officials could also impose demands for labor service as an occasional equivalent to payment. At the local level, "tax farming" was common, whereby the right to collect state taxes was in itself an exchangeable commodity. Some indication of the reasons for the unpredictability is provided in a study by Wang of land taxation in the last of the dynasties. In this he reports that the underlying system of taxation based on land was stable and apparently fair, except where late payments could lead to harassment and extortion. Where it became arbitrary was in the area of nonstatutory or informal surcharges which "made the management of the public economy fragmentary and even chaotic" (Wang 1973: 49).

The question of corruption must also be taken into account in considering the uncertainties to which the merchant was vulnerable. Lui's study of seventeenth-century corruption makes it clear that a great deal of bribery went on at the local level to which provincial officials turned a blind eye (Lui 1979). While much of this local squeeze may have been associated with avaricious local magistrates, much was also inspired by the class of underlings who actually collected and accounted for the money. Records of investigations at the time reveal such practices as: destroying receipts and extorting repayment; exempting those paying bribes and redistributing the tax elsewhere; changing information in tax registers; manipulating payment deadlines to extort late payment penalties; finding excuses (such as an army passing) for extra payments. Wherever a merchant could be held to ransom, such as at key progress points on the Grand Canal on which cargo ships could be frozen in for the winter if their movements were hampered, the ingenuity always possible with red tape was regularly exercised to the benefit of the minor officials. The merchants usually paid, and the loss doubtless passed down the channel eventually to the luckless, powerless, and phlegmatic peasantry.

A development which might have left the Chinese businessman less vulnerable to official and unofficial exploitation would have been the emergence of focusses of countervailing power. In Europe, the great bourgeois institutions of the guilds, and of independent city governments, provided strong institutional support capable of neutralizing central authority, and capable also of fostering a decentralization of responsible control which did not destroy the integrity or stability of the state.

China had major cities and also guilds, but they did not operate at all like their European counterparts. The tradition of centralized control in China has never changed, and the antique instinct for dominance from Peking, in maintaining the state's integrity, has always led to the sacrifice of its capacity for innovation and adaptation.

The mushrooming of trade in Europe from the fifteenth century onwards was closely associated with the emergence of cities such as Amsterdam, Paris, Hamburg, and London, which were free to set their own guidelines on the conduct of business. New forms of banking, new instruments of exchange, new business institutions, new techniques of commercial control were all, in this atmosphere, invented, tested, compared, perfected, and then dispersed for wider use.

In China, by contrast, the writ of the emperor penetrated everywhere to intervene in the creation and distribution of wealth. The idea of a free city was incomprehensible. Wherever the merchant operated, whether in city affairs, in local markets, in inter-regional exchange, in foreign trade, or in his guild activities, the state was there to keep an eye on matters. The pervasive and elite bureaucracy saw to it that financial muscle outside the emperor's control never emerged.

As Lucian Pye states the matter, the only legitimate power was limited to officialdom, and no other element of the population could claim any, regardless of social station. Family power was kept inside domestic boundaries and beaten back in if it looked like turning into wider social power. Merchants were politically impotent (Pye 1985: 88). For them to have achieved serious influence, they would have had to be corrupt: an early version of Catch-22.

The suffocating provisions of protection and stability in exchange for conformity and obeisance applied inevitably with the guilds, which never developed the kind of independent power they had in Europe or Japan. The traditional Chinese guild was a local association based on an industry, such as weaving or furniture making, and because of its being so localized came commonly under the influence of clan power, and especially that of clan elders. Compared with the elected officials of the European guild who would see themselves as promoting and protecting the occupation, the clan elders of the Chinese guild could treat their roles as largely decorative, social, and ceremonial. There were rarely any battles over political recognition of legitimate occupational interests, and instead the main activities remained the uncontroversial ones of local philanthropy (Jacobs 1958: 127).

The Chinese guild could never accumulate significant capital from its members, and would normally spend most of its fees on nonproductive rituals. Without real power in its own right, it could never discipline its members for occupational battles. It was a weak force, and without a protective charter, was open to intervention by political officials acting with police privileges, or with ulterior motives. An illustrative case is that of the *co-hong* established in the seventeenth century in Canton as a merchant guild with special rights to conduct trade with Westerners. Although prosperous, the size of the "contributions" it was forced to make to local officials caused it to go bankrupt in 1711. Reestablished in 1720, it survived by tax farming and by continuing to pay the mandarins, but was never able to generate independent economic power or protective rights. There were very many parallel cases.

Given the weakness of the guilds, the lack of city power to intervene protectively between the merchant and the central government, the lack of a codified law, and the inaccessibility of political power, the Chinese businessman for most of China's history was in a difficult, if not overtly hostile environment. In these circumstances, it should not be a matter of surprise that he came to rely on an institution which was the least vulnerable that could be devised and one moreover which the state stayed out of. He kept inside a structure he could control, using people he could trust in key positions, and relying for important supplies and custom on networks of trust or obligation. Without supporting institutions and structures, the organization could not be depersonalized. Long-distance transactions were severely hampered, for as Feuerwerker points out in a telling and still relevant phrase, "the actual presence of the principals was still required in order to close a deal" (Feuerwerker 1984: 318).

For his organization to grow beyond the scale implied by these restrictions would leave it open to attack from those whose trust had not been co-opted, and at the same time leave it without recourse to the protection of law or other guardian institutions. Even when China attempted in the late nineteenth century to create a more fertlle soil for the growth of organizations, the weight of tradition remained immovable without revolution, and business confidence continued to suffer from the political turmoils which have characterized most of the twentieth century for China.

For those who went abroad to the south, as we have already noted, environments were not always easy for the Chinese businessman. It is only in Singapore where he can relax from looking over his shoulder at those who would undermine his security.

The Chinese businessman has, in the event, emerged from the experiences of his ancestors with an instinct for looking after himself, and moreover, an instinct that officialdom is something you keep away from as much as possible (except when you need to co-opt it). In circumstances where government is genuinely supportive of entrepreneurship, as for instance in Hong Kong and Taiwan, he flourishes mightily. In other environments, where official interference of one form or another is always lurking, he is well prepared for it. The cost of this constant vigilance lies in the limitations imposed by the need for an organization which is, above all else, flexible and under trusted control. As we shall later note, moveable assets and deep reserves, and the avoidance of massive capital commitment in plant, typify strategy. Given a choice between commerce and industry, the instinct is still for commerce. It is much safer.

The Anatomy of Paternalism

Continuing to analyse the forces in traditional Chinese society which have sponsored the family business form of organization, we examine now the influence of paternalism. This arises in the nature of the patrimonial state, with its principal vehicle Confucianism, and is expressed particularly clearly in the absolute centrality of family. Noteworthy features, in supplement to those already discussed in the previous chapter, are: the special nature of this form of vertical power; the workings of nepotism; the impact of the traditional inheritance system.

Hamilton (1984) has provided a valuable revision to the classic description by Weber of how the patrimonial state worked in the case of China. In simple terms, Weber's position was that the Chinese state had become frozen in the mechanisms it used for the processes of domination, and these were similar to those adopted in ancient Greece and more especially Rome. The principle which

Weber saw applying to both was the power vested in the head of the household to maintain its internal peace, such power being enshrined in the formal legal system. If both Western and Chinese systems rest upon this common base, but the West developed out of it and China did not, then it becomes possible for a social scientist to build a general theory, and this is what Weber attempted. Hamilton, however, argues that the bases were in fact different. In the Roman case, the law, and eventually later Western interpretations of how society should be built, gave increasing emphasis to the responsibilities of the individual, and accordingly also to the rights of the individual.

In the case of China, however, the emphasis was, and has remained throughout the history of the Confucian state, on the duties which are part of a *role*. In effect, this depersonalized the structure and introduced a great deal of ritualistic role copying in which the individual's personal interests were sublimated. This produces a contrast between the Western emphasis on *power*, in which matters were looked at from a top-down perspective while at the same time allowing for individual interest to surface, and the Chinese emphasis on *obedience*, in which the person comes second to the order itself. Although analytically these can be argued to be two sides of the same coin, in terms of the institutions they produce they turn out in practice to be radically different. The West institutionalizes jurisdictions, China institutionalized roles.

The book of filial piety (the *Xiaojing*)—a key text in Chinese schools for two thousand years—is all about a person's duty to a role, and the way in which a total system can be sustained only if all those in it remain faithful to the demands their role places on them. In that case, power derives from role obedience, not from jurisdiction. All had to be dutiful for it to work, but as long as it did, as Needham (1956: 290) points out, "The notion of Order excluded the notion of law."

The notion of law in the Western case gradually lessened the power of the head of the household and replaced it with various forms of civic control, most dramatically, and quite early for instance, in the head's loss of the power of life and death over household members. In China by contrast, as late as the nineteenth and early twentieth century, brutal punishment of disobedience within a family was quite common and met with no official disfavor. This untrammelled freedom of the head of the family paradoxically became greater in China as role behavior became more tightly prescribed and understood. Infringements stood out more clearly, and the constraints laid upon the head to behave considerately were only part of his total set of guidelines.

In defining the family as the prime unit of society and then locking people into roles, the Confucian code created a myriad of self-controlling units. In order to do so effectively, it was necessary to ensure the inner coherence of such units, and thus facilitate the workings of the father's power. To this end, Chinese law, unlike Roman, gave legal status only to relatives and would not acknowledge strangers. Non-kin were forbidden household members. To be an outsider in

Chinese society was deeply threatening, and this in turn added further to the magnetism of one's own family unit.

It is now possible to discern some of the reasons why familism is so central a feature of Overseas Chinese society. Without the deliberate redesigns of society recently embarked upon in the mainland, the Chinese of the *nanyang* are acting out very deep instincts and long traditions. It is hard for a Westerner to understand the extent to which the Chinese depend on family; how they look out and see the vacuum of no-man's-land—traversed as it may be by the networks they construct—but no-man's-land nonetheless. Their traditions teach them that as individuals there is nothing out there to support any position they might take in opposition to the family head; and in any case, to even think of looking outside in such a manner is deeply contrary to their role requirements. Even so, their dependence and their conformity are not entirely due to years of being trained to think that family is what life is all about. There is a further ingredient, namely that there is genuinely nothing else to turn to. They are pulled to the family, but they are pushed also.

Given such a design for society, the role of the paterfamilias took on special significance. He was the fulcrum of the entire system. Given also the Confucian aim of a peaceful, harmonious, ordered society, much effort went into ensuring that the father figure role was not abused, as the cost of such abuse would have been the disintegration of the social fabric. As it was, it has lasted longer than any other social system. Thus emerged a form of paternalism which combined discipline with benevolence. The capacity for benevolence is related to the way in which the insistence on appropriate role behavior all through the system reduced the need for harsh dictorial methods. If society were successful in socializing people, then the son's behavior to the father was automatically deferential. The need for discipline was relatively rare, given all the surrounding influences which encouraged conformity to the order.

Largely because of this, paternalism for the Chinese does not carry the same stigma as in the West. It is even arguable that the word does not mean the same thing. As Lucian Pye notes from his study of power in Asia:

In most Asian cultures leaders are expected to be nurturing, benevolent, kind, sympathetic figures who inspire commitment and dedication. The Western concept of the leader as being the commanding executive, firm in decision making . . . is less appreciated in Asia. The relationship of power to the responsibilities of office accountability rests upon quite different concepts of power and authority (Pye 1985: 28).

How then does the paternalistic power relationship work in Asia, and particularly within the tradition carrying Overseas Chinese family business? Scholars who have addressed this question specifically include Robert Silin (1976), Lucian Pye (1985), and Frederick Deyo (1978, 1983), and their findings, corroborated in many smaller-scale reports of empirical research by others, may be condensed into the following themes:

(1) Dependence of the subordinate, as a mind-set.
(2) Personalized loyalty leading to willingness by subordinates to conform.
(3) Authoritarianism modified by sensitivity to subordinates' views.
(4) Authority not divisible when it has become so clearly identified with a person.
(5) Aloofness and social distancing within the hierarchy.
(6) Allowance for the leader's intentions to remain loosely formulated.
(7) The leader as exemplar and "teacher."

It was noted earlier, when discussing child rearing, that the early stages of up-bringing in the years up to age five or six, are ones in which children are commonly indulged. It is one of the few areas of Chinese life where open displays of emotion and affection are encouraged, and it creates in the child a strong sense of dependence. Having been once at the center of the universe and having once been able to influence authority by exploiting the atmosphere of indulgence, the child grows up to seek a similar psychological bond in later life. The same effect with the same causes has been noted for the Japanese by Takeo Doi (1973), who argues that dependence is the key to understanding the Japanese character. Although the Chinese case may not be quite so extreme, it is without doubt similar in nature and effect.

The leader or manager, and certainly the owner of a business, can look to his workforce and to his immediate subordinates also for a degree of deference unusual when compared to that found in other cultures. Their dependence on him is more than simply economic, and he may well take on the role of surrogate parent. To play this role to the full requires a knowledge of the Confucian rules for maintaining vertical order, the acting out of which will produce responses of conformity and acceptance of the domination. The hidden key to the workings of this stable pattern is that the subservience implied is in fact sought. Chinese hierarchies are perhaps better understood from the perspective of followership than of leadership.

Such subservience is also the outcome of a highly personalized relationship, as such bonding cannot occur in a depersonalized system. The Chinese are loyal to people, less so to principles or ideas. It is people who can most easily give them what they want in exchange for the highly focussed form of loyalty which they are prepared to offer in exchange. Given a "fixing" on a father-figure boss, and given that his authority is exercised with a civilized benevolence, then the conformity to his will offered by the subordinates is of a kind likely to transcend any formal definition of its limits. The organization chart and the formal job description become irrelevant as reflections of the power relationship, and redundant as guides to action, except in the crudest sense.

Mention of civilized benevolence suggests a further crucial feature of domination in its Asian form which requires that the normal assumptions about authoritarianism, as it is understood in the West, be suspended. In the West, it is normal to think of domination as a matter of deciding directions and then commanding. In this case, contributions from below may easily be taken as challenges, and there is an inherent competitive tension between authority and participation. Also Western authority is commonly associated with the programs and policies which the leader is implementing, and should criticism of the leader surface, it may thus be deflected onto the policies themselves. In the Asian case, policy is much more an extension of people rather than of principle, and it is harder to separate the persona of the leader from the policies he is following. Such a separation is almost never made. In this context, criticism from below is even harder to cope with, and some leadership situations can give the impression of a form of dominance which verges on the despotic. These however are not the norm, as a heavy battery of values are in place to support the considerate leader and to deny legitimacy to the one who abuses power.

The common form of relationship expresses mutual dependency. As Pye (1985: 37) points out, "paternalism is meaningless without participation, for there can be no father without children." Unlike in the West, where inferiors are in constant danger of being manipulated by superiors who are pursuing their own interests, the Oriental matching of patrons and clients vertically locks the two parties together in a way which inhibits exploitation. Subordinates' views may not be overtly sought, or formally taken account of, but ignoring them will undermine the commitment of those below, and bring about a whole array of subtle and often invisible denials of cooperation.

One of the difficulties of paternalistic power is that it can take on a sense of omnipotence which can eventually become a handicap. All matters great and small tend to keep gravitating to the boss's desk. When authority becomes so bound up with a person, it becomes very difficult for others to exercise it on his behalf. It remains indivisible. This is one of the great limiting factors to the growth of Chinese organizations, and a cause also of much middle management frustration.

It should be added that much behavior among Chinese bosses tends to exacerbate this potentially debilitating feature. The maintenance of a position of dominance is often achieved by preventing other executives from making highly visible contributions which might symbolize their quality as leaders. Also, it is common for a boss to surround himself with a nonthreatening clique made up of people whose talents are not such as to pose a threat, or who are too young to challenge the established order.

It is commonly a matter of fascination among Westerners observing the Japanese that their society provides for periods, usually off-duty, when all the defences can be dropped, and bosses and subordinates can go out even getting drunk together, and in the process exchange valuable "home-truths." They can also indulge in often emotional gestures of mutual support, making commitments which underlie the rigid formalities of the workplace. Such dropping of one's guard, as it were, is inconceivable in the Chinese case, where the vertical order is maintained by the consistent playing of superior and subordinate roles, consistent that is in all contexts. Noting the importance of dignity as an element of authority for the Chinese, Silin (1976: 66) remarks that "Superiors must convey an impression of aloofness. . . . the boss is preferably a person of considerable stature and reserved, taciturn deportment." Familiarity is seen as threatening in these circumstances, and excessive closeness unwelcome. Certainly there is socializing, and certainly the boss may laugh and joke and often be the life and soul of the party, but nowhere in the Chinese context will you find the slightly tipsy colleague bending the boss's ear with risky advice on how he should discharge his duties. Such behavior would be seen as dangerously subversive.

Given this sensitivity, it is common in the work situation to find a surrounding coterie of people with whom a boss interacts regularly. These are likely to be reflectors and extensions of his will rather than challengers of it, but despite the implication that they are "yes men," they may nevertheless have influence far greater than their formal authority or title suggests. This comes about because they can claim understanding of his intentions. Few are normally privy to such intentions, and given a lack of overt goal setting otherwise, the coterie can form a powerful defensive wall inside which the boss can retreat to concentrate on the unusually opaque, intuitive, and constantly shifting creation of strategy typical of the Chinese business. Let us, in saying so, not forget the effectiveness which such an instinctive process can lead to, nor the fact that the intuitions are usually exercised by a mind deeply informed about one particular area of business.

That the leader's intentions remain loosely formulated is a common observation in Chinese organizations. Equally common, and related, is the capacity for surprise leaps into unrelated ventures which speaks of a very open-ended view of an organization's mission. There is a real sense of being untrammelled, of being uninhibited by the so-called logics of decision making.

In the traditional Chinese family, the concerned but distant father is free to keep his own counsel and to have his private plans. As long as the good of the family remains his central mission, he is not constrained to sharing his thinking, bearing his breast, or going over past mistakes. As Pye notes,

The Chinese father is expected to be aloof and distant, invulnerable to all but the most subtle hints of criticism. To challenge the father's decisions would be equal not just to questioning his judgement, but worse, to suggesting that he has been disloyal to his family . . . Children learn early that it is not wise to question their parents' conduct (Pye 1985: 199).

Silin uses the word "didactic" to convey something of the character of the boss–subordinate relationship. The implication is that the boss is exemplar or teacher, and that he passes down information in small pieces, retaining to himself the mastery of the total subject, and using his special knowledge as the coinage of power. In a sense, dividing and ruling.

This will, of course, only work if the boss can retain his record of successful decision making, or at least not make obvious mistakes. In these circumstances, the high need in such a hierarchical society for clear leadership will then serve to keep him invulnerable to attack, and the interests of the collectivity to remain stable will be served.

It was noted earlier that an important component of the paternalism so common in Chinese companies is nepotism. As the word has odious connotations in the Western context, being normally associated with favoritism and the carrying of inefficient people, it will bear some scrutiny. It is important to see whether it really is limiting for the Chinese, and also whether it provides any special strengths to their systems.

Let us first be clear that we are not simply talking about the grooming of the eldest son to take over the business. It extends more widely than that in normal practice, and companies are commonly manned, in key positions, by offspring, brothers and sisters, uncles, nephews, nieces, and more distant relatives. A wife may also play a key part alongside a husband, as, say, financial controller, or personnel director.

In all this, however, there would appear to be an iron rule at work, which is that performance has to be good for real responsibility to be allocated. Social duty is still clearly tempered by pragmatism of a high order, and the deep-seated need for economic viability remains non-negotiable.

In the Overseas Chinese context also, the urge to acquire education serves to prepare the aspiring younger generation in ways which suggest that the granting of power to them has to be deserved. They are commonly better informed technically than their parents, and many second-generation chief executives will bring masters degrees, or doctorates, to the boardroom, almost always gained in a field relevant to the role they will assume.

The preparation of the young entrepreneur is an elaborate and lengthy process (Limlingan 1980, Redding 1986). It is based on the insight that formal education is not a guarantee of entrepreneurial skill and that this latter has to be identified and encouraged by trial and error. It is common for a chief executive to allocate the business education of his son to a trusted friend, often in a separate company. By encouraging involvement in a series of increasingly weighty "deals," the skills necessary are honed, the principal ones being negotiating skill, financial sophistication, and marketing judgement. As a trainee's judgement and confidence are developed, he gradually becomes capable of running a company, at which stage he would be returned to the family business, to await developments. This may entail a long and frustrating wait, but is more normally a matter of assuming a key role placing him close to the father. A further component in this apprenticeship is the tradition of leaving the trainee relatively poorly paid, and close to the working conditions of those at the base of the system. This provides him firstly with a desire for the wealth which success can provide, and which the owner clearly enjoys, and secondly with a sensitivity to the viewpoint of those on whose work that wealth will be based. The key aspect, however, is the identifying and developing of entrepreneurial judgement, and without success in this field, the young person is unlikely to be given senior responsibility later unless he has no rivals. Given the size of Chinese families, complete reliance on a sole heir is unusual and competition between candidates might be fierce. First choice is always the oldest son, but the condition is clear that he must be capable and tested.

In these circumstances, it is clear that nepotism does not necessarily sponsor weakness. It will do so where no effective heirs are available, or where the screening process has not been used, but if the safeguards are used, it can in fact be a source of substantial strength.

There are a number of senses in which using family members can add to an organization's efficiency. In the first place, identity with the organization's goals is very powerful. If the key people in the company are all dedicated to the accumulation of family wealth, and if that is the hidden rationale behind much decision making, then a great deal of communication is already taken care of. Secondly, motivation tends to run high, especially if extra effort is being called for and the availability of an intensely dedicated set of executives in key positions has incalculable value. Thirdly, confidentiality of information is easier to guarantee if it is a matter of keeping it in the family.

Nepotism, for the Overseas Chinese, is a means of counteracting the problem of trust in a minimally integrated society. It is both a reinforcement of and a result of the family business form. It does not, however, automatically entail inefficiency. Although there are inevitable failures due to it, and the "third generation problem" is an issue of great concern reflecting how difficult it is to maintain the entrepreneurial momentum, it must be remembered that the companies concerned are small-scale structures normally, and that they are in a sense built for it. The large-scale corporation, in which nepotism can be very damaging, is rare.

The final aspect, under the general heading of paternalism, which has contributed to the retention of the family business form as normal, is the system of inheritance traditional in China, and perpetuated among the Overseas Chinese. In this, property passes by equal division to all legitimate heirs, normally the sons. The most significant consequence has always been that wealth keeps on being broken up. If a family accumulated wealth, it tended to be able to use it in a coordinated way during only one or two generations. Even when a family remained highly cohesive, the dissipation of the leadership role into perhaps four or five separate hands tended also to dissipate the central purpose and replace it with new directions for effort. Thus potential dynasties are constantly dissolving.

A second feature of this system, and especially significant in contrast with European traditions, was that as wealth was evenly distributed, the numbers of the dispossessed remained smaller than in societies with inequitable inheritance systems. In Europe, the system of primogeniture, while keeping intact the family wealth, also released into the economy a stream of ambitious younger sons,

for whom entrepreneurship and commercial empire building became common
outlets. Conditions for this stimulus in China were far less favorable.

The Endurance of Personalism

It was noted in the preamble to this chapter that the third major force in
Chinese culture which has created a predisposition towards family business is
personalism. The argument is that this denies the emergence of the kind of objectivity and neutrality in which truly rational and professional bureaucracy can
flourish. In saying this, no assumption is implied that bureaucracy is a necessarily superior form of organization. It is simply the only one well understood and
considered normal for large-scale enterprise.

Personalism is the tendency to allow personal relationships to enter into decision making. In feudal societies, where power is highly concentrated in the
hands of key people, the workings of society reflect that particular distribution
of power. It is not what you know, it is who you know, and the "who" are people
with the right connections. At the extreme, it becomes impossible to make anything happen without access to the blessing of those in the key positions, and
successful organizational life comes to be based on the building and maintenance
of the appropriate contacts. The holding of a key position carries with it inordin-
ate influence and can be used to advance the security of its occupant as he shows
patronage and favor to individuals capable of repaying obligation with deference
and loyalty.

In all of these matters, the judgement of a person's worth, and particularly his
or her appropriateness to fill a certain role, becomes a question of loyalty rather
than technical ability. The possession of skill may not be totally ignored, and in
many cases may be an object of concern. The point is that in such a system it is
not the prime, or sole, criterion. The obligations which accompany such networks may also come to influence other features of business life such as investment decisions, borrowing and lending, and buying and selling.

There is an enduring myth that bureaucracy was perfected in China, and has
been a natural feature of life for centuries. It is certainly true that the creation of
a elite civil service in the form of the mandarinate, and the rigorous selection of
its members based on examination performance served to depersonalize government in a way which made it into a massively professional machine. It was never,
however, possible to extend those principles outside the governmental sphere,
and there were also large parts of the classical Chinese bureaucracy which were
rife with petty corruption, nepotism, and inefficiency (Sterba 1978). In a way,
the purity of the mandarinate itself was an anachronism and that may explain
much of its potency. The society to which it was applied remained concerned
with survival, with mistrust, with family welfare, and under a government more

concerned with stability than with institutional progress, more inclined to control than to protect, the Chinese people have built their own devices to make progress feasible. One of these is *guangxi*, or personal connections, and it remains the key to progress in the system. China has always needed more bureaucracy, in the technical sense of the word—the practical implementation of rational-legal authority—but has never been able to spread it far (Boisot and Child 1989). To understand why, and to see the limitations caused to organizations by this inhibition, requires some analysis of the social origins of personalism.

Inevitably in this analysis, one is faced with questions of why certain things did *not* happen, rather than why they did. It is rather like the problem of science, and arguably has the same ultimate determinant in the lack of rationality. The bureaucratic form of organization which is the norm for the West, the center piece of the entire field of management theory and very much the dominant economic mechanism in today's world, rests on certain values which its practitioners espouse, and which its creators especially believed in. These may be simplified into the following precepts:

(1) The organization of economic activity should be based on the logical pursuit of defined aims, which in turn will make necessary certain activities. Economic efficiency will determine the nature and structure of these activities, the choices being mediated by executives pursuing the goals rationally.
(2) The roles required for the managing of such systems should be filled by those most competent technically to carry them out.
(3) The achievement of cooperation, and thus of willing work, from the main operatives in the system should be based on creating a reward process which is objective and neutral, thus eliminating favoritism. Individuals then choose to contribute rationally.
(4) The creation of a neutral system requires extensive standardization either of work processes, or of outputs, or of skills. This standardization creates the order in which the neutrality may be grounded, and acts also as the base for specialization of work.
(5) All relationships and exchanges should be subject to some separate and authoritative body of law, recourse to which will ensure decisions accepted as reasonable by the majority.

The function of this combination of features is to allow people to transcend the limitations imposed when trust is circumscribed. Especially crucial is the availability of a recourse to law. This replaces the need for personal trust and produces a quantum leap in the kinds of relationships and exchanges which become feasible. Without it, life in general, and commercial life in particular, is kept within a smaller compass. In China, law was never really available as a practical recourse for the merchant, and without such a backing, all relationships remained personalistic. This in turn produced a barrier to the scale of enterprise, as important transactions could only be made face-to-face, and it made redundant any need for the professional executive who would rationally pursue goals on behalf of others as part of a contractual exchange.

The inhibitions which lay in the way of large-scale coordination of economic activity may be observed from an analysis by Lillian Li (1981) of the development of the silk industry.

In industries such as this in Europe, a critical change is discernible in the late medieval period when the "putting-out" system brought previously independent craftsmen under the control of merchants who provided them with raw materials, equipment such as looms, working capital, and a means of selling their production. This fostered a change from feudalism to merchant capitalism, and although the process of change was slow, it spread widely in Europe from the fifteenth century onwards.

Later, a further transition took place as the gathering together of production into workshops gave rise to industrial capitalism and set off a string of events which released increasing efficiencies in the production process as more complex technology was added, capital investment was increased, profits flowed back into plant, ownership of the means of production separated from labor, and a bourgeoisie emerged. In these circumstances, the spirit of capitalism was eventually made manifest in the managerial revolution which saw the emergence of a professional class devoted to the efficient managing of large publicly owned corporations. Such a spirit took efficiency as its central theme, and it has been accompanied by dramatic economic progress.

The development of industry in China, assuming the silk industry to be representative, displayed major differences from that in Europe. The universal use of silk in China dates back a thousand years to the Sung period, when it was produced for both wear and as currency in all but two of China's twenty-three provinces. It has since then always featured extensively in internal and external trade.

Originally in the hands of the state, whose Imperial Factories dominated the organization of the industry, new developments in the sixteenth century, and in particular the rise of urban markets, the growth of inter-regional trade, and increasing foreign demand, led to the rise of new and independent commercial weaving. Among this set of private commercial ventures, new ways of organizing developed and centered on the coordinating device of the *chang-fang*, or account house. Li describes these merchant enterprises as operating putting-out systems to distribute raw materials and looms. The weaving of silk fabrics would then be done in exchange for piece-rate wages and some kind of living allowance.

This system of loom households tied to an account house was normal into the twentieth century. The usual number of looms per household would be around four, thus making it a workshop and not a factory. The account house would normally control somewhere between a hundred and three hundred dispersed looms.

An important distinction now needs to be made between the way of organizing in China and that found in Western countries. The *chang-fang* were really merchant houses that became involved in manufacture mainly to ensure regular supplies for their principal function of trading. Although they were involved extensively in the financing of various stages in silk production, and were thus able to facilitate the flow of goods from one stage to another, their coordinating role stopped a long way short of bringing together the units of production into a more capital-intensive factory. Production thus remained small-scale, separated, and eventually based in a large number of single-family households. Similarity to European putting-out systems is then superficial, and the difference in organizing principles suggests that the development of capitalist-type production systems was not a natural part of the Chinese approach, which instead remained highly diffracted and family based. After considering parallel evidence from other industries, Li concludes that

Wherever putting-out existed in China . . . its fundamental purpose was to contract out work in a production process that was too complex to handle alone and to make a middleman, or series of middlemen, responsible for seeing that it got done . . . "Pao," "to guarantee certain achievement" was a fundamental concept which pervaded all such economic relationships in China . . . Financial management and production remained separate. The ultimate purpose was the diffusion of risk and responsibility among several different people, rather than their concentration in the hands of one entrepreneur. In short, it was totally contrary to the so-called spirit of capitalism (Li 1981: 61).

As Elvin also noted from a study of business history in China, rather than coordinating production into units which could release economies of scale, and substitute more efficient technology for hand labor, commerce rather than management continued to be the dominant theme (Elvin 1973: 277). Arrangements "congenial to the merchant temperament" meant that, for instance, cotton cloth merchants were not directly involved in production; the dyeing and finishing industry "seems to have been deliberately designed to prevent direct merchant participation in production"; cloth wholesalers were separated from finishers by contractors; merchants continued to play contractors off against each other; the merchant looked at the market, the artisan looked at production; the merchants only became involved in production when they were forced to, usually to protect supplies. Even when dense market networks grew in the nineteenth century, the integration of all these processes was not achieved by growing large coordinated organizations. Whatever linkages took place remained the temporary couplings of the market place. The fundamental economic unit remained small and almost always overlapped with a specific family.

We see then a society lacking in large coordinated economic structures, a society in which the only large-scale organization is government based, a society built for pre-modern growth but not for modernity. A number of contributing causes have so far been identified to explain why such a plethora of small institutions is preferred, and why they remain the limited extensions of what can be achieved when interpersonal trust is the principal connective tissue. We have noted the vicious circle of the high-level equilibrium trap in which the inefficiencies of hand labor and the inability to invest surplus capital in productive technology serve to perpetuate a muscle power economy. We have noted the lack of positive government intervention to foster the economy. We have acknowledged the insecurity of the businessman's environment and taken account of the traditional mode of domination-paternalism.

Beneath these, however, lie deeper influences, and they exist in the base layer of culture—that layer of mental life where a society's most elemental formulae are worked out. The institutions, laws or lack of laws, government behavior, economic activities, all reflect these prior understandings. It is at this level that insights may perhaps be most usefully gained, although doing so introduces the risks attendant on speculation.

Although subject to refinement by later writers, it is worth noting the classic treatment of this topic by Weber (1951: 277), whose view was trenchant: "in the magic garden of heterodox doctrine (Taoism) a rational economy and technology of modern occidental character was simply out of the question." Weber's reasoning was that all natural scientific knowledge was lacking, and its place taken by a crude, abstruse conception of the unity of nature, with the bulwark of magical tradition maintained by "chronomancers, geomancers, hydromancers, meteoromancers." Confucianism conspired with Taoism to preserve the magic garden, and at the same time to reduce tension with the world to an absolute minimum, seeing man-in-nature as ethically good and capable of unlimited perfection. Pious conformism became the guarantor of harmony. Nature was to be blended with and accommodated to; it was not to be controlled.

The importance of this "tension" between religious ideals and practical reality lay in its capacity to explain why some cultures strive to change the world and others (those without the tension) see the world as unchangable. For Weber, Protestantism particularly was all about change and control, whereas Confucianism was all about the preservation of the status quo.

The workings of these influences diverge particularly in the arena of personal relations. In the Confucian case, certain relationships are obligatory and hallowed, and as manifestations of the harmony of nature, they take on primacy. By contrast, Protestantism gave precedence to a person's relationship with God. Trust in men could endanger the soul. A superior community of faith and a common ethical way of life were set against the community of blood relationships, and even against the family itself. In Weber's view, the great achievement of such an ethical religion was to shatter the fetters of the clan. This achievement operated in the economic sphere by basing business confidence upon the "ethical qualities of the individual proven in his impersonal vocational work." In the Chinese case, reliance on personalism was a matter of building specific trust-bonds in a context of ubiquitous mistrust. Weber adds darkly, "the economic ramifications of universal and mutual distrust must probably be rated high" (Weber 1951: 237).

Noting the great cohesion of Chinese family organizations, Weber nevertheless observed that "to a striking degree they lacked rational matter-of-factness, impersonal rationalism, and the nature of an abstract, impersonal, purposive association." Economic and managerial forms of association or enterprise which could be identified as "purely purposive" were lacking. Kinship relations penetrated all communal action, including occupational associations. A stark contrast is evident:

Whereas Puritanism objectified everything and transformed it into rational enterprise, dissolved everything into the pure business relation, and substituted rational law and agreement for tradition, in China, the pervasive factors were tradition, local custom, and the concrete personal favor of the official (Weber 1951: 241).

As the constant reference to rationality indicates, this particular element is crucial, and yet it is not entirely obvious what is meant by it, in practical terms. It requires a little explication.

Robert Bellah (1965: 145), in his discussion of Asian religions and economic progress, makes the observation that the main vehicle of progress, which is technology, can only create a modern society when it is harnessed to two kinds of rationality: the rationalization of *means*, in which the insistence on technical efficiency is the typical case; and the rationalization of *ends*. This latter comes about when society achieves a sufficiently rich communication density to make it possible for rational goal-setting to take place based on assessing the needs of all parts of the system. It is in the arguing out of these latter priorities that religion, in representing core societal values, continues to play a central role. If the Protestant Reformation made all the world a monastery and channelled ascetic religious motivation into economic, scientific, and political roles, thus stimulating capitalism technology and democracy, what does Confucianism do in terms of defining desirable ends?

Arguably what it does is, by retaining such heavy emphasis on the family form of society, to sanction a family based economic system. It is then necessary to contend that this is not in fact rational, as it denies an "abstract, impersonal, purposive association."

The rationalizing of means in the Western case is visible in the drive for productive efficiency, in such fields as management science, microeconomics, production engineering, organizational design, etc. The rationalizing of ends is visible in the societal debates over appropriate wage payments, consumer rights, profit sharing, social responsibility of the corporation, environmental protection, and in fact any arguing out of the question, "What is industry there for?" The annual reports of corporations are replete with explanations of what their efforts are all about, and therein lie the rational intentions of the economy.

The most highly developed economic manifestation of such twin rationalities is the Western business corporation. It is designed for efficiency and constantly redesigned in pursuit of improvements. It is also designed with certain intentions in mind, and these are reflected in its shape and content. If its intention is to sell refrigerators, it will contain important sections which work on productive efficiency, on consumer needs, on distribution and marketing. If its intention is the mass retailing of food, it will accord emphasis (i.e. people, money, plant) to stock control, to purchasing, to retail operating. The huge variety of organizations which result reflect the workings of a vast proliferation of aims.

Such variety is less apparent in the Overseas Chinese case. Organizations are smaller, more similar to each other than are Western ones, and do not normally expand to follow the logics of design implied by their purpose. The small scale may well reflect the defensiveness, problems of trust, and paternalism already discussed. One further factor, however, may have a bearing on the hesitation to move to the neutral, objectively designed bureaucratic form. It is a contentious matter, and offered here only hypothetically and almost by way of a footnote, but it derives from a key word in Weber's description of the nature of modern organization. As well as the terms "impersonal" and "purposive," he used the term "abstract" to describe them. It may be that Chinese thinking does not naturally operate at this abstract level. Such organizations may be quite genuinely inconceivable.

We have noted in chapter 3 the way in which the Chinese language, by relating directly to sense-dependent impressions of tangible reality, builds a world picture to which the individual connects directly. The striking lack of abstracts in the language is further evidence of a quite different thought process from that normal in Indo-European languages. Western rationality rests heavily on Greek and later Cartesian logic and makes extensive use of abstract notions. The large Western corporation and even many medium-sized companies could not have been formed as they are without prior imagining of abstract concepts such as "the marketing function," "financial control," "divisionalization." What if such notions are not just foreign, not just obscure, but are actually somehow unnatural, even perhaps unthinkable? What if the organization can *only* be people and things?

Footnotes

[1] For a critique of Elvin's model, see also Huang 1978.
[2] The argument about city growth limits is:
    (1) Mortality rates in cities were higher because of disease;
    (2) an excess of young unmarried males caused lower urban fertility rates;
    (3) thus preindustrial cities had a negative demographic balance;
    (4) they required a continual inflow of rural people which could not increase until better agricultural productivity released it.

[3] This "southern metaphor" of escape into imitation of the landed aristocracy is held by
     Wiener to be still a powerful motivating force for many British executives (and a cause
     of much decline in manufacturing industry).

Chapter 7
The Chinese Family Business

An organization, especially when it is the dominant type of organization in a particular setting, may be seen as a cultural artifact. To understand the way in which the Chinese family business is a creature of Chinese tradition requires (a) a means of making valid comparison between it and other types in such a way that differences requiring explanation are illuminated, (b) that the ideas about organizing held by the key actors, in this case the entrepreneurs themselves, are explained and linked to their cultural sources, and (c) that the way the organization normally works in practice is explained.

The chapter sets out to meet those requirements. Before turning to the detail of those connections, however, it is necessary to make clear some warnings about over-simple models of cause and effect.

It is not possible to wrench a thing out of its context and understand its workings fully. The Chinese family business comes to be the dominant form for the coordination and control of economic activity in the societies where the Overseas Chinese flourish, because of a whole series of causes. More complete comprehension of why such a form becomes a standard and habitual response requires the analysis of a wide variety of factors present in the environment (Redding and Whitley 1990). These are partly sociological, partly political, and partly economic, and they will vary widely in detail from one national environment to another. Explaining this would be too grand an undertaking for our present purposes and for the present state of research in the field. Instead, this analysis concentrates very specifically on one line of influence—that running from the culture into the mental frameworks of the key actors, the entrepreneurs, and then on into the kinds of organization they create. In thus concentrating, it is necessary to acknowledge the liberty being taken, and to ask the reader to accept that in reality a full explanation requires more complexity. It would have to take far more variables into account, to allow for multiple and reciprocal determinacy, and to allow for a variety of forms within the general types discussed.

There are two main aspects of organization which will serve here to describe the nature of the Chinese family business: the structure of the organization, in terms of shape, size, and basic framework; and the way it is managed, seen in terms of the main managerial functions such as personnel, finance, etc. The way in which these features are influenced by the managerial ideology is outlined in Figures 7.1 and 7.2 and these will serve as the frameworks for this chapter.

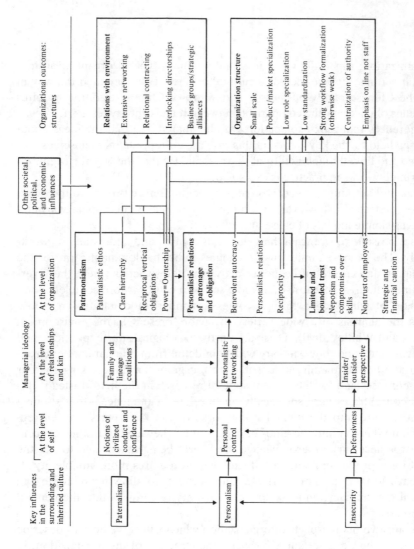

Figure 7.1: The Chinese family business: ideological determinants of organization structure

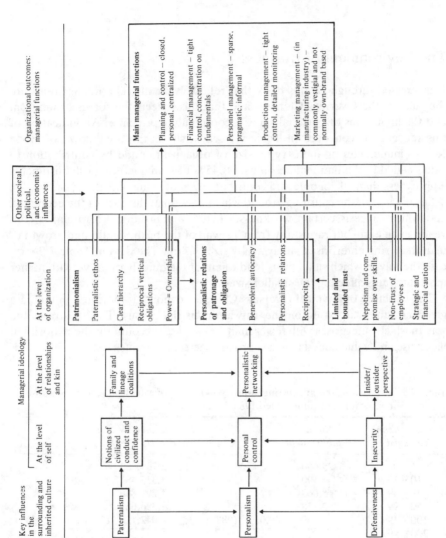

Figure 7.2:   The Chinese family business: ideological determinants of managerial functioning

Before considering the inner workings of such firms, however, it is necessary to have a sense of the setting in which they operate, and to that end, the business environments of Hong Kong and Taiwan, both archetypally Overseas Chinese in their make-up, will be briefly analyzed.

The Environment of Business

It is stressed throughout this book that relatively small-scale organizations are the rule for the Overseas Chinese, and that this reflects the forces of familism and the limitations of personalism as a coordinating principle. An indication of this tendency is conveyed in Table 7.1 which shows the breakdown of Hong Kong's manufacturing industry by size of organization and by contribution to value added in the national accounts. 98.45% of manufacturing establishments employ less than 200 people and contribute 63% of value added.

Some sense of the churning around which goes on at the base of the economy, and which suggests certain weaknesses in the organizational formula, is conveyed in an early but rare study from Taiwan of the birth, death, and growth of manufacturing enterprises, analysed by size of firm. The data in Table 7.2 indicate the way in which small firms tend to either die quickly or grow, with higher mortality rates affecting the smaller sizes.

The structure of a typical Overseas Chinese economy is indicated in the data given in Table 7.3, based on the Taiwan industrial census. This illustrates the way in which enterprises with fewer than 100 workers account for the majority of labor use and value added across a broad spectrum of industries.

Table 7.1: Hong Kong manufacturing industry—number of establishments by size and contribution to value added 1983

No. of Persons Engaged	No. of Establishments			Nat. accounts Value added HK$ 000's		
1 – 9	25,650			2,764,283		
10 – 19	6,190			2,335,481		
20 – 49	5,063			4,299,846		
50 – 99	2,138			4,396,663		
100 – 199	989	40,030	(98%)	4,042,128	17,838,401	(63%)
200 – 499						
	466	40,496		4,622,940	22,461,341	
500 – 999	117			2,960,616		
1000 +	45			2,908,951		
	40,660			28,330,888		

Source: Census and Statistics Department, Hong Kong Government

Table 7.2: Birth, death, and growth of manufacturing enterprises, Taiwan, 1961–66

	Distributed by size (workers) of enterprise				
	10 – 19	20 – 49	50 – 99	100 – 499	500+
Number of enterprises in 1966, T_1	3,912	2,510	758	643	131
Number of enterprises in 1966 less than 5 years old, B	2,107	1,408	420	339	24
Number of enterprises in 1961, T_0	3,872	1,851	426	318	69
$T_1 - T_0$	40	659	332	325	62
$(M-X) = (T_1-T_0) - B$	−2,067	−749	−88	−14	38
$(B/T_1) \times 100$	54%	56%	55%	53%	18%
$[(M-X)/T_0] \times 100$	−53%	−40%	−21%	−4%	158%
Workers in enterprises in 1966, N_1	52,012	75,614	51,301	133,560	205,019
Workers in enterprises less than 5 years old in 1966, N_b	27,656	42,527	28,356	69,548	21,605
Workers in enterprises in 1961, N_0	63,985	53,781	29,052	63,723	128,961
$N_1 - N_0$	11,973	21,833	22,249	69,837	76,058
$(N_m-N_x) = (N_1-N_0) - N_b$	−15,683	−20,694	−6,107	289	54,453
$(N_b/N_1) \times 100$	53%	56%	55%	52%	11%
$[(N_m-N_x)/N_0] \times 100$	−57%	−49%	−22%	.4%	252%

Notes: M is the number of enterprises 5 years or older in 1966 that moved into a given size category from other size categories during 1961–66. X is the number of enterprises that exited from a given size category either by death or by movement to another size category. N_m and N_x are the number of workers in M and X, respectively. For consistency, repair establishments and tailor shops are included in 1966. The underlying data are from *General Report, 1961 Industry and Commerce Census of Taiwan* and *General Report on the Third Industrial and Commercial Census of Taiwan, The Republic of China*.

The data indicate that in 1966 new firms (B, surviving firms formed during 1961–66) accounted for over one-half of both the number of enterprises and number of workers in every size category except for the largest (500+ workers). As expected, there were large negative net movements into the smaller size categories and large positive net movements into the largest size category. During 1961–66, 2,067 more enterprises left than entered the size category with 10–19 workers, probably because of the very high death rate among small firms. The net movement of enterprises during 1961–66 as a share of the number of enterprises in 1961 was −53 percent for enterprises with 10–19 workers, −40 percent for those with 20–49 workers, −21 percent for those with 50–99 workers, −4 percent for those with 100–499 workers, and 158 percent for those with 500 or more workers. In other words, the evidence suggests that death and movement to a different size category occurred frequently among small enterprises.

If it is assumed that during 1961–66 no firm with 500 or more workers died or moved to a smaller size category—that is, X = 0 for enterprises with 500 or more workers, then it can be deduced that, during 1961–66, 38 firms moved from a smaller size into the largest size category, and they contributed between 25 and 72 percent of the increase in employment in the 500+ size category. In other words, the growth of small and medium scale firms may have contributed substantially to the increase of employment in enterprises in the largest size category.

Source: Ho 1980

Table 7.3: Taiwan industries in which small enterprises[a] employed 50% or more of the workers in the particular industry in 1971 by type of industry

			Workers in small enterprises		Value added in small enterprises	
		No. of small enterprises	Persons	Share of industry workers	Million NT $	Share of industry VA, %
IA.	**Resource processors**					
	Meat processing	158	1,014	74	21.8	84
	Dairy products	327	1,760	58	39.8	41
	Vegetable oil	521	3,751	80	31.0	44
	Rice milling	6,899	18,031	100	389.3	100
	Tea processing	234	3,715	95	56.3	96
	Tanning & leather finishing	115	1,016	53	26.7	63
	Sawmills and planing mills	1,291	12,222	52	338.6	30
IB.	**Market-oriented industries**					
	Animal feeds	1,078	3,921	64	76.7	a
	Food, n.e.c.	2,401	13,562	81	208.6	81
	Furniture and fixtures	909	6,212	67	148.3	63
	Agricultural insecticides	65	1,496	68	49.7	59
	Glass and its products	147	4,514	53	95.8	29
	Structural clay products	1,066	22,347	90	332.2	88
	Cement products	633	4,490	67	89.3	58
	Nonmetallic mineral products, n.e.c.	379	5,512	60	133.2	77
	Metal furniture	147	1,572	100	35.2	100
	Tin cans and boxes	76	1,315	82	30.9	76
	Aluminum products (e.g., door, window frames)	282	4,262	71	93.4	61
	Manufactured ice	658	3,610	58	114.4	74
IC.	**Service industries**					
	Printing	1,261	13,201	85	345.7	64
	Metal processing	414	3,183	100	72.4	100
IIA.	**Separable mfg. operations**					
	Iron and steel products for industrial use	1,650	14,802	70	347.2	64
	Manufacturing and repair of machines, and equip., excluding electrical	4,161	40,882	67	1,031.4	58
	Transport equipment, n.e.c.	272	3,058	68	73.5	61
	Metal products, n.e.c.	288	3,798	92	74.3	77
	Special electrical apparatus	59	1,289	56	23.8	47
	Professional, scientific equipment	165	2,359	50	52.9	51
IIB.	**Simple assembly, mixing or finishing**					
	Flavoring exc. monosodium glutamate	528	2,828	79	62.2	72
	Products of wood, bamboo, cane, n.e.c.	1,399	15,024	78	300.4	81
	Processed paper & its prods.	304	3,928	72	74.3	92

Table 7.3: (Continued)

	No. of small enterprises	Workers in small enterprises		Value added in small enterprises	
		Persons	Share of industry workers	Million NT $	Share of industry VA, %
Bookbinding	159	1,554	94	34.7	92
Acids and alkalis	185	3,693	52	98.9	42
Paint, color, ink	176	2,676	75	77.0	77
Medical, pharmaceutical preparations	544	8,456	72	228.7	49
Soap, detergent, cosmetics	412	4,255	55	126.1	73
Chemical products, n.e.c.	300	3,841	66	27.5	19
Textile products, n.e.c.	108	1,791	57	25.0	51
IIIB. Small total market					
Canning, preserving of meat	36	716	87	9.1	75
Animal fats	19	148	100	3.2	100
Mills, n.e.c.	334	1,810	94	20.0	97
Silk textiles	51	934	67	14.4	70
Leather apparel	1	25	100	1.3	100
Wood preservation	2	181	100	14.0	100
Paper bags	55	493	62	11.2	48
Publishing	2	19	100	.3	100
Engraving and etching	77	695	100	16.0	100
Inedible oils and fats	54	426	70	2.6	99
Coal products	6	78	100	2.2	100
Asphalt materials	3	43	100	1.3	100
Rubber and synthetic rubber	54	705	100	13.3	100
Rubber sole	43	783	65	8.8	77
Copper	59	761	61	14.4	b
Basic metal, n.e.c.	13	126	100	2.6	100
Electric insulators and insulation	1	14	100	.2	100
Motorized tricycles	84	836	72	17.2	92

[a] Those with fewer than 100 workers.
[b] Industry's value added was negative in 1971.

Source: The Report of the 1971 Industrial and Commercial Censuses of Taiwan and Fukien Area, *Republic of China*

Reference appears regularly also in this book to the processes of networking which tie organizations together, and which reflect the instincts whereby personalism is used to counteract the limitations brought about by trust being so circumscribed. Data illustrating this phenomenon are available from a recent Hong Kong study of almost three hundred small and small/medium-size firms (Sit and Wong 1988). The nature of these connections is visible in Figure 7.3 which shows the extent of local buying and selling relationships in five representative indus-

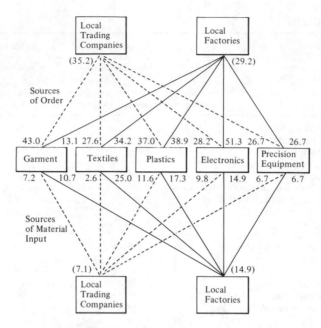

Figure 7.3: Purchasing and selling relations between local trading companies and local factories

Note: Figures are percentages of firms selling to or buying from respective sources from each industry; bracketed figures are same percentages for total small and medium industry sample.

tries. The formalization of these connections in contracts is illustrated in Figure 7.4. Companies making finished products, such as garments, rely heavily on local trading companies as sources of orders. Companies making components, such as those in the electronics or plastics industries, rely heavily on local factories for their orders.

The move into subcontracting as such, which introduces a degree more rigidity into the system, affects about a quarter of small and medium-sized firms in both selling out and buying in. Dependence on subcontracting is marginally higher in smaller firms, but the striking feature in this survey is that the majority of firms did not use the subcontract option. They appear to prefer the freedom of buying and selling in a less structured manner. 23% of those in that freer category said they thought it unprofitable, and 23% said they had enough orders anyway. We shall note later how this flexibility in making economic transactions brings a substantial source of efficiency to the economy when analysed at the level of a particular industry.

Among those firms receiving subcontract orders, the tendency is to manage that relationship with a degree less formality than might be the case in other cultures. 31% of subcontracting firms were in that position because of "personal

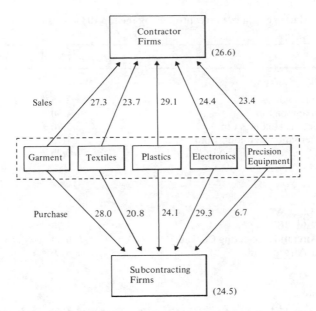

Figure 7.4: Frequence of subcontracting arrangement

Note: Figures are percentages of firms in the industry with subcontracting arrangements for buying from and selling to relevant sources, bracketed figures are same percentages for total small and medium industry sample.

Source: Sit and Wong 1988

relation" with the firm they supplied. In 53% of cases, price was fixed by negotiation between the two parties rather than unilateral offer, and in 34% of cases only verbal contract existed. The majority of orders were for delivery inside one month, and this indicates the flexible market response in operation. Despite the unstable and irregular nature of subcontracting described by 71% of respondents doing it, nevertheless 81% were satisfied with the formula.

Networking of a quite different form operates also in the field of ownership among the Overseas Chinese and is illustrated by research on the control of companies on the Hong Kong stockmarket (Wong 1989). Table 7.4 shows how 54% of the stockmarket capitalization is controlled by ten family groups, seven of them Chinese, one Jewish/British, and two British. This process of creating informally allied business groups has strategically useful outcomes for capital raising, competitive behavior, and political cooperation, and is done by an elaborate net of interlocking directorates. Although this is networking writ large, it is nevertheless symptomatic of the web of relationships tying the economy together through to the base of the system where either partnerships or trust bonds serve to maintain the potent balance of flexibility in meeting market demand, and reliability in seeing economic transactions completed.

Table 7.4: % Market capitalization controlled by the top 10 families in Hong Kong as at 31.3.88

	% Market Capitalization
K.S. Li Group	
Cheung Kong (Holdings) Ltd.	3.15
Hutchison Whampoa Ltd.	4.80
Hongkong Electric Holdings Ltd.	2.76
Cavendish International Holdings Ltd.	1.75
Green Island Cement (Holdings) Ltd.	0.26
	12.720
Swire Group	
Swire Pacific Ltd. "A"	3.19
Swire Pacific Ltd. "B"	1.78
Hong Kong Aircraft Engineering Co. Ltd.	0.44
Cathay Pacific Airways Ltd.	3.86
	9.280
Keswick Group	
Jardine Matheson Holdings Ltd.	1.45
Hongkong Land Co. Ltd.	3.53
Hongkong Land Co. Ltd. - Preferred Ordin	0.23
Jardine Strategic Holdings Ltd.	1.13
Jardine Strategic Holdings Ltd. Preferred	0.06
Dairy Farm International Holdings Ltd.	1.12
Mandarin Oriental International Ltd.	0.50
Zung Fu Co. Ltd.	0.19
	8.200
Kadoorie Group	
China Light and Power Co. Ltd.	4.17
Hongkong and Shanghai Hotels Ltd.	0.75
Hong Kong Carpet (Holdings) Ltd.	0.03
	4.950
Y.K. Pao Group	
World International (Holdings) Ltd.	1.28
Wharf (Holdings) Ltd.	2.25
Harbor Centre Development	0.35
Hongkong Realty and Trust Co. Ltd. "A"	0.31
Hongkong Realty and Trust Co. Ltd. "B"	0.04
Realty Development Corporation Ltd. "A"	0.21
Realty Development Corporation Ltd. "B"	0.02
Harriman Holdings Ltd.	0.03
Allied Properties (HK) Ltd.	0.17
Lane Crawford Holdings Ltd. "A"	0.12
Lane Crawford Holdings Ltd. "B"	0.08
	4.860

Table 7.4: (Continued)

	% Market Capitalization
T.S. Kwok Group	
Sun Hung Kai Properties Ltd.	2.72
New Town (N.T.) Properties Ltd.	1.11
Kowloon Motor Bus Co. (1933) Ltd.	0.72
Manor House Holdings Ltd.	0.11
	4.670
S.K. Lee Group	
Henderson Land Development Co. Ltd.	1.34
Wing Tai Development Co. Ltd.	0.28
Hongkong and Yaumati Ferry Co. Ltd.	0.21
Hongkong and China Gas Co. Ltd.	1.41
	3.240
Y.T. Cheng Group	
New World Development Co. Ltd.	2.14
New World Hotels (Holdings) Ltd.	0.64
	2.780
T.H. Chan Group	
Hang Lung Development Co. Ltd.	1.05
Amoy Properties Ltd.	0.78
	1.830
T.V.B. Group*	
Bond Corporation International Ltd.	0.32
HK-TVB Ltd.	1.14
	1.470
% OF TOTAL MARKET CAPITALIZATION	54.000

* Until recently, this was the Run Run Shaw group.

Notes: All the Chinese groups are first generation. The non-Chinese are much older in lineage.
Control does not mean total ownership, but ability to control a firm's strategy, via sufficient ownership.

The Firm's Internal Structure

The basis for this account is a parallel study to that analysing the beliefs of managers. It is part of the Aston series of organization studies, and as the account of it presented here is written for the non-specialist in organization theory, some introduction to its aims and methods will be justified. A note should perhaps also be injected here that this book is principally about the spirit which moves these organizations rather than about their detailed mechanisms. Even so, that spirit cannot be seen in context unless some basic understanding is also available of the economic instrument which such a spirit gives rise to. Chinese capitalism has a special way of coordinating and controlling economic action. It can best be understood by reference to the ways adopted in other economic cultures. The Aston research method facilitates this comparison. A total of 94 companies were studied in Hong Kong, Taiwan, the Philippines, and Indonesia, each with an interview schedule of 114 pages.

The language for describing organizations, as it has been refined through the Aston studies, sees them as varying along five major dimensions. [1]

(1) *Centralization*, which conveys a sense of where hierarchically in the organization the majority of decisions are taken.
(2) *Specialization*, which reflects the extent to which labor is divided. It includes dividing an organization into specialized units, and also allocating tightly defined roles to people.
(3) *Standardization*, or the extent to which rules and definitions are used to regularize procedures and roles.
(4) *Formalization*, or the extent to which activities are formalized through paperwork systems.
(5) *Configuration*, which conveys the balance of line vs. staff personnel.

There are fairly obvious connections between specialization, standardization, and formalization, in that they all reflect the degree to which a company is "organized." If they are clearly evident in an organization, it suggests that somebody has designed the system to allow people to focus on specialist activities, somebody has laid down a set of guidelines, and somebody has designed a paperwork system to keep track of what is happening. These managerial activities commonly go together as they are all parts of the same momentum to get things under tidy control. It is possible thus to combine these three, calling the result "structuring of activities" and allowing it to represent the degree to which the behavior of employees is overtly defined.

In contrast with this tendency to have work systematically designed, there is another organizing principle which, put at its simplest, is telling people what to do. If people can get on with their work without being told what to do, it is another way of saying that authority has been decentralized. For this to happen, the authority figures at the top usually want some assurance that the authority delegated will be exercised within certain understood boundaries, and with some defined discretion. For this reason, a higher degree of structuring of activities usually goes with more delegation. If, on the other hand, a boss wants to retain the complete say-so in everything, he does not need elaborate structures to control subordinates' discretion because they don't have so much. High centralization of decisions usually means low structure. Delegation requires structure.

It is also intuitively obvious that as an organization grows larger and more complex, there will need to be a process of delegation if the top is not to become overloaded with decision making. Research findings demonstrate this clearly, so that larger size means (a) more structuring of activities, and (b) less centralization of decisions.

The way in which the structuring of activities proceeds to grow as the organization expands divides into two alternative paths. Some organizations bureaucratize everything relating to employment, and they tend to have central recruiting, selection, discipline and dismissal procedures, formally constituted committees, appeal procedures, and the like. The way they organize concentrates more on the employment contract than the daily work activity itself. Such an organization is called a *personnel bureaucracy*, and they are typically found in government structures or in smaller branches of large corporations.

An alternative route is found in much of manufacturing industry and in big business generally. This is based on the idea of structuring activities around the flow of work and is based on the use of such control devices as production schedules, quality inspection procedures, output records, etc. This combination produces a *workflow bureaucracy*.

It is also possible for both of these forms of organizing to be combined into what is termed a *full bureaucracy*, and this is normally found in organizations which are at the same time large, complex, and decentralized.

The data will lead us to the conclusion that the typical Chinese family business remains small and relatively unstructured. Because of cultural restraints on the sharing of trust, it does not develop decentralized decision making, and this acts as an inhibitor to successful growth. It therefore forms a type of its own, with low structure following the universal tendencies of the size/structure relationship, but with the reason for staying that way having much to do with a particular social psychology. Where it does exhibit higher structure, it does so selectively and usually in the field of control of basic workflow operations.

In order to connect the social psychology and the organizational outcomes, we may now bring back into the account the views of the chief executives, and use them as a framework, as in Figures 7.1 and 7.2, to organize the comparative data.

The overwhelmingly consistent theme in discussions about their organizations by Chinese executives is patrimonialism. That word as such is not used by them, but it is the only word which captures adequately the themes of paternalism, hierarchy, responsibility, mutual obligation, family atmosphere, personalism, and protection. Out of it flow three related themes which are in some sense expressions of it, namely: the idea that power cannot really exist unless it is connected to ownership; a distinct style of benevolently autocratic leadership; and personalistic as opposed to neutral relations. Given the working of these three influences and of the paternalist climate, a number of organizational outcomes are discernible: problems over high-level skills; small scale and product/market concentration; the repression of organizational talent.

Paternalism

Let us begin by considering the paternalism *per se* in the sense in which it is discussed by Chinese executives. We shall then proceed to analyze the three consequent topics which flow from it.

To be able to say, as did *Shek*, "My staff is my family" requires not just a knowledge of how to turn such a view into an economically efficient system of relations, but also a set of inner convictions to sustain the chief executive in making often hard decisions which affect such an organizational culture. Firing or not firing someone, determining rewards, dealing with discipline and control are all tests of an executive's inner morality as well as his economic pragmatism. The sustaining of familistic organizations on the scale that is evident in the Overseas Chinese case suggests that these inner convictions are strong.

Perhaps because Chinese morality is based in relationships rather than in more abstract ideals, one might anticipate the enhancing of a sense of responsibility towards workers. *Hoi* in discussing whether there was a moral base for authority, observed that "'Moral' is perhaps a misnomer. It does not represent the quality of being always on the straight and narrow. It is more a matter of respect in treating workers and the company."

Or, as others put it,

Hsien:
The Chinese mentality is to have the tax rate low and let the owner be benevolent to his surroundings.

Teng:
In a smaller business, affection and relationships between boss and staff is important for good working. The human factor is very important, even though the sole purpose of management should be growth. I pay a great deal of attention to such interpersonal relationships with staff, and every year I will hold a party for all my staff and their families first to feel close with them like one family.

Hu:
I believe I was doing the staff a good deal [growing the company]. All the staff that are under me, they served me well and I look after them. That is a very well-known Chinese way. I believe in it so much that I feel if I have more people—I haven't got that many, only sixty or seventy [note professionals]—it's not that many, but I've built up from ten people, so my success is more or less based on the people, so I provide happy employment. That may seem a little bit philosophical.

It is of course inappropriate to isolate such a component from the culture in which it is embedded, and necessary, in consequence, to acknowledge that this view, as it were, from the top, tends to be balanced by and in tune with the view from below:

Huan:
The best factory of all I know was the one my mother worked for. The reason is that the boss had managed to extract a lot of people from the same village. He helped a lot of people and their livelihood, and he used a lot of his earnings, his money, and distributed it

to his relatives—buying houses, flats for them. I admire him a lot. The thing that has a shaping influence on me is that kind of caring. It's not exploitation as such.

Hioe:
Generally the Chinese employees normally respect managers. They are mostly rather obedient type of people. It's from the traditions and from the educational system. The first thing you have to do you have to listen to the leaders—to do what the leader tells you to do—until you have experience and know-how and try to do what you want to do—but not until then. I see many young graduates and they are very respectful, very obedient in the first place. But psychologically you have another burden—that means that you have to take care of these guys. They keep holding your hand.

Responsibility comes thus to be exercised partly from moral purpose in the Confucian humanist tradition, and partly in response to a somewhat deferential and dependent mentality on the part of many workers. The responsibility spreads over both task and welfare aspects of employment. Managers expressed regularly a view that they were responsible for fitting people into the right slots, for stewardship of resources, for helping the inefficient, providing security for the older ones, for being understanding.

Hap:
In any incident which might involve firing, my advice to supervisors is to assess the blame. If you assess 10% to the company and the worker 90%—I call it even—you don't fire. . . . I walk around my factory—my symbol is a bottle of beer in my hand, no glass— my workers drink Blue Riband, I order San Mig, the cheaper price. I think I'm very paternalistic. I think I have an obligation to look after my men. But I know that if I look after them eventually I look after myself. That is my philosophy.

Our normal staff bonus has averaged nine months per year over the last three years, paid twice yearly. If we paid it monthly they would spend it. . . . At the time of a recession, the first bonuses cut are the directors' and senior managers'.

Reporting very similar approaches in Indonesia, *Ip* noted that the function of the family atmosphere was to foster cooperation, a matter discussed from inside a very large financial corporation by *Han*, who described the chairman knowing about the staff's families, giving out the red packets at Chinese New Year, joining the singing at Christmas.

There is something which goes beyond a staff and superior's relationship, and they like this working environment. And, erm—dictatorship—is seldom needed in the company. A lot of people would tend to think if the boss wants it done this way, he must have some reason for it, it must be good for the company. Not many people will think about whether this is right or wrong. Chinese are less inclined to face an issue direct. It's more related to family training.

In a consideration of the contrast between relationships based on contract and those based on personal obligation, *Hsien* expressed the opinion that "More medium-sized firms—even very large firms—in Hong Kong—if you are looking at the contractual at one end of the scale and the extended family at the other end—I would think probably it tilts toward the extended family. It still is, I think, in Hong Kong."

The cooperation which results in these structures, although clearly a major contributor to organizational efficiency, is bought, as are most organizational features, at the cost of something else, and there are inevitable weaknesses in paternalism acknowledged by several observers. The most obvious target of the familial approach was nepotism, a problem illuminated by a number of dramatic corporate collapses in Hong Kong, Singapore, and Taiwan. But very little was said about the need for a more neutral and professional approach. In fact, only one respondent said, "You should run a company like a company and not a family" (*Sit*), an exception which may be left to prove the rule.

The cultural legacy of Overseas Chinese business has caused to emerge a distinct view of power and legitimacy. Power derives from ownership which is in turn vested in family rather than an individual. While this does create the kind of unquestioning obedience just noted, it also introduces one very distinct, and particularly Chinese, organizational defect. This is that nobody outside the owning group can generate for himself truly legitimate authority. This becomes a very significant handicap to the grafting on of a middle and senior management group made up of competent professionals, and it becomes an important component of the explanation of why Chinese family businesses are unable to escape from the formula of family domination. Although there are occasional exceptions, and although change is possible and occurs in many fields, the overwhelming impression is that the status quo as regards authority being legitimated only through ownership is proving remarkably resilient and resistant to the forces of modernization. What is happening fits the culture, and some of its most deeply embedded features change at a rate which can only be described as glacial.

The matter is put clearly in a conversation about the nature of authority, which went as follows:

Hsien:
The staff would naturally look towards the highest source of authority, who is the boss, the real owner of the company. He will take commands from that level. Even though a manager tells him to do this and that and he knows that is probably the right track—the boss can come around and overrule the manager, and the lower level would listen to the boss instead of the manager—because he knows where the paycheck is coming from. Even though the boss may not be right.
Hwa:
I think most people would say it's the ownership that gives the authority. In the old days, the emperor said that he owns the entire country. In many Chinese organizations, deep inside I think the boss thinks he owns everything—you are my people, my subjects.
Question:
If the natural form of legitimacy is ownership, that must make it almost impossible to create an alternative form of intermediate authority, correct?
Hwa:
That makes the life of a manager very difficult. That's right.
Hsien:
That is the case.

Hwa:
I think for many managers the criterion for making a decision is to ask how would the boss react to it. Would he overrule it? You have to avoid loss of face.

This very revealing conversation, with all its overtones of a somewhat stifling atmosphere for a really talented middle manager who does not belong to the family, provides a further reason for the obsession to control which was noted in chapter 4 and which fuels the constant upsurge of entrepreneurial talent. The reason is that anybody really good is just as much pushed out as tempted out, a point which will be returned to.

The idea of the *eminence grise* standing behind all decision making is noted in Chinese as well as French. As *Hsu* noted, "If you're talking the Chinese family business, definitely ownership and managerial responsibility overlap—and the owner carries far more status than ever—he is the real boss (*Lau bak*)." This "realness" is explained by a number of respondents, often with the brutal simplicity of *Huen:* "Maybe they are aware that I sign the checks," or of *Hsia,* "We own the company, so we have the authority."

The big boss also may have his surrogates, and the line between responsible involvement and meddling may become blurred.

Tin:
In a family business, the family and especially the older generation can't help interfering in decision making in the business.

There are no really viable alternatives in normal use. As *Heung* says, "I don't think we have the concept of a public company." "Being a son of the founder is a logical mandate in Chinese society" (*Siu*), and will always bring compliance even if not always respect.

There are also protective devices which help to preserve such authority from being undermined, one of the most insidious being reminiscent of the old Chinese tradition of some other unfortunate taking your punishment for you:

Har:
My father taught me that in a situation where, say, the owner of the company is at logger-heads with the staff, then someone in management is to take the blame. It's not going to be him. There has to be a scapegoat, because the Chinese believe in a very untarnished reputation. . . . It is important that he remains the god. In fact, his nickname was Jesus in Chinese, because he preaches a lot. He would take them out to a restaurant, or a cooked food stall, to take the air, to take food and also preach at them.

Such an Olympian perspective does not, however, prevent realism, and it is not unusual now for companies to offer shares to really crucial non-family executives, in partial acknowledgement of questions of legitimacy, and also questions of commitment. The hoped-for outcome is the kind of influence able to be exerted by, for instance,

Hap:
We had a big order and needed three floors of the factory to work from the third day of Chinese New Year instead of the seventh. The factory manager asked and 65% agreed. It was not enough. So I wrote to everyone and the response was 98%. And the three workers who could not, came to me in person to explain why.

The retention of power in this way, at the top of the organization, is of course only conducive to overall effectiveness in certain kinds of organization, and perhaps at certain stages of their development. The cost of autocracy, whether or not it is benevolent and responsible, is that fewer people are doing the organization's thinking for it. As *Ho* puts it:

As an owner, no one will challenge what you say. They accept. They do what you want. But in a way I don't find it very healthy, because they don't become responsible people. They just let you make the decisions.

Evidence for these forces at work is available from the Aston data about organization structuring given in Table 7.5.

The main elements of structure are described statistically in Table 7.5, using a comparison of Hong Kong and UK companies within the same size range. From this, it is clear that the degree of organizing which takes place in the Chinese case is less than in the British case.

Role specialization indicates the extent to which an organization has taken the

Table 7.5: Main elements of organization structure described statistically using the Aston measures comparing Hong Kong Chinese companies and UK companies

			mean	*SD*	*range*
Role specialization	UK	(n = 34)	26.2	13.8	0–62
	HK	(n = 53)	18.5	14.4	0–69
Standardization	UK		74.4	20.4	30–117
	HK		59.8	23.0	11–111
Formalization	UK		19.8	9.9	4–41
	HK		19.7	10.0	1–41
Centralization	UK		80.9	13.9	57–116
	HK		109.9	15.2	70–139
Configuration	UK		29.7	17.2	6–72
(percentage nonworkflow)	HK		13.5	12.5	0–75
Size	UK		727	435	241–1,749
(no. of employees)	HK		512	494	50–2,600

Note: For details of Aston methodology, see Pugh and Hickson (1976)

trouble to specify precisely what people are to do. It is evident in such practical manifestations as organizations charts, titles on people's office doors, job descriptions given to people to make clear what they do, whom they report to, whom they are responsible for. It is particularly an indication of the organization's wish to organize a concentration of skill on some aspect of its work, and to leave that concentration more or less undisturbed. In this regard, the UK score is 30% higher than that of the Hong Kong companies, and is compelling support for an earlier description of Overseas Chinese organizational behavior by Silin (1976) in which he describes the allocation of managerial responsibilities as diffuse and shifting, with responsibilities kept deliberately open to change and reinterpretation by the chief executive.

In a sense, giving people clearly defined roles is a way of decentralizing authority. It makes it more difficult to impose new or alternative requirements on them and thus reduces the discretion of bosses to impose their will differently later. There appears to be resistance to placing such a limit on managerial discretion. Instead, the paternalist ethos, with its non-negotiable definition of authority residing in ownership, means that the boss can still intervene. The subordinate needs still to adjust. To exaggerate the point, there is no job definition to hide behind, or at least less of one. As *Tsai* succinctly put it, "There is too much stupid loyalty to the boss."

Standardization displays a similar pattern. The UK score is 20% higher than the Hong Kong score and again indicates a lower level of "organizing" for the Chinese. Here the question is one of the regularizing of procedures and again indicates the difference in the balance achieved in each case between the pull to use a neutral bureaucratic system and the pull to rely on a more personalistic over-ride. The latter with its capacity to fit with expectations about specific bonds of reciprocity, and also with the urge for centralized control, would appear to be preferred.

Formalization is the only dimension where scores are the same, but a closer examination of the detailed scales reveals that this is because the Chinese organizations are particularly strong on the use of paperwork to control the workflow process of the organization, stronger than the Western counterpart. This sense of urgent control of things such as production scheduling, the keeping of detailed records related to the work process, are indicators of the intensity with which attention is brought to bear on the managing of the lifeblood of the organization—productive efficiency. Here is a glimpse of the hard-nosed pragmatism of the owner-manager, standing guard over the efficient use of his personal capital, concerned to a special degree with the real fundamentals of the business. Reflected here also is the problem of trust outside the inner circle, and the very basic tools needed to motivate a workforce whose loyalties inevitably lie with their own families to a degree unusual in many cultures (Redding and Wong 1986).

The Chinese score for centralization is 27% higher than for the UK, indicating that there are more decisions made at the top in the Chinese case. This accords well with expectations of a paternalist system, and with the fact that virtually all Chinese family businesses are headed by a dominant paterfamilias who becomes deeply immersed in the minutiae of daily operations.

The configuration score is an intriguing index of pragmatism. It measures the percentage of people in the organization who are not directly concerned with producing the output, what used to be called "staff" as opposed to "line." In the UK case, the figure is 30%, whereas in Hong Kong only 13.5%. Some acknowledgement has to be made that the complexity of the UK environment, and the imposition of government regulations, etc., will demand the employment of more specialists to handle such matters, certainly compared to the non-interventionist, unregulated atmosphere of Hong Kong. Even so, the difference cannot all be accounted for thus, and it remains striking. One is tempted to see it as a sign that Overseas Chinese organizations contain no frills and carry no fat. If you are not helping directly to produce profit, there is little room for you.

Another influence reflected here is the suspicion of professionals. To have a personnel department, for instance, or a financial analyst, or work-study function, is to bring into the organization a possible challenge to managerial authority. Expert power can undermine the power of relationship or patronage, and this may also account for the apparent reluctance to build up the "staff" side as opposed to the "line." There may thus be several reasons for this feature: an unwillingness to spend money on organizational "frills", a suspicion about the threat of being undermined, a simple lack of examples to follow, or organizations being too small for such finesse. In reality, no doubt all features are present.

What has been said so far about paternalism will have imparted some of the flavor of Chinese leadership style, a style summarized in Silin's monograph on the topic as "didactic"—retaining power by rationing information and assuming the superiority of the teacher. As this appears to be a core component of leadership behavior, it will bear some scrutiny before looking at other related aspects of style. In all this, it is inevitably necessary to acknowledge that individuals will interpret such norms via their interpersonal behavior in ways which display wide variation, and that not all will fit into this pattern. There is, however, a chorus of comment about it which suggests that across the respondents the interpretation of how power is best exercised does take on a certain coherence, and that this is not understandable unless the socio-cultural surroundings are taken into account.

It does not come as a surprise that decision making is not an open affair. If it were, many more people would feel the right to become involved and that, in turn, would threaten the hierarchy. In any case, there appears to be a consensus among subordinates that their duties do not include taking on the responsibility normally resting with owners. It is not the subordinate's job to make decisions, and his reaction would be a conflation of (a) he has no right to, without ownership, and (b) he is not paid to, so why should he?

The mixture of power with ownership, nobody else being responsible, and accustomed deference, allow the leader, in the Chinese tradition of the paterfamilias keeping his own council, to quietly ruminate over the issues until he arrives at a strategy by a process most conveniently, but not necessarily accurately, labelled "intuition." Such a label does insufficient justice to the accumulation of information and experience in the chief executive's head, and the clarity with which he normally perceives his goals.

But whether he commits himself openly to a public declaration of his intent, is another matter entirely. In fact, he is very unlikely to, for open communication is a taken for granted side effect of a democratic style, and these are not democratic organizations.

Hsu:
I think communication is a Western concept. It's never been a Chinese concept. We never talk about the skill of communicating. If you're smart, you learn to feel it. You learn to be very observant. You look at the face of your boss—the little actions that he does—and you pick up the hints, you know. You would be very bloody stupid if—until the boss told you, to do certain things. Although you know how to do it.
Question:
What's the function of that?
Hsu:
It's the art of ruling that I put you in a situation where you have to keep guessing what I'm thinking. So I put you in a role where you are always trying to please me . . . In the older Chinese style, quite often what is not said is more important than what is said—and they just deliberately leave little hints without being explicit—to test you. And this is said to be the highest art of leadership and management.

As the superior—subordinate relationship is a crucial building block of organization, it will bear further scrutiny:

Hwa:
In a Western system, people can argue and disagree—openly. If the decision is made by someone higher up, then you follow but you can make him know that you disagree. But with the Chinese then, it's different. You try to think what the top man is thinking and then you tend to agree. You say something that he would agree—
Hai:
Otherwise you lose your job—
Hsien:
Well, that's part of the Chinese culture as such—trying to avoid confrontation.
Hwa:
The culture itself is the submissiveness. The Chinese are so used to it generation after generation.

Given a style of decision making as introverted as this, and given the parallel willingness by subordinates to accept it, it is not surprising that a senior person would allow himself the indulgences of (a) unaccounted-for changes of direction, and (b) interference. Changing direction may, of course, be a strength in that it provides the organization with a sometimes remarkable level of flexibility—a feature which in many industries can be crucial to survival. It can also, however, lead to wasted resources and much lower level frustration. The astute executive would not wish to be judged erratic and would control that impulse, but there is much evidence that such astuteness is not universal.

Interference, a version of the same possessiveness over strategy, and an index of the inhibitions over delegation which are equally a part of the leadership style, is also commonly reported. As *Hu* confesses,

I have a lot of trust in my own staff. I believe they will not do anything bad which brings harm to the company. But I do not trust them well enough to just let go, and let them run the business, or run departments in the business. I still want to interfere in most of the decision making.

This is not to say that a more democratic style is not seen as an ideal. It undoubtedly is at the level of "I would *like* to be able to do it that way." There are also rising and subordinate expectations about participation, as better educational standards and exposure to alternative societal norms make such notions seductive. But old habits die hard and if the majority of subordinates are unwilling to accept the responsibility which goes with full participation, there will be an automatic brake applied to the process of transformation. That they are so unwilling is a consistent and long-standing lament in multinational corporations operating in Asia where this particular clash of expectations is a permanent battleground.

Further down in the Chinese family organization, at the level of middle management and first line supervision, leadership style tends to reflect the combination of personalism and hierarchy which typifies the whole. Although this was not a central concern in a study of chief executives' beliefs, a number of reflections on it came to the surface when discussing Chinese leadership behavior.

It has been noted a number of times that avoidance of confrontation is a normal part of the Chinese make-up, as indeed it is for most collectivist cultures. It has also been noted that leadership style would tend to be more autocratic than participative, although such autocracy may be benevolently exercised. The style of decision making would lead to a distancing between the ranks, and this would be exacerbated by Confucian deference to superiors and emotional aloofness with those outside the personalistic circles of family or clique. Power, moreover, only really derives from ownership.

These features would predispose the supervisory system to certain weaknesses, and may explain further why "interference" is felt to be necessary by chief executives. The weaknesses are likely to surround the combined difficulties that (a) ownership of the company's problems cannot easily be transferred outside family membership, as information about problems is likely to be closely guarded and real trust limited and (b) supervisors are likely to repli-

cate on a smaller scale the paternalism and personalism in which they are embedded. This latter feature may well result in priority being given to keeping
relations smooth rather than to disciplined pursuit of company goals, a softening of emphasis which will be reinforced by the wish to avoid disciplinary
confrontations. Such inhibitions were a focus of occasional chagrin, as in *Hsieh*'s
outburst about the comparison of supervisory quality between the Western-
managed Star Ferry Co. and the Chinese-managed Hong Kong and Yau Ma Tei
Ferry Co., the latter being regularly complained about for a lack of cleanliness,
inefficiency, and the former the opposite.

The special feature of Chinese face also introduces barriers which occasionally
inhibit supervisory involvement, as association with certain tasks is a matter for
finely tuned demarcations. The idea of rolling up your sleeves and pitching in
with the boys on the shop floor is not looked upon favorably, and perhaps understandably so when authority beyond the family itself is only delicately maintained and easily undermined. It is protected by a certain hauteur and aloofness
which can become dysfunctional.

Im:
We had recent production problems because the supervisors did not check directly on site
where problems arose. They felt embarassed to work with their subordinates on the site.
They see themselves too highly.

Constantly referred to as "old style," this form of organization is clearly
understood for its weaknesses. Chinese owner-managers know that their organizations arc inhibited. They see examples of major successes by, for instance,
Mr. Li Ka Shing, Mr. Fung King Hey, Mr. Liem Sioe Liong, Mr. William
Suryadjaya, and they know that one of the elements in those successes is coming
to terms with the delegation of trust. In such discussions, however, the exceptional nature of that capacity to trust is always acknowledged. They know their
weakness but are seemingly unable in most cases to surmount it. Centralized
decision making is easier to manage, and democracy very trying for those in
power. As long as the workforce is both dependent and conformist, there is little
incentive in most industries to change, and companies are likely to continue with
a style which, while being culturally adapted, also eventually chokes the organization's long-term growth. Deference to "modern" management methods and
espousing of the notion of delegation may remain matters for lip service in the
majority of cases.

The feature of Overseas Chinese organizations identified as "personalism"
makes up a third element in the set of subsidiary features within the overall
paternalistic corporate culture. It means that personal relationships and feelings
about other people are likely to come before more objectively defined concerns
such as organizational efficiency, or neutral assessment of abilities. It turns the
organization into a world where who you know is more important than, or at
least as important as, what you know.

Personalism lies on a continuum with extremes of favoritism at one end and cold rationality at the other. Clearly at each end, there are dangers for any organization. Favoritism will destroy it in time, and cold rationality will equally drive away most people in normal circumstances. The kind of personalism in question is not of the extreme kind, but it certainly veers towards that end of the continuum rather than the other.

It was argued earlier that the Chinese person carries his relationships round as part of his persona. Social needs are comparatively more significant than in the Western case. Friendship is an especially important item of currency. Also authority is based largely in the exchange of balancing obligations, and these are transacted through subtle processes which are at once interpersonal and highly personal.

It is almost impossible to find any chief executive anywhere in the world who would not make some statement equivalent to, "What this company is really all about is people." The experienced boss will inevitably acknowledge that he can do nothing without others. Where this human universal is taken to a more extreme point by the Chinese is in allowing it to displace more neutral means of coordinating effort, such as formal control systems. In saying this, however, it should be noted that more formal control systems may be redundant (and therefore an unjustifiable cost) in a society where strong hierarchical discipline is imported into the organization in the heads of its members. People will tend to do as they are told, they will not answer back, they do not need to be controlled to the same extent as in many other cultures. Qualities of diligence and what Kahn (1979) called "seriousness about tasks and responsibilities" are inbred, and are available as a feature of the majority of personnel. Given this feature, the managerial job is to create an atmosphere in which work may be directed towards organizational purposes. In the intensely social world of Chinese people, this is largely done by social means.

This is patently not how the textbooks say it should be done, and there is therefore a degree of reluctance in acknowledging it, but it occasionally comes to the surface in statements which appear like the tip of an iceberg.

Hwa:
People are more loyal to people than to an organization. I like people to be loyal to me. People down below should be loyal to the superior rather than to the firm itself.

Hon:
A Westernized company will be run with a very organized manner, will move people as in chess—it doesn't matter who is the man.

For many chief executives, as *Hap* observes, "I'm people-oriented. Making money is not enough for me." Or,

Har:
I don't know why I've got a love for it and a lot of loyalty whenever I work. This firm I've already worked for, for fifteen years. I have seen it grow from small and become a big

company and now growing bigger and took over a lot of subsidiaries. I don't know but I think if I work for myself, I can earn maybe four times more than my salary. [2] But I've got the love of the company and also the joy of our colleagues with me.

Such people orientation, while not being universal in the world of the entrepreneur in any country, is perhaps unusual in the Chinese case for the inhibitions it may bring with it, especially over matters of discipline. In this the Chinese abhorrence of confrontation, with all its overtones of incivility being uncivilized, comes to the fore:

Huen:
In my organization, we have many different performances, but I would still be reluctant to fire the one who is ineffective. I would try to keep him and maybe try to help him improve. I just cannot bear to fire people. I don't think we have ever fired anyone in the company, except one accountant who was cheating.

Huan:
We decided to fire a production manager in the San Po Kong factory and my partner was trembling. He simply could not do it because he was so bound up with this man.

Some of the atmosphere of the organization run in this way is captured in *Hu*'s description of his father's way of working as an owner:

He owned the largest Chinese-operated facility in Hong Kong. He would report to work at about seven, and he would talk to all the workers; the painters, the mechanics; he would stand next to the panel beaters and talk and offer cigarettes to them. He did not worry about finance. Human relationship was important.
Question:
When you say he wouldn't worry about the finance, he would still presumably be fairly good at finance?
Hu.
He left it to a trusted accountant. He had some very simple form of monitoring. All the rest of his time was spent on building up the relationships.

When personalism radiated to and from the chief executive in this way, it may well be a positive force, in that it is likely to extend his influence into the body of the organization and stamp it with his vision. If, on the other hand, one examines personalism at lower levels in the hierarchy, one begins to see in it potentially divisive features. These arise because of the taking of positions on personal grounds, and the forming of factions and cliques, something for which Chinese social life is notorious.

Cliques can form on a number of bases, and examples would be, say, a Chiu Chow or other regional group within an organization, or a group doing the same work such as the drivers, or the messengers. Cliques can also develop between organizations, for instance that of secretaries coming from one foreign city, or members of one family playing the stockmarket jointly but operating from individual bases in large company corporate planning departments. The point about such hidden networks is that they are capable of placing their own interests above those of their organization, and this can become damaging if undetected or unchecked.

Hui:

I joined a firm of professionals but was not satisfied with the structure of this firm because it was so loose. It was very Chinese style. The interpreters had a firm grip.

When there is competition between cliques, then dissension begins to destroy the cooperative framework on which day-to-day operations depend. The chief executive finds himself lobbied by one group against the others.

Har:

And another thing is the camps. . . They've got different camps. Things are fed back to the boss, and he can learn who's been doing this. And things like that. I think this kind of situation even makes it worse. Maybe their whole philosophy [i.e. bosses guilty of encouraging this] is they think, you know, people come to see you and talking about "This

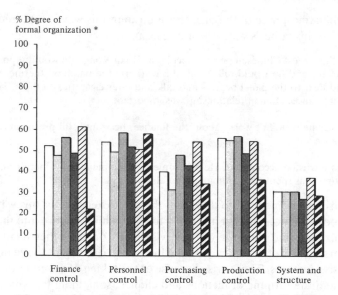

* Composite of formalization, specialization, and standardization, with 100 %
  as the maximum possible scores on the Aston instrument

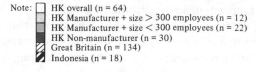

Note: ☐ HK overall (n = 64)
       HK Manufacturer + size > 300 employees (n = 12)
       HK Manufacturer + size < 300 employees (n = 22)
       HK Non-manufacturer (n = 30)
       Great Britain (n = 134)
       Indonesia (n = 18)

(Key to Figures 7.5, 7.6, 7.7, 7.8, 7.9, 7.10)

Figure 7.5: Degrees of formal organization in different managerial functions thing, he's not doing it right." He can appreciate this, it's right, that's why you create the camps. Modern bosses, Chinese bosses, they've got the foreign education. They can see things better.

If cliques of this nature are tolerated on the grounds that "divide and rule" will loosen up the channels of information flow to the boss as one group watches another, there is one other clique which has formal approval and which should be noted. This is the in-plant subcontracting group. Common in the Chinese manufacturing context is the "gang leader" who brings in his own people and takes responsibility for a part of the manufacturing process. His group may be ten or twelve people and, when observed on the factory floor, they look just like other workers. They do not, however, have a direct authority relationship with the factory owner. This is an indication of the common preference in Overseas Chinese organization to generate predictable behavior by trusting people (i.e. the gang leader), rather than adding systematic control procedures. Again this goes back to the endemic problem of limited trust, both a cause and a consequence of the reliance on personal bonds of obligation, without which willingness to cooperate can not be assumed.

So far, this discussion of the Chinese family business has been conducted at the level of the general principles likely to permeate the corporate culture of a typical company of this type. In simple terms, it has examined what patrimonialism means in a present-day organization.

It is, however, also necessary to consider aspects of management of more common currency, features which are more tangible, and for that purpose, discussion will turn briefly to financial management and management control, production, personnel, and marketing, as outlined in Figure 7.5 and supported by data in Figures 7.6 to 7.10. After that, some general conclusions will be drawn.

Management Control and Financial Management

The degree of system and structure in Chinese organizations, although overall less than in the UK, nevertheless varies in intensity from one field of managing to another. In production, control appears to be tight, and also relatively so in personnel, although in the latter case, the tightening up is in the area of controlling people, rather than their development. The production emphasis is an indicator that the core activity of the organization is a matter for intense managerial concentration, reflecting as has been noted earlier the power of ownership as a stimulant to taking care of the use of the assets.

Formal control in the fields of purchasing and finance with somewhat lower scores than in the UK may reflect the extent to which these aspects of the firm call for personal involvement by senior executives with consequently less need for structuring the work of subordinates.

Interesting light on financial management behavior among the Overseas Chinese is shed by a study of 250 of the largest companies in the Philippines (Hicks and Redding 1982). The companies were divided into ethnically Chinese owned, and those owned by others, principally non-Chinese Filipinos. The differences in financial behavior are striking and are illustrated in Figure 7.11. It was evident in that study that Chinese financial strategy is based on the following principles:

(1) Low margin and high volume as a means of penetrating markets and of guaranteeing a steady flow of profit.
(2) Rigorous control of inventory to achieve low capital investment and high rates of stockturn.
(3) The reduction of transaction costs by use of networking within the Chinese community.
(4) The use, where possible, of capital available from sources outside the firm, to improve gearing potential.

Other aspects of managerial strategy will be discussed shortly under the heading of general management, but it can be contended that the soundness of these finance principles has done much to account for Overseas Chinese success throughout the region. They could have been taken from a standard textbook, but have in fact been accumulated as folk wisdom passed on from father to son over generations, and not normally committed to any Chinese literature on the subject.

Personnel Management

A first glance at the data in Figure 7.6 suggests that the management of personnel has a distinctly harder edge to it in the Chinese case than in the Western. The use of control and of penalty is universally stronger among the Chinese. Appraisal of performance is accorded high importance relatively, and recruitment is an area which also requires and gets extensive management attention. What one might see as the more sophisticated personnel functions of selection and development are clearly given lower priority. While much of this difference may be due to environment differences and differences in worker expectations as well as labor market pressures, it is nevertheless arguable that a degree of Chinese pragmatism is at play here, refusing to spend money unless absolutely necessary, and concentrating on the discipline of making it above all else. The impacts of paternalism, and the relatively low emphasis on professionalism, are also visible in the priorities assigned.

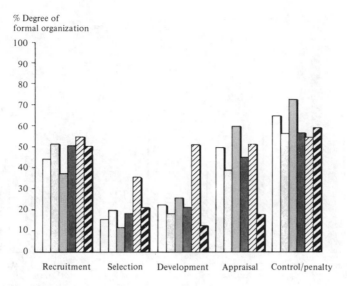

% Degree of
formal organization

Figure 7.6: Degree of organizing of the personnel function

Marketing Management

Marketing for the majority of Overseas Chinese manufacturing companies in Hong Kong and elsewhere is largely a matter for others to worry about. The amount of organizing which takes place to support it is low compared to the UK equivalent (Figure 7.7). Standard trade marks are less used, displays are less standardized, catalogues are only used to half the extent, there is almost no sales policy as such, there is little market research, and there is less organizing of distribution.

Much of this is a result of geography, as most markets are a long way away in Europe or North America. The marketing process outside the context of the developed world is in any case different from that in the advanced countries and relies on different channel structures (Ford et al. 1986). Much of it also comes from an inhibition about extending the boundaries of the organization beyond those controllable by the core executive group, a point which will be returned to. Some of it may be due to caution about the acceptance of risk, because, although margins may be low in the normal OEM [3] system of much Overseas Chinese industry, the risks are far less. It is up to the purchaser to worry about the risks of stock-holding and marketing. Finally, it must also be seen that the ties of personalistic networks, and the loyalties which develop in societies where mutual obligation is common currency, take an important part in explaining the marketing process (Redding 1982a).

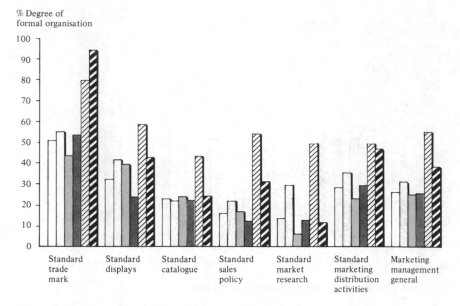

Figure 7.7: Degree of organizing of the marketing function

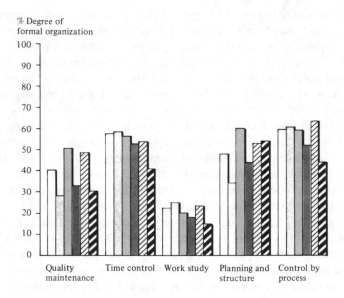

Figure 7.8: Degree of organizing of the production function

Production Management

It has been remarked already that management gives priority attention to matters concerned with production, and this is evident in Figure 7.8. Here the scores for the degree of organizing which goes into the process are close to the norms for the UK and regularly exceed them in the detail which lies behind the chart.

Concern with managing the time aspect of production is marginally greater on average than in the UK and suggests the urgency with which Hong Kong industry adapts to market demand. Although quality control presents a mixed picture, it is at least capable of exceeding UK levels for the attention given to it, as is also the planning and structuring of the production process. Work study also reaches close to a Western norm. Again the criticality of getting right the fundamentals of the business for an owner-manager using his own capital is suggested.

General Management

The planning of future events in the organization in any kind of structured manner as illustrated in Figure 7.9 is a matter of low priority in both the UK and Hong Kong, and the resistance to formal planning is not thus a specially Chinese characteristic. It may nevertheless take on its present attenuated form for specially Chinese reasons, which add urgency to the drive for accumulation.

Tam:
It's difficult to communicate with the board of directors, as they don't have any long-term investment ideas. They want a quick return. That's the trouble with this company. So I have tried very hard to convince them about long-term planning.

Tai:
I feel that Taiwanese businessmen are usually holding a short-term view of business. That gives flexibility, but the result is that Taiwan's business development is short of long-term objectives.

Production planning is naturally accorded a somewhat greater amount of attention, given the fairly obvious need for it to be a managerial concern. It is only in the field of research and development where UK organizations do noticeably more, and even here the difference is not great.

A great difference does appear, however, in the field of internal communications, where the UK score is almost double that for the typical Chinese family business. This reflects both the high level of centralization in the Chinese case, and the impact of a high power distance culture with expectations of paternalistic treatment. Such an attitude to authority does not carry with it subordinate expectations about being informed or consulted by those in senior positions.

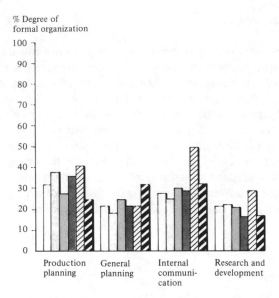

Figure 7.9: Degree of organizing of planning, internal communications, and R&D

There is thus little point in building organizational systems to that end. The contrast is clearly illustrated in Taiwan:

Tai:
I would like to be remembered as an integrator of East and West management . . . I can justify my authority by lessening the degree of dominance of the boss and increasing the flow of information.

The tendency to centralize decisions is illustrated clearly in Figure 7.10. This shows that in virtually all areas of concern to management in the Overseas Chinese case, it is the more senior levels which handle the decisions. This occurs in the production process, in the area of organizational planning, in marketing decisions, in the control of purchasing, and in research and development.

Data given earlier in Table 7.5 have already suggested the tendency for the more patrimonial flavor of the Chinese organization to show itself. A finer breakdown of the centralization scales has revealed that the tendency to make decisions centrally is more marked in the field of questions connected with people than for questions connected with more neutral aspects of organizing.

Tse:
In the States, 70% of my job (company president) is execution, 30% communication, but in Taiwan the reverse is true. I feel the level of management technique here is still quite far behind that in the States.

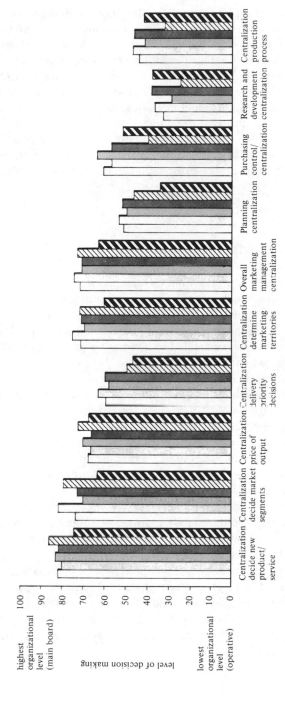

Figure 7.10: Centralization of decision making in various fields

This echoes a description by Deyo (1978, 1983) of the flavor of the managerial process used by the Overseas Chinese. The retention of discretion by the chief executive to make decisions in the field of people and their employment is used as a means of sustaining authority. Much else is delegated within a tightly controlled system of producing output, and supervisors are kept thus under a tight rein in which their role is to maximize productive efficiency. As they do not have discretion over key personnel decisions, their power is limited, and they remain dependent on the chief executive. This produces at the same time a willingness to comply but also a lack of initiative and some difficulty in growing the skills necessary for larger responsibility. The system thus stabilizes at the scale which such decision processes are built for, i.e. relatively small, and growth meets a number of barriers.

Dilemmas of Growth and/or Stability

Although there is great variety within the sample, it is nevertheless possible to see certain tendencies which reflect on the patterns of growth described earlier. Firstly, the use of centralization rather than structuring of activities as a way of controlling behavior in the organization indicates that the normal growth process is operating with a brake applied to it. In other words, for the Chinese the typical textbook growth process is not "normal."

The second conclusion is that where structuring is taking place, and a certain amount is inevitable given the anarchic alternative, it tends to take the route of tightening control of the workflow process, rather than by specifying the parameters of the employment contract (in its widest sense). Thus a workflow bureaucracy is favored over a personnel bureaucracy. The lack of evidence for the existence of full bureaucracies suggests that the inhibitions to true decentralization of control, to the delegation of trust, to the full-scale employment of professionals, are such as to make it a deviant organizational type in this culture. The first professionally managed and publicly owned Chinese multinational is still waiting somewhere in the shadows, and may, in any case, be a fantasy of minds which assume all enterprises contain the same essential dynamics, and are not really cultural artifacts.

This chapter began with the general characteristic of paternalism and has subsequently considered three related outcomes of it, namely (a) the inability to separate power from ownership, (b) a didactic leadership style, and (c) personalism. It is now necessary to bring together the organizational implications of this set of forces for the notional "average" Chinese family business. These may be stated in three propositions:

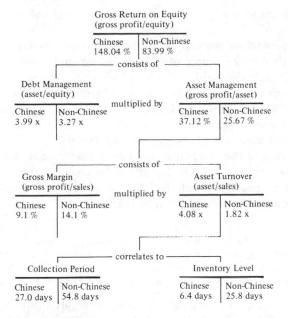

Figure 7.11: Comparative financial performance of Chinese vs. non-Chinese commercial
firms in the Philippines

Note: n = 33 Chinese firms; 40 non-Chinese firms

Source: Limlingan (1986: 75) after Hicks and Redding (1982)

(1) Maintaining talent at the top is difficult without open competition.
(2) The leadership style adopted is repressive of talent at the base of the organization.
(3) Organizations under these restrictions survive either by concentrating or by
remaining small.

The problem of talent at the top of the company is naturally one of great
concern to Chinese chief executives, and nepotism a matter for strong opinion.
On the one hand, there is acknowledgement that the commitment which goes
with ownership is the only thing which will guarantee the combination of incentive and guts required in taking risks. On the other hand lie the problems of
inbreeding and the eventual dilution of talent.

The most elaborate education is not an answer to the question of entrepreneurial skill, and was held by a number of respondents to produce mismatches.
Very often the son becomes alienated from the world of business. Alternatively

he may finish up with a doctorate in nuclear physics, but have to run an ice cream factory.

The third generation problem is visible in too many examples to be a myth, and it is clearly not just a piece of folklore. Although the burn-out of the company is not entirely due to the dilution of senior talent (much else to do with horizontal cooperation needs also to be brought into the account), there is clearly a major difficulty in pushing a Chinese family business through what became in the West the managerial revolution—the transfer of power to professional executives and the divorce of control and ownership.

The resistance to the competent non-family executive is still fierce and the field even potentially dangerous for him if he comes to be seen as a threat. Although not necessarily typical, the following comment is revealing for its view of the occasional paranoia which can be reached:

Har:
I think some of the bosses—I don't say all but maybe a majority—they won't like the company secrets going out. Meaning they can only entrust their sons. Meaning any staff who has worked too long and knows the inside story about something, he may chuck them out or something. I don't say majority [sic] but this can happen. I have seen it.

In acknowledgement of the pressures on the family's own executives, there was a chorus of agreement from respondents over the essential need for technical competence in the boardroom as a basis for legitimacy. Without that, ownership *per se* was dangerous. Authority comes from both skills and ownership. This is in the long run, of course, fudging the issue and displays the tendency to compromise at its most vulnerable. The attempt to live by this hope is the determinant of much eventual malaise for the organization, and normally the final cause of its decline.

Nor is it at the top that the propagation and maintenance of high levels of talent run into problems. While their humanism and paternalism make it inappropriate to label them repressive, nevertheless Chinese business organizations, in the manner of all centralized systems of power, find it difficult to foster talent within their own boundaries. It could be argued that their small scale, and heavy reliance on the center, make it unnecessary and that the consequent leaking out of talent into new ventures is good for an economy. Nevertheless, the climate for innovation inside the organization must be understood for its limitations.

Hui:
I think that one of the weakest parts of the Chinese organization is that they do not have much respect for the employees, and there is very little employee participation—not like in Western companies. That is why, if something goes wrong, the business will go away. There is very little input from employees. The employers think that they are superior. That is part of Chinese philosophy.

The number of chief executives who could trust employees was noted by several for its sparsity. *Han* praised his former chairman because "he could trust employees who were not relatives and that is rather unusual." *Hong* described how he had developed a company within a larger Chinese family business as a professional executive.

I started to think I need something more challenging that's really of my own. That's why I moved out and joined XY. With the present company, it is as if it were my own. I have that much discretion. This is very rare, I must say. In a Chinese family business, it is very rare, and I appreciate this very much. I would say this is a very rare case the reason being our chairman is in Singapore. He's a sort of remote control, he's semi-retired . . . I'm now having a cooperation with my parent company to have a joint venture in Taiwan, and there I'm really a shareholder because they need my expertise.

The more normal organizational climate is suggested by these exceptions and, especially at lower and middle ranks is characterized by an air of obedience, of deference to authority which have predictable results for real commitment and involvement, unless these be stimulated by fear.

Hung:
The relationship is contractual—but informally (sic)—even without formal signing. People work because they have no protection. They'd be kicked out.

Shang:
My ideal of leadership is to tell people what and when things should be done but not how—but in Singapore you have to explain how also.

The repression of organizational talent, and in consequence of much potential innovation, is not a conscious matter, but an outcome, not normally taken into account, of other postures. There is a fundamental fear of letting go, and this is the price paid for it. Responsibility for the organization's adaptiveness is shouldered by the owning group, and nobody else. That becomes one of the key underlying rules of the game, and it pervades the organizational climate of most Chinese family businesses. It explains much of their traditionalism and also the way in which they reflect so clearly the wishes of one person. It also contributes much to understanding the limits to their growth.

The vast majority of Chinese family businesses are small, and the vast majority specialize in one field of expertise. There are admittedly exceptions. Large organizations have appeared, but they have done so normally under either or both of two conditions, namely, (1) concentration on one sector in which the chief executive is deeply immersed and immensely knowledgeable, thus allowing a gearing up on his very finely tuned intuitions; (2) a "soft" environment in which a largely monopolistic position can be enjoyed, usually based on political patronage, and where the full force of competition does not penetrate and the organization can run with considerable slack.

The alternative route to growth which is the building of a complex multi-product or multimarket organization, fully integrated under a complex bureaucratic control system, and professionally managed, does not appear to be a normal route.

In any case, large Chinese family businesses are so rare, and the large concentrated ones still run as though they were small, that it is better to conceive of a small one when trying to imagine the core characteristics most likely to be encountered by outsiders. The "typical" case would be a company with between fifty and four hundred staff performing a specialized activity such as garment manufacture, or component subcontracting. The person running it would most likely be the majority shareholder, and he would be deeply committed to the generation of a return for the risk he feels personally responsible for. As *Heung* disarmingly put it, "It's not that easy to get rich—it's not easy to earn the first lot of money."

Perhaps on account of the "blood, sweat, tears, humiliations, demoralizations willingly put up with" (*Shek*) to make a business successful, the fear of losing something built at such a cost acts as a brake on further unnecessary risk, and introduces also a caution which can verge on the parsimonious.

Huen:
[discussing a successfully grown Chinese company] Maybe he had budgeted enough to pay higher salaries to buy managers he can put his trust on. Many of the local companies are reluctant to do that.

Sung:
The sacrifices I have made have been time, stress, and income. I could earn much more elsewhere, in a multi-national. This is a traditional Chinese organization. We just don't pay exorbitant salaries—myself as MD included.

Such caution applies too in the field of financing. We have noted earlier the way in which Chinese financial management skills, and the sense of reverence for money, lead to especially efficient use of working capital. It is, however, also noteworthy in considering caution that the borrowing of money is commonly an area for inhibition. Several chief executives spoke of a policy of never borrowing money, or of the golden rule of never being over-stretched. References to this as an old Chinese principle are reminiscent of the asceticism of their ancestors, and it is clear that, although such austerity is not universally practised, the fear of getting into debt with banks must act as one more restraining factor when organizational size is being considered.

Caution is also visible on the question of areas of expertise. Chinese chief executives tend to know what they are good at and to stick with it—again another conservative force.

Sit:
I've had opportunities to diversify into property, construction, etc., but I want to stay in my own line, the one I'm most familiar with. Maybe I'm conservative but if I diversify, I have to start all over again learning everything.

Hung:
It's best to stay in areas you understand—for me spinning and weaving. . . I went into property just to use assets. In unfamiliar areas, I can be a partner, financier, a colleague, but not a boss.

Hwee:
My judgement is better in textiles. I cannot go into other fields without knowledge.

The knowledge in question is not always articulate. It is judgement. "You carry the paper and pencil in your head" (*Hsia*). But knowing that you are "a factory person" (*Hsing*), having plenty of funds but being "very cautious over expansion" (*Seow*), suggest a view of the world which is full of deliberation and reticence. Once you have the wealth, conserving it becomes a priority. Again, organizational growth *per se* may not be best served in these circumstances.

It is apparent from this consideration of the Chinese tendency to think small that a certain possessiveness grips all Chinese organizations. Although some examples of success in organization building are visible, their common denominator—a capacity to trust—stands in some way as a pointer to all the rest who can't. In consequence, cooperation between organizations, in any structured sense, is limited: "they don't like the good things to go to others," and this inhibits joint ventures. The infusion of new stimuli is thus also restricted, and the organization remains in a form where arguably its characteristics are most potent—the village with its seignior, the feudal condition.

Footnotes

[1] These descriptions of the dimensions are in summary form only and do not do full justice to their complexity. Full details are available in the four-volume series of Aston papers, the key volume of which is Pugh and Hickson (1976).

[2] His company has been bought by a large conglomerate but he was retained as the salaried chief executive.

[3] "Original equipment manufacturing" in which the goods and brand name are owned by the purchaser not the manufacturer, whose function is simply production to a set quality standard.

Chapter 8
Society at Large

The outer perimeter of our set of concentric circles of values is the one representing the view of society. We have observed the perception of the self, of relationships, of organizing, and now we turn to the larger context in which these are all embedded. How do the Overseas Chinese see the societies in which they live? What position do they take on the issues which occupy the attention of most societies, even though not always openly addressed as such? With what common understandings do these societies work?

Life among the Overseas Chinese contains a fundamental paradox. As a society, it is essentially non-cooperative; as Lau Siu Kai points out, of Hong Kong, it is "minimally integrated." Horizontal cooperation is problematic. And yet enough is generated in Hong Kong, Singapore, and Taiwan to make society work noticeably well. The paradox is resolved if one attributes the stability achieved to the combination of (a) an unusually powerful vertical order, and (b) certain pragmatic drives which foster and protect the limited but adequate horizontal linkages.

As questions of limited horizontal cooperation have already been considered when analyzing relationships in chapter 5, this chapter will take the major problem of trust as already given, and concentrate on the two main themes just noted: the strong vertical order and the drives which lie behind the carefully delimited cooperation. Figure 8.1 illustrates the main features of the value set, and their linkages.

Vertical Order

Clearly with the chief executives the most strongly felt and most commonly discussed idea relating to Overseas Chinese society is that of discipline and social structure, and predictably in a Confucian setting the structure is predominantly seen in vertical terms.

The core principle is respect for older people, especially within the family, and coupled with this, obedience to those on whom improvements in life may depend, such as the employer who controls income, and the teacher who strongly influences vertical mobility.

The origins of this vertical discipline, or more accurately of the ideological

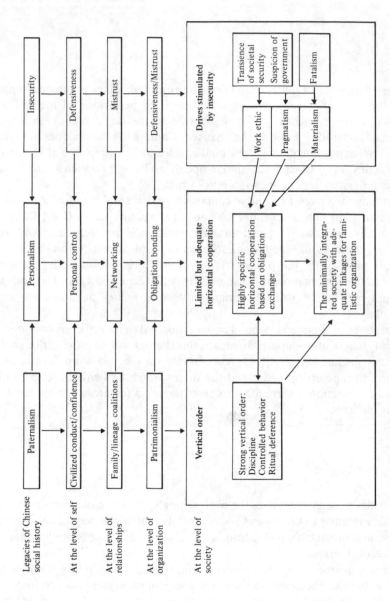

Figure 8.1: Main features of the societal value-set

base in which the discipline is grounded, lie inside the family and in the very powerful socialization mechanisms employed by the Chinese. A partial contribution to the consistency and universality of this training is the enormously long history of the Confucian doctrine and the virtual impossibility of challenging its credentials as a template for society. Another perhaps less immaculate motive, the real power of which can only be guessed at, is that parents protect their own futures by inculcating the powerful obligations of Confucianism in their children. While this may lack nobility, it is nevertheless understandable given the insecurities and unpredictable fortunes of life near the subsistence level or life under conditions of threat or turbulence. Confucian cultures are no strangers to either of these conditions.

Respect for vertical order, initially in the family context, is induced early. *Hsui*, in discussing the willing acceptance of the authority structure, observed:

I think this has something to do with Chinese tradition. Everyone as a young child is brought up to be an obedient person, in a sense. In my earlier days, you could not be otherwise.

Children are taught to be polite to elders by such signals as never eating before the seniors start, escorting them to the lift and not the apartment door when they are leaving (*Han*).

Hsiang:
In the Chinese family, they always have to respect their parents and all elders, including the uncles and all this, anybody older than you, you know. And we have some traditions, more or less: have respect for the elders, be friendly with people who are the same age, and also help to bring the youngsters up by setting up a model for the young.

The perpetuation of this model, clearly over centuries, is suggested by *Hoi:*

We were brought up as a strict family—always certain guidelines—we can do this; that we cannot do. It's modelled after our parents, and they probably model after their parents. It is a familial tradition and behavior pattern handed down from one generation to another.

The notion of unquestioning obedience, reserved in the Western case for unusual circumstances such as the parade ground or the protocols of a court of law, is still common in much of Chinese life. It extends to a wider range of circumstances than it does in many other cultures, and this perhaps reflects the rigor with which it is induced in childhood. This is not to say that childhood is barren of affection as it most certainly is not. The Chinese commonly display great affection for children. The pattern is such, however, that the first five or six years of indulgence, and the consequent building of a dependence relationship, gives way after early childhood to a clearly rule-bound and more strongly disciplined atmosphere.

Har:
I think for Chinese we normally worship the grand-father or the father. We cannot argue with our parents ever. Everything they tell us we've just got to follow. We can't answer back. It might not be a good thing but that was the way we were taught.

As the circle of contacts widens, and especially in education, the child is taught to extend the same principle. The view by a boss of an employee is:

Hua:
They basically do whatever you tell them to do. In the education system, at school, the teacher is the ultimate god and you sit there and take it. This has been hammered in—the psychological respect for authority.

The outcome is predictable.

Hsui:
We employ a person. He comes in. Right there, that moment, that person already is ready to obey. It's his mind set. People accept authority. It's not a big deal.

Hioe:
Generally the Chinese employees normally respect managers. They are mostly rather obedient types of people. It's from the traditions and from the educational system. The first thing you have to do you have to listen to the leaders; to do what the leader tells you to do, until you have experience and get trained. Then you can show off your experience and know-how and try to do what you want to do—but not until then. I see many young graduates, and they are very respectful, very obedient, in the first place.

The sense of vertical order, the natural obedience and willingness to follow the guidelines—perhaps even a need for the guidelines—result in the incorporation of societal order into business organizations. This is a subtle, invisible process and has substantial ramifications for efficiency if it means that much normal (i.e. for Westerners) vertical control can be dispensed with. It is perhaps one of the least replicable and least visible organizational secrets of the post-Confucian cultures, and is certainly one of the least understood. A hint of it is provided by *Heung:*

I think people have an understanding of organization structure. Everybody will understand this kind of system. For Chinese we have more obedience than Westerners. When the structure tells you this, we are more obedient.

The naturalness of hierarchy, echoing as it does the major cross-cultural differences in "power distance" identified by Hofstede (1980), brings to the organization a high degree of stability. As *Sung* pointed out, "The hierarchy provides the legitimacy." For the Overseas Chinese, the giving and taking of orders is not a field for the emergence of resentments, as long as the proprieties are maintained, as long as the vertical order is being followed, and as long as the design of the order is understood by all involved. This latter constraint may well provide some limits to organizational size, but that point will be returned to later. It is now necessary to address the first point concerning the proprieties and to understand the importance of ritual restraint as a check on the possible abuse of such a potentially autocratic system.

Sensitivity to others emerged as a key component of the person's survival kit for life in Chinese society when this analysis was focussing on the self. It is clear also that confidence can be built into people's characters via the assurance which comes from following clear guidelines. If appropriate behavior is prescribed carefully and in detail, then conformity with it is able to induce a degree of self-righteousness (albeit not so overt or so unwelcome as it can become with more individualistic Westerners). This inner core of confidence rests on conformity and the espousal of gentlemanly or ladylike conduct and comportment. An outcome of this is the softening of social conflict with the rituals of polite interpersonal behavior. Aggression must be suppressed as it would prove especially damaging in a structure where horizontal cooperation is at best fragile. The proprieties have a clear and important function.

Hsien:
Although you're in competition, you still talk to each other, you know.

Hsia:
I have no religion. I came from a Catholic school but insisted to the last day not to be a Catholic. But the key influence is the Chinese language. It influences me quite a lot. I always tell myself to be a respectable man—a gentleman. Suppose I'm waiting for a bus, I line up, even if people take advantages.

Hap:
In twelve years I've only fired one staff, because he used foul language to the female workers. I make it very loud and clear—nobody uses foul language under the factory roof, and since this is my warning then I have to fire him reluctantly.

The suppression of aggressive tendencies is suggested in this description from the childhood of *Hu*, who was found at an early age fighting with his brother:

My mother said, "you shouldn't fight and if you are, I will beat you both. I don't want to know what's wrong. I won't ask questions. It's just that brothers should not fight." Since then, you know, we dare not because we'd get beaten . . . I think maybe my mother was quite fair. I think even today we still are good brothers. We really treat each other very nicely.

It is noteworthy that overt socialization of this kind is restricted to childhood and that the filtering of such values as politeness and nonaggression through the society is rarely a matter for open discussion. The Confucian order is rarely based on preaching. As *Hu* observed, on this theme:

It was never very explicit to me. And also I have a feeling that if I have to tell my son about all the virtues and so on it becomes hypocritical. So a lot of these are implied, and a matter of leading by example.

It may now be asserted more confidently that Overseas Chinese society, as a kind of offshore version of traditional Chinese society, preserves its verticality, and its distinct form of order, and preserves also the legacy of weak horizontal cooperativeness. People remain in the walled encampments of their families. Larger-scale communities, and even perhaps politics, are of secondary consequence in themselves. Lin Yutang (1977) pointed out the absence of the Samaritan ethic in Chinese thought and described the family as a form of "magnified selfishness," poor material with which to build a united community.

Rampant self-interest will never of course be espoused as a respectable philosophy and can only be suggested as another facet of the materialism which will
be considered shortly. Before doing so, however, it will be salutary to take note
of the rather diffident and conditional position taken on social responsibility by
these representatives of the Chinese capitalist ethic.

Perhaps not surprisingly, it is only in Singapore that strong declarations
emerged about the social responsibility of the businessman. After several decades of very open publicity and exhortation about "nation building," Singa-
poreans in leadership positions are prone to orate upon the topic. In Hong
Kong, the response is decidedly more muted and in tune with the jungle-like
atmosphere of its business world. The response there is one of regret that people
are so selfish, but balanced by some pride in occasional displays of a soul, as long
as it can be afforded financially.

The Singaporean response is typified by *Sit* who viewed his success in selling
40,000 home air conditioners over the years as something to be proud of, in that
it was a major contribution to improving the life-style of the people. Similarly,
Sun clearly believed that the kind of work he was doing in applied natural science was for the betterment of mankind and that was one of the driving forces
in doing it. *Sit* was proud of having sons who were "civic minded," and he took
great personal pride in his own charity work with a paramedical organization.
Sung was quite clear that societal respect was destroyed by the selfish pursuit of
profit and pointed to a recent dramatic object lesson. Echoes of these noble
sentiments were evident also from *Iek* in Indonesia who considered it "not really
respectable" to think only of money and better to be dedicated to other people.

These, however, are exceptions to the generally materialistic and pragmatic
view of life held by the Overseas Chinese businessman, arguably of necessity,
and to be examined more fully in the remainder of this chapter. Social responsibility in the business world of Hong Kong is generally noticeable by its scarcity.
Cynically, one might add, also by its flamboyant and perhaps essentially self-
serving occasional presence, as family reputations are enhanced by visible public
service.

The reasons for this are explained by *Hai* in terms of the deep mistrust of
government resulting from the experience of Chinese history:

Because of this mistrust they rather look at themselves, do things for themselves, for their
own family, for their own future. This is my observation. And that becomes a very selfish
motive. This is very apparent in Hong Kong even, you know, even though it's a British
government, they have certain mistrust. And they don't care about public—you see people spitting in the streets, throwing garbage on the street—somebody will take care of it.
They take no pride in citizenship, in public life, no pride. If they are benevolent and
philanthropic towards other people, it's because for their own good—because they want
to make a name, or they want to have good reward, or they want to command respect.
The Chinese become so self-centered. They rally round their family, their own people,
and say at least I'm doing something for myself.

Pragmatic Co-operation

This reminder of the vertically fixed but horizontally loose structure of society will serve as a backcloth to the analysis now to be made of the pressures which drive the essentially pragmatic capacity to create limited but adequate horizontal linkages; adequate that is if one abandons notions of a society of large-scale efficient organizational forms, and substitutes instead a society of small but connected organizations.

The pressures in question, in other words, those forces which make it possible for people to get over the barriers of mistrust and form workable linkages, are the three interrelated forces of (a) the work ethic, (b) pragmatism, and (c) materialism. Behind these in turn lie the much less obvious but still powerful effects of life in a transient society and of fatalism. It is proposed to examine each of the three main forces and then the latter two underlying influences.

The centrality of work in the consciousness of the Overseas Chinese tells us much about their society, as so much flows out from this core activity. The drive is of course the result of an amalgam of insecurity and opportunity, and this comes out in the descriptions of it. But there is also a sense of its taking on a momentum of its own, a phenomenon which sweeps people into it, arguably reaching its most intense manifestation in the maelstrom of Hong Kong, a place where the activity of working saturates the air in a way which makes it almost tangible. People rush about their business, talk fast, transact at high speed, seethe in fast-moving crowds, make much noise, and generally take life seriously. It can make New York seem sedated by comparison.

Hwang:
Hong Kong businessmen work very very hard. Twenty-four hours. They don't think about a holiday when they are busy making money. They would rather give up leave. They are working Saturday, Sunday, evenings. If they are the owner, they couldn't care less about time spent. If you miss a phone call, you may miss the chance of getting so much money. Western people think without a proper holiday that's no way to live, but here it's different.

Hui:
My staff turns up at 8 a.m. and are often still there at 7 p.m. You may say that I'm a slavedriver, but these people—one person starts—my assistant comes in very early—one person comes in and its sort of associated cross-psychology. Everybody don't like to be outdone, so they come in very early. It's teamwork. It works like a family.

Hsieh:
Much success in Hong Kong depends on the ordinary people, middle management, professionals, foremen, skilled workers. These are dependable people. They don't absent themselves for minor reasons.

Har:
In my younger days, I worked very hard, but now I still work hard. I think it's mental.

This almost narcotic effect which work has is partly understandable in terms of reward and partly in terms of threat. It would perhaps not be such a powerful drive except that success feeds it. The Overseas Chinese societies are replete with examples of the direct connection between hard work and wealth.

Hui:
It's contagious. If you see that he is driving a Mercedes, and if you want to drive a Mercedes, then you've got to work hard. Chinese people by nature work very hard. Unless you are very good, you don't come to Hong Kong—that's why we have the cream of best people coming to Hong Kong. . . and now with the opening of China, the best of people from the multi-nationals. And that is why this spirit and drive to make more and more money.

The capacities of these societies to provide aspirants with their Mercedes requires little elaboration. From positions of average third world poverty in the 1950's, Hong Kong, Singapore, and Taiwan have leaped several league tables in terms of wealth, with average annual g.d.p. growth over more than two decades running at nearly 10%. The two city states have overtaken some European nations in average personal wealth, and Taiwan has stored currency reserves second only in world terms to those of Japan. At the level of the businessman, it is possible to become wealthy, and work is likely to find its reward.

But the reward is not always entirely material. There is clearly some exhilaration in the work itself, especially for those in charge of their own organizations.

Hwee:
I simply like to work as much as I can, to become as big as I can.

Shek:
I often work fifteen hours a day in the office. I'm totally work obsessed, and I still look forward to work every morning.

Tseng:
Sacrifices? My family and personal life. There is no Saturday and no Sunday.

Even so, the workaholic in the Far East pays a similar price to that paid by his Western counterpart, for such addiction. The sacrifice of time and family life was reflected upon ruefully by a number of the respondents.

The work ethic of a people both driven by insecurity and tempted by open opportunity operates on the processes of cooperation by the simple means of raising the importance of successfully transacting business. People who let you down by missing deadlines, people who promise a certain quality of product but can't meet the specification, people whose advice proves worthless, are not connected with again. The price of staying in business is giving people what they want. The inadequate is not tolerated.

In this unforgiving atmosphere, cooperation is fostered by the sharing of understanding that the end product matters, and the work ethic thus takes on an extra dimension. It is not work in itself which is so "right" for this society, but the efficient production of wealth. This is a matter which is tacitly understood by all. It causes no dispute, and gives rise to no jealousy. It is one of the basic rules of the game, and if all are playing by the same rules, the fostering of necessary linkages is greatly enhanced.

A second driving force, which makes it possible for a minimally integrated society to cohere, is a shared sense of pragmatism, seen here as the tendency to judge matters in terms of their practical outcomes. This tendency to focus on ends serves to loosen up possible inhibitions about means, and thus smoothes the flow of interactions.

In this atmosphere of guileless and uninhibited pursuit of worldly success, usually measured in terms of possessions, concern with ethics becomes a luxury not affordable by all. The Confucian strictures about decent behavior towards those whom you *know* are seemingly followed. One's own, in the widest sense, are looked after. But the rest, and that includes society at large, are fair game.

Hsu:
Insider trading uses an unfair advantage, but if you really want to be successful, you don't obey the rules. You be bloody minded. Some people say if you're being fair, it's so-called "womanly-kindness." It's not a real man's behavior. . . . Expediency is very important. As long as you succeed, never ask how.

Hung noted that in a "very mean society" moral obligation does not come naturally. In both Hong Kong and Singapore, business ethics have had to be imposed by strong measures, and for good reason.

Hui:
Without the ICAC[1], for instance, people who would like to get patents and so on would buy you a good car. This is an element where the Chinese will excel in more ways than one. Ethics and morals rate very low as far as businessmen are concerned. The morals are very low. If they can cheat, they'll cheat. In Hong Kong, we owe the society nothing. There is no identity. It is a colony, a transient place. You are here to make money.

The pursuit of riches is the unashamedly open intention of a population without the luxury of alternatives. Understanding the pragmatism of the Overseas Chinese in Hong Kong, Indonesia, Malaysia, the Philippines, and Thailand is to understand the narrowing of goals of a people who are largely disenfranchised.

Heng:
Thinking in terms of Maslow, there is just no outlet to show success in Hong Kong. Political power? Artistic or even scholastic? These routes do not exist.

Before turning to a consideration of money as such, it is necessary to note the way in which pragmatism influences relationships, and to consider also the element of opportunism.

The hard edge of an unsentimental society is displayed in this reflection on the workings of the cocktail party machine. The commentator is in a powerful position politically but understands the rules of the society in which many relationships can be instrumental and little else.

Hui:
There are too many parties in Hong Kong, and this is not good for your health. Last night I was at two parties before dinner, and as long as I am in Legco there will be parties, in Exco more parties, but I know that when I retire—no more parties. You know, people are very pragmatic. I recognize the fact and I consider that it is a good thing. If I am a chief executive, a lot of people will come to me and the moment I step down they will forget me. Look at X. Once he stepped down, he is forgotten. Hong Kong's memory is very short.

The instrumental view of relationships, the opportunistic "using" of other people, is likely to lead to friction only when one of the partners is naive, and the naive do not survive in this environment. More typical is the working out of a cautious, watchful accommodation, each being aware that both buyer and seller should be wary of each other. If social compatibility is high, then it is possible that the mutual dependence will cause a real obligation bond to be forged. Social compatibility may however be low, and it is in these circumstances that the power of Overseas Chinese pragmatism to foster linkages comes into play. They avoid making enemies. It is a drastic matter to lose control of a situation to the point of creating an adversary. Results matter more than personal sensitivities. The connections to produce those results are instruments; they are important, and are to be seen as such.

Hap:
Friends come and go, but enemies accumulate.

Hsui:
Hong Kong people are very practical. You may be very harsh on your buyers but you will still do business. Even if he's tricky, and you need to be cautious, you would still go back to him. If you try to make an enemy of that man, people will think you're not a businessman in Hong Kong.

Two things must be remembered about what at first appears cold and calculating opportunism in business networking. In the first place, the Overseas Chinese businessman grows up in a world of extremely secure family relationships. These provide him with an emotional bedrock, and from this secure base he can view many of the tensions of the business world with equanimity.

Secondly, the element of opportunism is at least partly attributable to the amount of opportunity. It will grow in fertile ground.

Hsieh:
The Chinese are opportunistic. You cannot stay in one profession all your life and do very well. You have to do many things. Grab at things and prosper.

Hsia:
It is just that there are a lot of opportunities. You have a lot of stimulation if you open your mind. The reason why my desire to get rich is so potent is that looking around I see just ordinary people like me can get rich in a day, so why shouldn't I? Someday maybe it comes to me, who knows, as long as you get yourself prepared.

Being prepared for the eventual entrepreneurial leap is the drive behind three commonly noted social phenomena in the Overseas Chinese. The thirst for education is very much related to career preparation and displays little of a deeper thirst for knowledge for its own sake. Secondly, the quite ruthless "use" of large, usually foreign, companies as training grounds in which to absorb techniques, is a regular cause of complaint in the labor market. Thirdly, the tradition of moonlighting flourishes, and many executives in apparently secure employment have another role on the side, capable of sudden expansion as a full-time occupation when the need or opportunity dictates.

Pragmatism, the concern with the practical consequences of action, suggests the ascendancy of ends over means. It contains the implication that if the means serve an end as ignoble as getting rich, then they cannot at the same time serve ends such as morality. The moral base of Chinese business behavior requires some scrutiny if their apparently opportunistic activities are to be seen in context. Not surprisingly there are strong opinions on this issue. Not surprisingly either, the tone of the responses is that immoral business practices have been common, even traditional, but in only one or two cases does a respondent propose that bribery is simply oiling the wheels of commerce. Condemnation is normal, combined with a rueful acknowledgement that the "game of business" has always been played by its own rules, not society's.

Hon:
Before they made a big fuss about insider trading it was a way of life in Hong Kong.

Hioe:
Insider trading is not considered as a-crime. Chinese people don't take it so seriously.

Hai:
Do you know why there is so much corruption among Chinese people? Because in business, the master of the game is the person who is most ruthless, who uses all ways and means—to look at the end but never mind the means—as long as you get there you are the king. . . . That's the whole game of business. That's why corruption is tolerated as long as you are not caught. But that's only a belief among businessmen. More generally it's not accepted. And that's because businessmen tend to employ this sort of means for doing things. That's why they are never respected in Chinese history.

The result can justify either cynicism or regret, depending on your standpoint.

Hai:
The wealthy people tend to be philanthropic when they get older, so that they can buy some of their debts off—what they have cheated from others.

Heung:
Insider trading is evil. The stockmarket is ridiculous—educated people trying to make money from uneducated people.

As a final comment on pragmatism, and perhaps a pointer to hard reality rather than wishful thinking, here is a statement made late one night, when the cosy intimacy and bonhomie of the research method was able to tempt truth to the surface. It will be given here without even an alias, but it comes from an experienced executive who had worked in several of the countries of concern to this study. The topic was bribery.

It's more serious in the XX industry, and still practised. They put a stop to it at the cost of losing business. As a businessman, I don't mind paying HK $ 2 million "commission." That means I get a contract of HK $ 2 billion. If I have to rebate $60 I wouldn't do it, but if it comes to 2m I would have to do it.
The ICAC has cleaned up the small fry and that is beneficial. You are no longer hassled by the police, the customs at the airport. But the top is still doing it, and that is not really harmful. In a way, it's good for business.

We observe at work here the compartmentalized mind, the mind which can deal elastically with matters of good and evil because it is not trammelled by some ultimate black-and-white sense of right and wrong. Good and bad are contingent, they depend on the circumstances. Morality is based on what serves the welfare of a specifically circumscribed set of people, i.e. one's family. This allows for considerable flexibility in determining good from bad. The classic riddle in Chinese moral philosophy is "If your father steals a sheep, do you tell the policeman?" and the answer is "no"; it is your father who has committed the offense and it is thus no crime. The contrast with the absolutes of Western thinking is dramatic.

It is this capacity to suspend judgement, even perhaps to see judgement as irrelevant; this lack of concern with societal good and its replacement by a family-serving (i.e. essentially self-serving) focus on results regardless of their means of achievement; this loosening up of constraints, which lie at the heart of Overseas Chinese pragmatism. The freedom which results, and the cooperation which is thereby facilitated, contribute much to the dynamism and efficiency of their organizations.

The third major societal drive which supports cooperative effort by clarifying shared purposes is materialism, more specifically the pursuit of money. Enough has been said already to indicate the salience of wealth for the Overseas Chinese, but there is a danger of judging this from a Western perspective, of perhaps being somewhat supercilious about it, and as a core feature of society, it requires some comment. More particularly it is necessary to elicit some sympathy for the plight of a people wrenched from their extremely deep roots and plagued by two insecurities: that of being in essence sojourners; and that of being businessmen in environments which have normally been either threatening or hostile, and have only recently in some places become supportive. The old defences remain, the old methods work. You trust your own, you keep things to yourself, you save and accumulate, and you fight to protect what you have for the use of future generations. The name of the game is wealth and it is a surrogate for security in a decidedly insecure world.

From the interviews it is possible to discern three themes which represent the thinking of Chinese businessmen about money. Overwhelmingly the strongest and most consistent was the view of money as an instrument for the growth of an organization, a view which suggests that money simply for the sake of money is not a central pursuit. Supporting this is a second common perception, namely a traditional frugality, an ascetic self-denial, especially in favor of future generations. Thirdly is the somewhat peripheral acknowledgement that money is society's yardstick, the key determinant of respect.

The notion of money as instrument for the growth of a business, and not an end in itself, is clearly and firmly fixed in the mind of the Chinese entrepreneur, and perhaps explains the finesse with which funds are managed (see chapter 7). A corollary of this is that money should not be allowed to lie idle. Capital comes to be imbued with the work ethic just like labor.

So:
The purpose of wealth is to build up a business. It should be *used*. Pure accumulation is no use.

Shing:
Wealth is valuable not *per se*, but for the extra gearing which is possible.

Hsing:
Capital accumulation is to keep the company running. That was my father's philosophy. It is not personal property. It belongs to all contributors, the staff included.

Heung:
What I earn money for? I feel I have the capability to do more things but without money you just can't do anything. Of course I can buy luxuries. But right now I own two companies and I'm setting up the third—to me I think I have the capability to do more but I need money to do more. Money makes me such that I can expand my capability. After the first million the living standard is the same but from then on you have money to expand your business.

It must be remembered here that the great majority of respondents would have discretion over the funds of their companies, and the option to siphon off surplus into personal channels. Although this unquestionably happens, and has happened dramatically, illegally, and regularly in a long running series of scandals affecting major companies, on the evidence of these seventy-two interviews, it is not normal. Money is too important, for the generation of more money, to allow it to be misdirected into personal indulgence. No respondent referred to such misdirection by discussing third parties and certainly not in terms of him or herself. Although it generates much publicity when revealed, it would appear to be deviant behavior rather than normal. There are of course extravagant lifestyles fed by family businesses, but these are either restricted to the temporarily callow younger generation, or excused by the need to maintain a confident image. The more normal and representative tone is that of modest display, with for some the occasional flashes of symbolic affluence—the Mercedes (and chauffeur), the Balenciaga, the real Cartier, the emerald necklace—to remind the observer that inner reserves of indeterminate quantity are available.

Reticence is of course a Confucian virtue, but in this context it is combined with the deep-seated traditional frugality of a people whose not-so-distant ancestors, and in many cases they themselves, have known life at the subsistence level. Frugality, asceticism, and saving are common norms and are clearly being transmitted from generation to generation.

Han:
The question of facing poor conditions came up time and time again when I was young, but the whole family is not a big spender. My mother in particular is very cautious in spending money. So I've never been exposed to a situation where money is of no importance.

The majority of respondents who mentioned the tradition of frugality laid emphasis on the role of the mother of the family in instilling it, but there was clearly a general consensus anyway, as indicated in this exchange of experiences.

Hsieh:
You learn this at home.

Huang:
My mother always taught me to save.
Hua:
It's an old tradition at Chinese New Year—all these laisee packets—and all the money—we never get to touch it. The parents always put it in the bank for us.
Huang:
I could only touch something like 10%. The rest had to be saved.
Hua:
You're lucky!

Hsieh:
My mother was very frugal—with herself mostly, and with the family. My father was frugal. Everybody I know is frugal. The Hong Kong people if they own two apartments, one in North Point, and one in Mid-levels, they would stay in the North Point place and rent out the more expensive Mid-levels one to renters, so that they can accumulate savings.

Such traditions are still perpetuated today despite a dramatic increase in affluence.

Hioe:
When I wanted to buy a new home, my parents said why not stay where you are and save money and not worry about being more comfortable?

Shen:
My younger brothers went to university but with part-time jobs to earn money, to appreciate the value of the dollar. Last week my daughter spent a hundred dollars (US$ 50) on a swimsuit. I nearly died—so disappointed that I've not taught them the value of money.

Sung:
My parents would not allow me to own a car while I was at college, and I will bring up my son in the same way.

Great wealth, and possibly a capacity for great philanthropy, do not appear to alter the basic asceticism learned in the early days. The wealthiest respondent, extremely rich by any international standards, revealed his adherence to folk wisdom in saying, "I have always believed in the Chinese saying 'pickled turnips with rice is the cup of tea for everyone.'"

If money is to be treated with such care and reverence, it is then not surprising that it should become an important yardstick, the talisman of a materialist culture.

Hsu:
In this society, people measure you solely by money and nothing else. Even if you have so much that you don't need the extra millions, you still go for the extra millions. This is Hong Kong. They measure by something which is visible.

Seow:
Money is not important personally but as a yardstick of achievement.

Given the obvious ascendency of such materialism as a societal value, it cannot go unobserved that the earlier Confucian tradition of lofty disdain for the businessman which had begun to break down in the nineteenth century has now been replaced with a new set of criteria for prestige. When *Huang* observes that "I picked up from the social norms in Hong Kong that having money is a respectable thing. I found in the social setting that it is quite respectable to be associated with the term 'a businessman,'" he is indicating that the earlier Confucian order has passed. What the Overseas Chinese preserve from traditional Chinese culture is partial and subconsciously selected. An important effect has been that the businessman has moved from the bottom of the social ladder to a place somewhere near the top.

This movement is associated with the loosening up of society. Whereas China was always, and still remains, controlled by an elite holding a monopoly on the interpretation of the state ideology and the retention of central power was and is served by downgrading the status (and thus the potential countervailing power) of merchants, in other societies of the Nanyang, central control has been less of a national obsession. In these freer environments, more confident perhaps politically, the power of business is not a threat. The government—business relationship is more of an alliance. These alliances will vary from the extremely close form in Hong Kong, where government is largely run by (and some would argue for) businessmen, to the watchful truce between government and Chinese business in Indonesia.

In finding host societies, or in creating their own economic cultures in Hong Kong, Taiwan, and Singapore, the Overseas Chinese have created social systems where the businessman can escape from the dead weight of Chinese tradition. His immense flourishing in these circumstances, although in part a tribute to what he brought from his cultural heritage, is at the same time an acknowledgement that parts of the Confucian tradition were abandoned as useless. In simple terms, he brought with him the legitimating force of paternalism, the coordinating magnetism of family, and a great respect for education. In the case of the latter, its focus was diverted from the ethereal to the pragmatic but the dedication retained. What was abandoned was a system of caste, an extreme conservatism, and an obsession with central political power.

The forging of this new culture, based as it is on creating an alloy of old and new elements, has taken place in environments which themselves have influenced the end result. Those environments are characterized by fairly high degrees of insecurity (except in Singapore) and often a sense of transience. This element must be seen as a deep-seated perception, not always openly acknowledged, but insofar as it has some explanatory power, it must be considered.

At its most extreme, it is overt in Hong Kong under the threat of the 1997 absorption into China. In Indonesia, the Philippines, Malaysia, and Thailand, the Overseas Chinese businessman must operate with care and may become a hostage to changes of host government policy at any time. In Taiwan, although political stability and economic success have encouraged a greater sense of relaxation, the permanent sense of threat from China cannot simply be put to one side and entirely ignored, and about a third of respondents mentioned this.

The problems of both the past and the present are most poignant in Hong Kong.

Hoi:
Our fathers' prime years were spent in turmoil—a lot of wars. And they understand the volatility of business, and they want their children to have something to hang on to when there's another war. Hong Kong is a transient place. People come here only to escape the turmoils of other places. My father bought property at the end of World War II in Canton and therefore lost it all. He told me not to do business because it would be a very hard life.

Hui:
Hong Kong is a transient place. We are sold down the river even by the British. More than half the population are people who escaped from China.

The view taken of China nowadays by the Overseas Chinese is an ambivalent mixture. There is identity with and obligation to the motherland, and at the same time a usually quite severe disgust and impatience with the inefficiencies of communism. There is much idealism in wanting to help, particularly in practical ways in the person's area of origin, and this is exercised on a large scale, with payment for the building of roads, the installation of power supplies, the gifts of technology, the building of schools and even universities.

There is, however, despair at the waste in the system and the slowness in progress. There is frustration at the delays and complexities caused by the elaborately patrimonial and personalistic networks of influence. There is cynicism about the unpredictability of government behavior. The wholesale slaughters of the cultural revolution, exceeding as they do those of the Nazis, lie buried in the memories of the population to guarantee for decades the perpetuation of traditional insecurities and familism. The Tienanmen Square massacre of June 4, 1989 was a reminder that ten years of subsequent liberalization had not changed the profoundest realities. As *Hai* observed:

I don't think that the average Chinese in China now has got much faith in the government at all. It's still like it was thousands of years ago.

As a result, there will remain among the Overseas Chinese a resistance to being embraced by China too closely. Romanticism about the heritage of Chinese civilization will always guarantee the emotional ties, but it will not guarantee relationships closer than arm's length. China remains more of a threat than a promise.

The resultant destabilizing of Hong Kong, although a special and narrow aspect of the world of the Overseas Chinese as a whole, nevertheless is having effects throughout their diaspora, and its nature is worthy of brief note. It contains three elements: the exit of talent, the exit of capital, and the breaking of networks.

The talent which is leaving is, by and large, that which can both afford to go and also persuade a foreign government to receive it. This means the professionals, the entrepreneurs, the middle class. Once the foreign passport is secured, some return to be ready for the opportunities which the opening of China may present. But many settle elsewhere and there is a net loss, important not so much for its numbers as for the sum of talent which it represents out of the original limited pool.

Capital flight varies with political mood, and money moves in and out of Hong Kong like the tide, a factor which makes consideration of the sums themselves pointless. What is more crucial as an indicator of attitudes and possible future scenarios is the hard realism of the Chinese businessman.

Hwa:
Taking money out of Hong Kong? Everybody's doing that these days. There's no shame in that.

A less obvious effect of the responses to threat is the break up of the social fabric, noted by *Hap:*

Long-standing friendship is more rare now because of the 1997 effect, but it is still a very valued sentiment in our scene.

These reactions to transience in Hong Kong are strong cases of traditional Overseas Chinese adaptability. They have successfully coped with such threats for centuries, although rarely on the scale currently affecting Hong Kong. In such cases, transience is a result of geography and history. There is, however, another aspect of transience not discussed so far and that is the one resulting from the life and death cycle of the family business, hence the family fortune. This is referred to as the third generation problem. They regularly speak of "rags to riches to rags in three generations."

The life-cycle of the family business will be considered as such in later chapters. Here it is simply necessary to note that the source of family wealth is itself transient. Upward mobility can be very fast and dramatic. Rags to riches has been a prevalent reality. But when you have come up from what may have been appalling conditions, there is often a sense that, in an uncertain world, you might one day have to return to them.

Many respondents reported parents or grandparents who were street-hawkers. One of the richest men in Hong Kong arrived with $ 14. Those who had been refugees themselves reported often harrowing circumstances.

Hsi:
For the first twenty years of my life, I lived in a squatter hut on Ap Lei Chau with nine people to a room. We were a refugee family from China.

Shang:
We were a poor family and I learned the value of money early, I remember my mother had to borrow money to feed us.

Hsieh:
My father's grandmother came from a village near Canton and was persecuted. Her husband came to be a regional minor lord and the Ching soldiers went to get him, so he and his family had to escape. She was very poor when she came, and had to take bread from the gutter. Her son was a scaffolding man. Her grandson began the family fortune.

It is perhaps appropriate here to recapitulate the argument being made about the Overseas Chinese businessman's view of society. It is that the high degree of social order provided in the sphere of vertical relations by Confucian ideals is in part negated by difficulties over horizontal cooperation. The family units remain essentially separate. For the cooperation needed in the economic process, three drives may be seen to underlie attitudes and to foster a sharing of goals. These are the work ethic, pragmatism, and materialism. The reason why these three drives are so strong is that the transience of both societal arrangements and of family fortunes fuel the sense of insecurity, and they are all three primarily manifestations of vulnerability.

There is one final societal feature remarked upon by respondents, which also helps explain behavior in conditions of instability. This is fatalism, with its corollaries luck and fortune.

About a fifth of respondents denied that they believed in luck, the remainder either espoused it openly or more typically said that they thought they should indulge the old superstitions just in case, and anyway it kept the staff happy. Typical of the majority are the following:

Hwa:
There will always be an element of luck in your success and you want that extra bit, and that's why you get the *feng shui* man there.[2] If you arrange the furniture the way the *feng shui* man says, you actually feel a bit more comfortable.

Tso:
I believe in luck and fate and have had many experiences to prove it works. There is an invisible hand shaping everyone's fate.

Heng:
I believe in luck but not to the extent of making the office ugly. I go to the fortune teller each year to have a quick rundown on what he thinks is going to happen.

Shek:
Feng shui for office arrangements? Very much so. I'm not obsessed with it, but you just don't take chances in business.

Tsim:
Two factors are important to success. One is fate, and that you are born with. The other is luck and you can only influence that a little, but you can't deny its existence.

Sung:
I would not fight it. I would not buy a home which was number 24.[3]

Huang:
I know a restaurant chain which uses palmistry in selecting staff and top management.

Ho:
When I resigned, my boss said I should not do so technically until I was 40, as 39 was a bad year for change. I finished up only giving 25 days notice as a result, although they knew well in advance that I was leaving. It was his advice.

More often than not, being tolerant of such beliefs was seen as a way of indulging staff. The senior businessman could get by without it, but one has to allow for the superstitions of others.

Tsui:
You have to go along with folk religion just to reassure your staff, your workers, or even your clients. They *trust* an investor in a construction project who has some belief like this. That means you have to act like someone who believes in it.

While it is possible to see the retention of superstitions as amusing reflections on a non-scientific and non-rational mental world, it would be naive to consider their effects as entirely superficial. Such a world-view, containing as it does the fatalistic belief that the events of life are not within the control of individuals, can infiltrate thinking about the capacity of a managerial group to influence the destiny of an organization. The following quote, devastating in its implications for the spread of professionalism in management, speaks eloquently for the influence of fatalism. The company concerned is a large and apparently sophisticated financial services organization but has been greatly dependent for its growth on the intuitive skills of a dominant founder. It is in many ways thus typical. The respondent is discussing the influence of luck.

Han:
We had a big debate on this in our company when a professional manager wanted to introduce organized training in the company. The opinion from the board is that training is not important. There is a Chinese saying, "the most important thing in life is whether you were born to be rich or not. But the second is your luck. The third one is *feng shui*. The fourth is when you accumulate a lot of charity." So they believe that luck is very important actually. Very important. More important than anything else.

Another way in which luck influences management is in sanctioning the use of intuition in strategic decision making. The business environments of many Overseas Chinese companies are especially volatile. They are so dependent on distant events in European and North American markets, many of their supplies come from the unpredictable field of basic commodities or raw materials, their buying power or production volumes are so small that they must often accept the dictates of others. In such circumstances, they must learn to cope with risk, and with decisions unsupported by masses of analysis and facts.

Hsui:
I always subscribe to the hypothesis that Chinese are great entrepreneurs but they are not great managers. They are very intuitive. They get a feel on the place and the market and they are most prepared to take risks in anticipation of tremendous rewards. They got a feeling for it but they are not 100% sure. And I think most of them believe in *feng shui*—it's my day—it's my time—so luck plays a tremendous part.

Tsai:
Chinese business culture means not being very scientific.

Huen:
Sometimes it's hard to get data so you have to take a risk. Money making is more a matter of luck than skill.

Hsieh:
It's 95% gut feeling. After you've done it, you ask your subordinates to prepare a reason for it! We are very fatalistic and believe in luck. Hong Kong is so small and so many things happening outside your control.

Seow:
Intuition influences my decisions. We feel what will work. I don't rely on market research, statistics, etc. There is a lot of ingenuity in our products and ventures. Luck plus ability are what matter.

Perhaps the real truth of the matter is that blame can be displaced. In a culture where control of the world is less a part of the belief system than is accomodation to the world, the idea of being able to dominate events does not occur naturally. Instead, the view is one of seeking opportunities, themselves formed by the workings of forces outside one's control or one's capacity to predict. Failure in such circumstances means not so much that your judgement was in error, but that fate was running against you. It is, of course, a good environment for the encouraging of entrepreneurship and risk taking, something for which the Overseas Chinese have a remarkable proclivity. That this is at least partly cultural in origin is suggested in this final quotation from an entrepreneur:

Hse:
We believe in good *feng shui*. This is how Chinese try to change their fate—fortune telling—which year is good or bad for you. That's why many Chinese can stand the hardship of failure. Even if they fail, they would put all the blame to the fate rather than to himself. Otherwise they blame themselves and the whole people would collapse.

In a study of the beliefs about society held by a Chinese community in Indonesia, Ryan (1961) identified three major components. These were (a) the problem of trust and cooperation, (b) materialism and money-mindedness, (c) Chineseness. Because the chief executives interviewed for this book were principally from the Chinese communities of Hong Kong, Singapore, and Taiwan, with only three from Indonesia, the latter component, the sense of Chineseness, did not emerge, as it would have been irrelevant in Chinese communities. It is, however, strongly relevant in non-Chinese host communities and must be noted as a special feature in Malaysia, Indonesia, the Philippines, and Thailand.

In these countries, as was noted in chapter 2, the Overseas Chinese are markedly successful in economic life. They also tend to remain unassimilated. There are exceptions to this, as for instance in Thailand, or with the *peranakan* people of the Malay Straits and Indonesia, but the general rule is that the Chinese band together to help themselves. In this process, the sense of Chineseness has an important function. It provides a language, a set of social norms, a set of beliefs, and a most subtle sense of cultural confidence; even, some would argue, a sense of superiority. Chinese civilization, and particularly the factors of its continuity and its early achievements, are sources of great pride. To be associated with it, in fact to be a member of it, is something to be conscious of, something to be taken seriously, something not be given up. The understanding of Chinese communities, especially in host cultures, can never be complete without an acknowledgement of the power of this unifying force.

Footnotes

[1] The Independent Commission Against Corruption, set up with special powers, has acted to clean up corruption in Hong Kong in both public and private sectors.
[2] *Feng shui* is the belief in propitious location, and embraces location of buildings, of offices, and of furniture. It also includes timing of events and requires a geomancer to advise.
[3] Number 24 in Chinese can also sound like the words for death coming.

Chapter 9
Sources of Efficiency and of Failure

That the Chinese family business is an efficient economic instrument is visible at the most simple level of understanding in the thriving economies of East and Southeast Asia. There is something inside those economies which provides them with their dynamism. We shall later consider what else, besides the entre-preneurship and coordinative skills of managers, makes for such success, and it is necessary to acknowledge that such managerial skills are only a part of the magical combination. Governments have to be supportive in the right way, world trade patterns have to facilitate the activities concerned, technology has to be accessible, etc.

There is, however, a need, before moving to that larger scale of analysis, to focus on the organization itself. Given the consistency with which the Chinese family business repeats the same characteristics of organizational style across industries and environments, it is proposed to take it as one type and to make comparisons with alternative recipes. Variation from the type is of course inevit-able, and allowance can be made for that when considering real world cases, but the core characteristics seem stable.

In this chapter, we consider the sources of efficiency and of failure, especially in the light of what is known of organization structures from chapter 7, and what is known about the reasons for them in the remainder of the text so far. The chapter will proceed by briefly summarizing the normal characteristics and then by analyzing what may be argued to be the strengths and weaknesses of such organizations.

The reasonably standard characteristics of Chinese family businesses are the following:

(1) small scale, and relatively simple organizational structuring;
(2) normally focussed on one product or market;
(3) centralized decision making with a heavy reliance on one dominant execu-tive;
(4) a close overlap of ownership, control, and family;
(5) a paternalistic organizational climate;
(6) linked to the environment with personalistic networks;
(7) normally very sensitive to matters of cost and financial efficiency;
(8) commonly linked strongly but informally with related but legally indepen-dent organizations handling key functions such as parts supply or marketing;

 (9) relatively weak in terms of creating large-scale market recognition for
     brands;

(10) a high degree of strategic adaptability.

It is, of course, reasonable to question how Chinese these characteristics are,
and whether one is not simply observing small-scale business anywhere. As has
been suggested earlier, the answer lies in the uniqueness of the *combination* of
features. There are for instance plenty of cultures with paternalistic organizations. There are very few, however, where that paternalism is combined with
strategic flexibility, and with cost-sensitivity, and with environmental networks,
and with narrowness of focus. The uniqueness also lies in the cultural heritage
which leads to such characteristics and which permeates the way they operate in
practice. The Chinese form of paternalism, for instance, is an expression of Confucian norms. External networking is in part a special response to problems of
insecurity and mistrust unique to the culture as they derive from Chinese social
history. Money consciousness and thrift have been part of Chinese people's collection of weapons to deal with a relatively harsh existence for centuries, and an
accumulation of traditions has accreted around the central notion, giving the
whole approach to money a distinct flavor.

    Identification of the strengths of such organizations begs a substantial ques-
tion about what is a strength. The question is not trivial because (a) a strength at
one point in an organization's development can be a weakness at another as the
organization outgrows one formula and requires novelty, and (b) a characteristic
at any one time can be both a strength and a weakness, as for instance with
centralized decision making which, on the one hand, can guarantee speed of
response but, on the other, destroy creativity. Strengths and weaknesses will
thus be discussed not as mutually exclusive categories but as characteristics
which display beneficial effects and inhibiting effects.

    Any business, at least any business in a market economy, needs to exhibit
certain fundamental traits to survive and grow, and these may be encapsulated
within four categories of activity which will serve as focusses for analysis. They
are

(1) *vertical cooperation*, whereby a stable hierarchy is established, in which at
    least some (and preferably much) commonality of aims is established;
(2) *horizontal cooperation*, whereby the work of various parts of the organiza-
    tion, and any crucially linked organizations, is coordinated smoothly;
(3) *control*, to ensure that some goal-based discipline is available to weed out
    inefficient and ineffective behavior;
(4) *adaptiveness*, to ensure that change is possible, if it is necessary, and to know
    when it is necessary.

The Chinese family business will now be analyzed to see how it deals with these
four requirements, to see what lies behind its strengths and weaknesses, and in

Table 9.1: Strengths and weaknesses of the Chinese family business form of organization

Organization Domain	Strengths	Weaknesses
Vertical Cooperation	Identity with goals of boss and organization	Danger of factions and cliques lower down
	Compliance by subordinates via work diligence and perseverance	Lack of innovation and initiative from below
	Long-lasting and stable key relationships	Limitations as to how far legitimate authority stretches
Horizontal Cooperation	Low transaction costs in economic exchanges	Limited field for cooperative relations, therefore tendency to small scale
	Reliability of networks and linkages	Mistrust and urge to control lead to capital starvation
	Maneuverability of linkages	Technical limitations caused by scale restrictions
Control	Intensity of managerial commitment	Lack of neutrality and professionalism
	Reliability of managerial commitment	Goal displacement possible when control is unclear
	Cost efficiency by reducing bureaucratic control	Coordination problems due to lack of focus
Adaptiveness	Strategic flexibility	Danger of non-rational opportunist leaps
	Speed of response	Possible diffraction of organization
	Personal vision can be operationalized	Lack of creative tension and debate on strategic issues

particular to take note of whether the formula adopted is culture-specific and thus not replicable as such elsewhere. A summary of the main themes to be addressed is given in Table 9.1.

Vertical Cooperation

Vertical cooperation, in the circumstances under consideration, works by incorporating many of the society's norms about social order into the business context. Because the society has an extremely powerful set of norms about vertical order, this makes it relatively easy for the organization to establish stable hierarchies. Because hierarchy is, in some sense, natural to the Chinese, this means that many of the systems designed into the Western bureaucracy to make hierarchy acceptable can be dispensed with. This may well explain the lower level of structuring found in Overseas Chinese organizations compared to Western. Discipline is already there; it does not need to be injected.

There are few societies in the world, one thinks most readily for instance only of Japan and Korea, where vertical order is so clear and so consistently supported by processes of socialization, example, and social sanction. The societies of East Asia contain people for whom the rules for behavior, as both superiors and subordinates, are very clear. Responsibility or paternalism from above and dependence and compliance from below are bedrocks of society, but rituals which reflect them daily allow for the maintenance of order without at the same time destroying all individual initiative or dehumanizing those at the base. It is part of the genius of Confucianism that its vertical stability is based more on morality than fear, and that its humanism, as long as it is operational, protects the lower levels from brutalizing exploitation.

In the organizational context, vertical cooperation is normally a question of workers fitting in with the requirements of their bosses. This means that there need to be some common understandings over purposes. In the Overseas Chinese case, this is made easier by the transparency of motives of those in power, and by the fact that those same motives are shared by all and identified with by all. The prime motive is the generation of family wealth and whether you are a boss looking for a favorable stockmarket flotation, or a worker looking for nine months pay as a Chinese New Year bonus, the motive is common. This is not necessarily to say that organizational loyalty of the kind visible in Japan is widespread. It is not. The worker's identity is primarily located outside the firm. Even so there is a sharing of views about the basic rationale of business and of the firm.

This shared understanding of what life is about serves to reduce what might otherwise be tensions, by eliminating the factor of jealousy. If a boss is successful and rich, then that causes no complaint. It simply points to what you might achieve yourself given hard work and luck.

Because of these features of the organizational psychology, it is possible to discern quite high levels of congruence between the ranks as to the purposes which lie behind the acts of working. At the same time, the society at large exhibits much evidence of upward mobility. This may not always take place inside the firm (although talent does tend to be spotted and used in such fast-growing economies), and access to real organizational power is inevitably going to be affected by nepotism. Even so, external possibilities are endless, and going out to run your own company, or moonlighting, are entirely normal behaviors for those with aspirations. As was noted earlier, the urge to control is a very strong one, and it finds so many outlets that there are no barriers to seeing yourself as a boss if you wish to.

This atmosphere is not, then, one in which workers and owner/managers naturally divide into two camps psychologically. They tend to be similar socially, in terms of their values, their behavior, their needs, and their aspirations. In consequence, one of the major weaknesses found in many Western organizations, that of the management/worker divide, may be largely discounted in the Overseas Chinese case. The contribution this makes to organizational effectiveness and efficiency may be more a matter of removing a barrier than of building a positive bridge. In comparative terms, however, that is still a significant feature.

One of the outcomes of this vertical cooperativeness is willing compliance. This tendency is also reinforced by early conditioning of people during childhood and education, and the respect for authority figures, deeply ingrained in the Confucian tradition, tends to be maintained through life.

An extension of this willingness to comply is willingness to engage diligently in routine and possibly dull tasks, something one might term perseverance. This nebulous but nonetheless important component of Overseas Chinese work behavior, a kind of micro form of the work ethic, pervades their factories and offices. It is visible in the concentrated frowns on faces bent over sewing machines, in the speed with which mounds of paperwork are dispatched from a desk, in the willingness to go to trouble over minor detail. It suggests an upbringing which inculcates an early acceptance of monotonous routine combined with a need to perform to a monitored standard. It was noted earlier that the huge diligence required to master the Chinese language has played a part here, as has also the strict order of a Confucian household.

A third feature connected with vertical cooperation and visible as an organizational strength is the stability of key relationships in the somewhat feudal context of Chinese authority. This is not intended to refer to family relationships, but to those which bind the "old retainers" in key positions. Very often, the office manager, the factory floor supervisor, the chief accountant, even minor guardians of key points in the organization's flow of activities such as the doorkeeper, have been brought into the organization by the paterfamilias, perhaps helped personally with a loan, or even in bad times simply with employment. They remain as loyal as they are dependent, and, if promoted, are likely, given Chinese pragmatism, to be also good at their jobs. This vertical network of the boss's own people provides him with a means of tapping deep into the organization to know what is going on, how people feel, and what to watch out for. As a conduit for communication, it is both efficient and reliable. As a resource to fall back upon when special effort is needed, it is always available. It is a strength not readily available in organizations which have neutralized the vertical ties of power and influence.

As has been noted, features which in one context can be strengths can in another be weaknesses, and it is now necessary to turn to the organizational limitations of the paternalist power structures of the Overseas Chinese business. There are three principal shortcomings: the danger of factions and cliques, the stifling of initiative, and the limited boundaries of legitimate authority.

The development of factions and cliques is inevitable when scarce resources are being contended for in a power structure which relies on personalism. The lack of objective criteria for assessing a person's abilities and worth means that influence is achieved by ties to authority figures, or to people who dispense resources. Such tied groupings may then become competitive, thus destroying horizontal cooperation, but more especially in the context of vertical coopera-tion they can result in the organization's needs coming second to those of the clique. This is visible when, for instance, a clique leader arranges for the promo-tion of one of his own people, perhaps without reference to the talent more generally available. The net effect is the gradual filling of the organization with mediocre people, compounded by ties of obligation which make their removal difficult.

The tendency towards compliance noted above as a feature of vertical coop-eration among Overseas Chinese subordinates, must now be seen in terms of its other face. Willing acceptance of hierarchy will tend to stifle initiative among those who are happy to conform to the status quo, and the stable Confucian order will not inspire a wealth of new ideas and initiatives bubbling up from lower ranks. In a sense, they see it as not their job to do so, and there is often an overwhelming sense that "I am paid to do as you tell me, don't ask me to do your thinking for you." Perhaps perceived less aggressively in the minds of many, it is simply an acceptance that the views of those above contain some form of natural authority and are thus not to be challenged or amended. At the ex-treme, in situations where subordinates do find an instruction unpalatable, there is a rich array of forms of passive disobedience which the aware leader will sense and adjust to, while the unaware leader will suffer the consequences for per-formance of his insensitivity.

The most vivid contrast in terms of the use of subordinates' creativity is with Japan, and it is in this regard that some of the greatest differences between Chinese and Japanese organizations are visible. In the Japanese case, a major part of the managerial role is concerned with creating an atmosphere in which subordinates are encouraged to think on behalf of the organization. This is achieved by extensive massaging of the subordinates' egos, by long-term socialization into identity with the corporate goals, and by a wide range of sys-tems and incentives. Such techniques as quality-control circles flourish naturally and prolifically in such a conducive atmosphere. The end results of the Japanese approach to vertical cooperation are very tight binding into identification with the organization and the release of much mental energy and creative talent.

In the Chinese case, a different approach produces a different result. Although both China and Japan were traditionally centralized states, the way in which power was exercised varied substantially. In the Japanese case, a stable aristocracy bound together with "its" peasantry through centuries of land holding developed a set of samurai ideals about leadership which inculcated a deep-seated respect for subordinates, the expression of which would cause loyalty to be returned upwards. Reinforced by the stabilizing and virtual freezing of societal relations induced by Tokugawa at the beginning of his shogunate and lasting almost three centuries to the Meiji restoration, the link between superior and subordinate in Japan developed a quite unique form. The central components of this are mutual respect, ritual deference, and strong obligations both ways. The social outcomes of history are still clearly visible in Japanese organizational behavior today.

And so, one might argue, are the Chinese equivalents visible, except that they run in the opposite direction. The aspects of Chinese social history which have a bearing on vertical cooperation in Chinese organizations, Overseas or otherwise, today, are the extremely centralized authority structure of traditional Chinese society, and especially the crucial role of the peripatetic mandarin.

Whereas in Japan, the average member of the population could look upwards for protection, the average person in China could not. What he saw when he looked upwards was control and order. There was nobody up there who felt an emotionally charged, personally based obligation to look after him. The mandarin who was in charge of his fate was austere, aloof, inaccessible, but above all else, the mandarin was only a temporary occupant of a role. He moved on every three years. No ties could be established. The Chinese system of vertical power traditionally contained an unbridgeable gap between the mandarinate and the people, and the legacy of that gap remains.

Because Chinese learned to see senior authority as difficult to relate to, they turned in defence to their own resources for support, being thus driven back into their own families, or into organizational relationships which were paternalistic, an extension in other words of the family atmosphere.

The outcome of this social tradition in China, added to also by other reinforcements of traditionalism and deference to authority, is an inhibition about thinking for one's superior. There is an inevitable inner core of anxiety about the vertical tie, an unspoken insecurity in dealing with all except one's own people. This stifles initiative and creativity and circumscribes commitment. At the extreme in the totalitarian state, as Zinoviev (1979) observed of Russia, the destruction of talent is not incidental to the administrative system, it is absolutely central to it.

The question of China will be touched upon in the final chapter, but for the Overseas Chinese family business, the encouragement of lower-level initiative remains an endemic reminder of a discouraging heritage. People who will "take responsibility" are constantly being sought by owner/managers, but always in fear that, unless they are closely tied in, they will leave and start their own operations. This inhibiting fear is inevitably a restriction on the process of encouragement, and the outcome is that the real responsibility for innovation usually reverts back to the family members and owners. The resulting restrictions on organizational size, scope, and complexity are easily visible and rarely mastered.

This brings us to the third weakness of the Chinese family business in the sphere of vertical cooperation, namely the limitations as to how far legitimate authority stretches. An inevitable starting point is the question of what constitutes legitimate authority, and here the clear answer is paternalism. If that is the case, then the limitation in essence is that of how far one person's decision making can be stretched.

Note that the point at issue is not one person's influence, but one person's decision making, in other words his or her direct involvement. Influence can be spread very wide if it is carried by policies and procedures. Decision making can not, unless there is some form of gearing which allows it to be amplified. It is clear, by way of example, that John Reed has extensive influence throughout Citicorp, Akio Morita throughout Sony, Arnold Weinstock throughout GEC. But they do not make all the key decisions. They establish a system and a culture which expresses their policies, and then other people can make large decisions within that framework.

In the Chinese family business, the building of systems and a culture to transcend the individual is exceptionally rare. Large organizations admittedly exist, but they have usually found a formula for gearing up on the strategic intelligence of the dominant individual. In shipping, and in property for instance, one man at one desk can continue to make all the key decisions, and he can also claim to retain a grasp of the fundamental features of the business environment which have to be taken into account. In product markets containing a greater variety of factors to be considered, this is substantially more difficult.

Because of this, the majority of Chinese organizations, even those which grow large, have tended to stay within one business domain. It is as if by intuition the chief executive knows what he is comfortable with and understands his own organizational limitations. Most of the organizational collapses in recent years, when not caused by the corrupt syphoning off of money, have been related to the strains of getting into unfamiliar products or markets. In such circumstances, a one man decision-making process will eventually yield decisions which are (a) late and (b) inadequately informed, either of which is enough to erode the company's competitive quality. Unless the business environment is unusually benign, decline will then set in.

Horizontal Cooperation

What is known of Overseas Chinese society, as discussed in earlier chapters, has suggested that horizontal cooperation is in general problematic. The society is composed of many thousands of relatively autonomous family units; connections between them are more or less utilitarian and somewhat limited. The idea of cooperation for communal purposes, over and above those of family survival, has not taken strong root.

Against this background, and in response to essentially self-directed needs, a limited amount of cooperation is established, adequate to serve the needs of families and firms. Externally in the firm, these needs are for supplies, labor, customers, and information. Internally, they are for smooth interaction between departments. Because of the critical nature of the external needs, and because of the traditional lack of a legal structure able to enforce agreements, a strong ethic of trust has developed, and would appear to serve the society well. It operates within very specific and limited boundaries, but a person's word is his bond, especially in business transactions, and without a sound reputation in this regard, it is difficult to function. One of the outcomes of this networked social structure is the efficiency of transaction costs in economic exchanges.

In practice, what this means is that many transactions which in other countries would require contracts, lawyers, guarantees, investigations, wide opinion seeking, and delays are among the Overseas Chinese dealt with reliably and quickly by telephone, by a handshake, over a cup of tea. Some of the most massive property deals in Hong Kong are concluded with a small note locked in the top drawer of a chief executive's desk, after a two-man meeting. [1] This is not to say that legal proprieties are entirely dispensed with. It is simply to say that they are not prerequisites to agreement, and for the majority of agreements they can be ignored.

When this principle of reliable personal bonds is extended down and through the economy so that it percolates through most of the buying and selling and agreeing necessary to make an economy work, then the size and cost of the legalistic and systemic infrastructure which can be dispensed with is inevitably large. The savings achieved by dispensing with it are an important contribution to the competitiveness of Overseas Chinese business in world markets.

Seeing the reliability of such networks and linkages as a strength requires some understanding of how the Overseas Chinese deal with the uncertainties they face in volatile environments. The importance of keeping old established ties comes from the fact that at one time A needs B, at another time B needs A. Ability to call in obligations is one of the means of dealing with uncertainty, a capacity for doing so being an important component of organizational survival.

This might be illustrated by observing the networking in operation in a volatile trade, and imagining the nature of the ties which bind the flow of activities. A telling description of the jade industry, from *National Geographic*, explains the illicit nature of much of the trade out of Burma and the way it is bottle-necked into four ethnically Chinese jade trading companies in the northern Thai city of Chiang Mai. They handle more than half the jadeite sold in the world.

The four act as brokers, bringing the Burmese merchants-owners-smugglers (usually of Chinese heritage) together with Hong Kong or PRC buyers. The trade in jadeite is, after all, a Chinese business. They bargain in a godown (warehouse) between Hong Kong-bound crates stacked to the ceiling. Besides a gooseneck lamp and a bucket of water, there is only the jade. If others are present, the negotiators are likely to hide their offers by using hand signals under a towel. None of the three parties—smuggler, broker, purchaser—wants any part of the transaction publicized.
A deal is struck, the rocks are flown to Hong Kong, the jade house's agent there is paid on arrival, the funds are deposited, a telex is sent verifying the payment, and the smuggler then gets his money, less a 7 percent house commission and any advances for expenses, food, mules, women, etc. (Ward 1987: 295).

One can imagine here the long-standing ties between the smugglers and the Chiang Mai jade houses, between the parties in such clandestine and virtually unrecorded negotiations, between the Hong Kong agent, his principal, and the customers. In no case is a contract signed, a witness required, a lawyer employed. And this is over half the world's wholesale trade in the most common source of jade jewellery.

It would, however, be deceptive to see the reliable and long-standing networks as a positive feature of horizontal cooperation, without at the same time observing that their reliable nature does not necessarily result in their being inflexible. A further strength here is the maneuverability entailed when millions of small-scale transactions occur between independent partners. Within the bounds of maintaining good relations, there is still a great deal of switching possible, and although there is much that suggests a fluid and constantly moving pattern of liaisons, some more repetitive than others, an equally valid metaphor is that of the interactions on the trading floor of a stockmarket.

This discussion of sources of effectiveness in the field of horizontal cooperation has concentrated so far on the external relations of the firm. Little has been said on the question of internal cooperation. This is largely because, by virtue of the small scale of the organizations, and the clear sense of who is in charge, there is not normally sufficient differentiation between sub-units for cooperation to be damaged. When the organization begins to grow, the Chinese capacity for mistrust begins to weaken the seams in the fabric, and it is now appropriate to consider the organizational limitations brought about by problems of horizontal cooperation. These may be seen in terms of three handicaps suffered by the Chinese chief executive in growing his business: firstly, the simple fact of limited trust which means the number of people who can be seriously relied upon is small; secondly, the outcome of this in terms of capital starvation, as the urge to control inhibits the sharing of power; thirdly, the technological limitations imposed on any organization which cannot generate large economies of scale, and the consequent restriction to certain forms of industry and commerce.

The patrimonial organization relies upon paternalistic ties between the owner-manager whose power is clearly perceived by all, and those who are dependent on that power. In the Chinese family business, such connections stem from either blood ties, in which case they reflect the external Confucian order, or from specific acts of bonding from which the subordinate owes the superior an obligation. One of the most obvious of these is giving a person employment at a time of need, or promoting a person in a context where it may not be justified in cold objective performance terms. This is not to say that performance would be weak, but simply that it is not measured, and left instead to be judged personalistically by the boss. Being promoted to be marketing manager, or quality control foreman, becomes a matter of personal gift.

There are many other forms of dependence-creation. Examples might be the financial support of a person's education, payment of hospital bills, soft loans, facilitating introductions, or giving references. In addition is the simple act of being interested in the private life of the employee—understanding why he needs to go and see his old mother in China, that he has a handicapped child, that he is going to risk buying an apartment. Eating lunch twelve to a table, bosses and employees all mixed together, and more often than not with food paternalistically subsidized, provides plenty of chances to know about such matters and to make permeable the boundaries of the organization.

By these social mechanisms is constructed a group of key dependents on whom the chief executive may then rely to hold the organization together. It is as if those that were not already family become honorary family. It is important that the heads of each of the organization's main units are connected to him in this way, that their loyalty has been secured. The organizational weakness derives from the fact that there is a limit to how many such relationships an individual can build and sustain.

There now enters into the picture a key problem connected with familism, and played out in the field of horizontal cooperation. It is that whereas the co-opting of non-family members into dependent relationships is always possible given a large range of individuals to choose from, the same is not always possible from the members of a large family. You cannot choose your relatives. They arrive into the organizational scene with certain "rights" and expectations, even perhaps the feeling of a certain amount of territory to defend, and as a family gets larger, it becomes more difficult to tie in its members by obligation to the central paterfamilias. They may by then be nephews, cousins, uncles, and may have strong opinions, untrammelled by feelings of deference to central authority, about the way things are being run. Rivalries and jealousies within an extended family are like the hairline cracks of metal fatigue in an aircraft. These insidious defects will eventually cause the structure to collapse. The notoriety of the third generation problem for the Overseas Chinese is universal, and there are few firms able to transcend it. This is not, however, to say that economic activity is destroyed. The end-result is more likely to be that a unit splits off and starts an independent existence as a new firm, until it, in turn, subdivides. The point here is that the kind of organization observable at any one time contains these limitations and displays them in its size.

A separate facet of the third generation problem is the decline of entrepreneurial talent among heirs, but that will be considered later under the question of control and professionalism.

Mistrust of others, even in an extended family, has particularly significant consequences in the field of finance. It is normally in this arena that battles over control are fought out, and as was evident from the interviews, the urge to control is strong for the Overseas Chinese. The sharing of ownership is only done reluctantly. On the other hand, investment is more attractive if it carries with it a "piece of the action." One of the results of this combination of inhibitions is the tendency for Chinese family businesses to be self-financing. Much of their cash flow is ploughed back into the company. Loans are used, but cautiously, and the preference is for forms of financing which do not entail loss of control, such as reliance on too much bank support.

Clearly in the field of finance, there will inevitably be massive variations in the pattern of behavior, and any generalization will be dangerous. It is, however, possible to argue when comparing the Overseas Chinese economies at large with those of Japan, Europe, and North America, that the way capital is used is different. The most noticeable indicators of a different strategic tendency are (a) the proliferation of small firms among the Overseas Chinese, (b) the avoidance of highly complex, integrated, capital-intensive structures such as are needed in car manufacture, heavy chemicals, iron and steel, and (c) the tendency to concentrate in property, banking, commercial trading, and small-scale manufacture.

Complex integration is avoided. The organizations subdivide, when they are large, into more or less separate units, each with its own products and markets. The creation of a single brand able to compete in world markets is not attempted. [2] This means that the complex coordination needed to integrate product research, market research, production, finance, human resources, marketing, international reputation building, is outside the normal range of Overseas Chinese business behavior.

Even the few Chinese organizations which have grown very large, for instance those in Indonesia, would be unlikely to withstand international competition without a great deal of help. They are in some sense artificial. The role of government in sustaining them has been crucial. As Limlingan observes of Indonesia from his study of large Overseas Chinese companies in ASEAN:

The government policies minimized the need for a change in the business and management structure of the Chinese businesses. The effect of government policies which assured profitability for participants in the industrialization program was to convert managerial expertise into a *desirable rather than necessary* component of economic performance. In other words, a company protected by tariff walls, subsidized by low-cost debt, and awarded a market monopoly does not need managerial competence to be profitable (Limlingan 1986: 100, Original author's italics).

If such large organizations are the exceptions they appear to be, and smaller-scale organizations are the norm, then some note must be taken of the implications of small scale for the absorption of complex technology. These implications can only be negative if the demands of that technology are for very sophisticated processes of coordination. This would, for instance, be the case in an oil refinery or a major chemical plant, if it be assumed that the managerial process is somehow divorced from the technology and not packaged along with it. In actual practice, of course, such technologies normally carry with them the organizational systems to make them operate, so the question of whether the Overseas Chinese would invent equally effective systems from scratch is a hypothetical one. Where these industries exist in the Far East, they are Western or Japanese derived, and although they might well employ large Chinese workforces, the control and the design of such organizations is not usually based in Chinese traditions.

Control

Control, or the process whereby organizational goals are achieved, starts with having goals in the first place, then operationalizing them, measuring performance against them, and applying managerial interventions to control the achievement of them. That is, if the process is handled in a Western "rational" manner. What is likely to happen in the Chinese family business is more nebulous, less programmatic, more personalistic, and it is likely to rely more on the sense of responsibility of key individuals.

In a small organization, such key individuals are likely to be family, or at least close relatives. They are working very much in their own interest, and their sense of responsibility and dedication can become intense. This is one of the less visible sources of organizational effectiveness, and the intensity of managerial commitment available to the Chinese organizations of Asia is an important competitive weapon.

To understand the nature of this process, consider the attitudes likely to be adopted by a "typical" senior manager in a family business, assuming that he is a member of the owning family. In the clearest case, he or she will be a child of the owner/chief executive. He will have learnt about the business and the industry from childhood, probably paying visits to the factory or office from a young age. He will have absorbed much information, a lot of it confidential, from family mealtime conversations. He will behave with great respect and deference towards the paterfamilias, especially if the relationship is a direct one. He will also feel a sense of family continuity and the need to perpetuate and enhance the family "name" or reputation.

There will also normally be a sense of obligation towards the person who built up the company and who went through some years of sacrifice, much information about which will have passed into the family folklore. Moreover, in time, the ownership of the company, or at least a perhaps significant part of it, will pass to him. Company success is therefore feeding directly into his own fortune.

He will find himself with a high level of legitimate power within the organization, as the workforce tends to identify ownership with authority. Unless he is in some way patently incompetent, he will find it relatively easy to influence others below his position.

Given resources of this kind, it becomes possible to leave control in the hands of certain key office holders and to rely on them to act as very realistic replicas of the chief executive, if not always in terms of behavior, then at least in terms of motives and attitudes. Such people will be influenced to work hard by both external obligations and internal motivation. They will be prepared to put in long hours, to worry about business problems, to think creatively about opportunities, to exert pressure on others to perform.

Given the availability of this resource and its extension perhaps in more dilute form in other more distant relatives or in honorary family members, much of the need for formal control systems is avoided. In a sense, the discipline is built in via key people, and to the extent that it is, more bureaucratic discipline can be dispensed with. This is not to say that control systems disappear entirely, as the information contained in them may be needed whatever the form of discipline used to make them work. It is to say, instead, that the "bite," the critical rigor, the insistence on standards, lies less in the systems and more in the relationships, persistently feudal as they appear to be. The end result is that managerial commitment, at least among key people, is intense. The problem of spreading it more widely is for consideration shortly.

Two other advantages to the organization flow from this scenario: a high level of reliability of managerial commitment from key people; and the cost efficiency of reduced bureaucratic control.

Reliability is itself an indistinct feature but nevertheless capable of making a contribution to an organization's survival. What it means is that key people remain available. This in turn means the retention of their accumulated wisdom, experience, and capacity to influence others. In organizations where important information is held privately rather than publicly and where crucial external networking is often personalistic, the long-term retention of a core of executives is in fact an important component of the set of attributes a business needs to remain competitive. The grafting on of new outsiders at a senior level in such organizations is particularly difficult, given the lengthy socialization needed for understanding the organization's core and often concealed features, but more particularly given the problem of time needed for the essential networking, not just outside but also inside the company.

Cost efficiency in the field of control does not stem entirely from a reliance on managerial commitment to replace bureaucratic system. It will in part stem from less stringent environmental demands, for instance those connected with auditing and reporting requirements, labor legislation, etc. In most of the Asian countries where the Overseas Chinese flourish, such forces have less of an impact on a company's record keeping than they would in North America, Europe, or Japan.

Having said that, it is still possible to make out a case that the lower level of formal control used in Chinese family businesses comes partly from the continuing reliance on personalistic methods of control. Regardless of the derivation, however, less paperwork and fewer formalities are likely to mean less cost. Whether this is, in the long run, more effective is a matter of whether the personalistic process, achieves an equal or greater amount of real control, something which can only be acknowledged as unknowable except in the aggregate. Given the thriving economies and their thriving organizations competing successfully in international markets, a *prima facie* case exists for claiming that the control process is in fact highly efficient.

Turning now to the weaknesses which Chinese family businesses display in the area of control, overwhelmingly the most crucial is the limiting influence of personalism. It is all very well having intense managerial effort and using it via the networks to engender loyalty, worker dedication, and stable external relations. But what happens when the organization needs to move beyond the boundaries to which that relationship-based network is being stretched? How does the company cope with the maintenance of control as it expands into new markets, new products, new technologies? Does it in fact accept such challenges? The answer is that, by and large, it does not. It stays within the domain it knows it can manage in its own way, and hence the vast majority of companies remain small.

For those few that venture out into large scale, there are two broad options open as far as control is concerned. Firstly, and more typically, an industry can be chosen where it is possible to extend easily the influence of the key executive group or more likely the key executive individual. These industries have the following characteristics:

(a) large but relatively infrequent judgemental decisions, as for instance in property;
(b) day-to-day operations which can be replicated using a standardized formula, and easily controlled or managed contractually, as for instance in shipping, or hotel management;
(c) financing which can be based in the headquarters city on an individual's reputation.

Examples of large Overseas Chinese companies with these characteristics are World Wide Shipping, based on the skills of Sir Y.K. Pao, or Cheung Kong Holdings, based on the skills of Mr. K.S. Li.

The other route is that of grafting on professional management and building a conglomerate. For this process, the entrepreneurial strategic thinking may well still be retained by family members, but the divisional operations left in the hands of professionals. Such operations are remarkable for their rarity. Those that have emerged have also tended to be unstable, perhaps a result of the unresolved power disputes dividing the professionals and the owning entrepreneurial strategists.

Returning now to the world of the more typical small-scale Chinese family business, and considering the weaknesses which counteract the advantages of a personalistic organizational structure, it is now necessary to assess what happens when an organization is unable or unwilling to break away from a reliance on obligation bonds and move to the kind of neutral, objective processes which form the foundation stones of the elaborate bureaucratic structures of Western companies. That the Chinese choose not to follow this route is perhaps an indication of their sense of a preferred alternative. For them, small works better. Even so, certain organizational weaknesses can be discerned in such personalism even within the small company, and these need to be acknowledged.

Looked at from the standpoint of a hypothetical consultant analyzing the workings of a department in a Chinese family business, it is possible to speculate that he might identify the following characteristics of the control system:

(a) the setting of goals is not done in collaboration with those doing the work;
(b) the intentions of the organization are only loosely understood by those doing the work;
(c) it is not normal to allocate individual performance criteria, or to assess performance on an individual basis objectively against any criteria.

The general tone of the work atmosphere is one where people follow procedures diligently and largely unquestioningly, but tend not to take a larger view of how their contribution fits into an overall scheme of organizational effectiveness. In the main, they receive little feedback which directly influences their own role performance. Instead, there is a need for them to please the boss and try to move in the direction they think he is also moving, although he may adjust his position from time to time. There are three main difficulties which emerge in this situation.

Firstly, good performers can become disenchanted and demotivated as they find that they are treated the same as the less dedicated or less capable colleagues. The system is not able to discriminate between the good and the bad, because it is not open enough and not objective enough. Maintaining a good position requires constant interpersonal work to keep the boss aware of one's loyalty, but it is difficult to make him aware of one's real performance compared to others'.

Secondly, given a lack of clear direction, a certain amount of effort is wasted as people try to work out for themselves where to put their main contribution. The person who thinks he should be concentrating on marketing activities might be better spending his time on quality improvement, but such issues are not thrashed out openly. Equally people are prone to protect their positions against criticism and to stay with doing things which are not risky.

Thirdly, it is difficult to sponsor close coordination across a group of people each of whom has been encouraged by the system to depend on his own boss for guidance and to protect his own role. The slight sense of insecurity engendered is enough to stifle the exchanges and collaborations which are needed if co-ordination across the organization is to flourish naturally and to occur spontaneously without initiation from above. This problem of vertical dependence and horizontal defensiveness is exacerbated by the absence of a system to clarify group objectives. People lack an adequate focus.

The control process, more than any other aspect of the Overseas Chinese organization reflects the heritage of personalism, although it also contains the influences of paternalism and insecurity. It is as though the creation of a social system based on the rational pursuit of objectively defined aims meets major resistance. A high level of neutrality was achieved in China in the system of the mandarinate, but this required the full power of the state in order to work and was constantly under attack from those who, by subverting it, might protect themselves. As we have noted earlier, the ruthless and aloof objectivity achieved in the mandarinate was a deviation from the Chinese interpersonal norm and could not be extended into society at large.

Adaptiveness

For an organization to survive, it must combine internal efficiency with externally related adaptiveness. It must be capable of change if the environment, by whose sanction it exists, places new demands or new opportunities before it.

It is a common observation that Overseas Chinese organizations are flexible and that this is a great strength. They can switch products quickly, chief executives can act decisively, the economies which contain them can display over time smooth transitions from one type to another: from, for instance, a concentration on semi-skilled assembly of consumer expendables to skilled manufacture of durable industrial components; from low tech to high tech; from commerce to manufacturing; from plastic flowers to wigs, to toys, to printed circuit boards. Each of these large-scale shifts of emphasis in an economy is the aggregate result of myriad strategic changes by single companies carried out without crisis, with little bankruptcy, and with often complex internal adjustments such as those of technology and labor skills. Such organizations are patently some of the world's most adaptive, and the sources of this strength, together with certain attendant vulnerabilities, require some elaboration.

There are a number of fundamental structural features of the Chinese family business which are conducive to strategic flexibility. The first of these is its small scale, and the second is the simple decision-making structure. A related factor connected with smallness of scale is the common tendency to avoid being committed by technology to one product market. If you are running a bauxite smelting plant, there is nothing else you can do with it. If you are running a factory using sewing machines to make wigs, the machines can be adapted to make underwear. At worst, the machines can be scrapped and replaced with new ones at manageable cost.

The strategic flexibility which flows from smallness of scale comes about because of adjustments possible in the spheres of both capital and labor. The capital invested in buildings is usually committed to buildings which are multi-purpose such as the flatted-factories of Hong Kong's dense urban industrial area, or the factory shell buildings of Singapore's Jurong industrial zone. These can contain many kinds of production systems and can thus easily change hands if need be. The machinery which goes inside them is commonly bought with a view to something like a four-year payback period. Financial strategy is such as to ensure normally that a company does not become locked in to a particular production technology for very long. If, however, it is able to use the machines for a longer period than that over which they are written off, then the benefits in profitability are likely to be preserved in capital reserves against the day when new investments are sought.

In the sphere of labor, the Overseas Chinese company employing Overseas Chinese labor finds itself with a workforce notable for its "trainability." This is based upon traditions of diligence and disciplined education, and also a high level of manual dexterity. At the same time, the labor markets have normally been fluid, and because geographical relocation has not normally been an issue for labor in highly urbanized industrial concentrations such as Hong Kong, Singapore, Taipei, Bangkok, many of the limitations on labor mobility found in other countries have not been found here. Families have not needed to be relocated. Children have not needed to leave home. Distances for travelling to work have remained manageable when jobs are changed.

Adaptiveness has thus been fostered by the suppleness with which both capital and labor can be managed in the Overseas Chinese business context. A further dimension of this is the speed with which change can be pursued, a feature which allows much Overseas Chinese industry to behave with an agility sometimes verging on the acrobatic.

This agility is perhaps best illustrated by the recent Hong Kong response to the opportunity of cutting production costs by moving manufacturing operations into China where labor costs are substantially lower. Hong Kong companies now employ about two million workers in China. The results of taking this opportunity on a large scale are that over a five-year period dramatic savings are being achieved compared with trends in other countries. What is significant here is not so much the single fact that the PRC labor is lower cost, but more the fact that releasing such efficiency has required major rethinking by hundreds of companies and the acceptance of substantial risk by them. Moreover, the process has inevitably involved complex negotiation across national boundaries and the construction of new facilities for production and transport. It is an indicator of just how much is possible in an economy made up largely of units able to seek independently their own best interests and able to act largely untrammelled in pursuing them.

More often than not, the pursuit of such interests takes place according to the vision of a single individual, and this feature must also be counted as significant in explaining the responsiveness of organizations. The Chinese urge to control ensures that most companies are firmly in the hands of a small and united group of related individuals. In turn, within this group is normally a dominant figure, and it is his vision which the company pursues. The authority which he has is not just a function of the streams of obligations accorded to him internally, but also the key relationships established externally, not least among which may well be the willingness of financiers to back him as a person.

Given such an authority structure, his or her ability to influence events within the firm is normally very great. The organization can be used to turn into reality something which is essentially a personal vision. In this case, strategic thinking can proceed intuitively and without extensive processes of rationalization such as the study of market statistics, or, the employment of analysts and advisers. Under no circumstances is this to say that such intuitive decisions are ill-informed. On the contrary, the distillation of knowledge in one person's head about a particular industry or business context, and usually extending back many years, provides that person with an instrument particularly well designed for such decision making. Add to that the fact that business decisions normally have a direct bearing on the person's own wealth and family security, and the likelihood of careful judgement is enhanced.

Such circumstances do not, of course, guarantee good strategy, as judgement may still be distorted by features of personality, and not all can be known about an environment. There are, nevertheless, grounds for supposing that in the field of small business the level of strategic intelligence achieved in many Chinese family businesses is at least the equal of, and possibly superior to, that achieved by larger organizations elsewhere using formal analytical logics to deal with similar questions.

The strengths of single-person dominated strategies, namely the gearing up on deeply informed intuitions, the speed of response, the flexibility made possible, are inevitably counterbalanced by weaknesses. Reliance on one individual contains substantial risk, both in terms of possible personal flaws, but also in terms of the denial of alternative perspectives and the stifling of debate. There are organizational strains also possible if opportunism undermines the logical coherence of a strategy and causes the organization to chase ideas which are more capricious whims than soundly analyzed options.

The danger of non-rational opportunist leaps in the dark is always present when one person can dominate a boardroom, even more so when the boardroom is largely irrelevant. It is, of course, exacerbated with new technology changing industries rapidly or creating new products and markets, and it is also more likely to occur when an inexperienced chief executive, perhaps the son and heir, takes over and feels it necessary to prove his dynamism. Nor can the role of luck and fatalism be ignored, as chief executives are still found who believe in portents to guide their fortunes.

It would of course be possible to argue that such non-rational stimuli to new ventures serve to create a stream of innovations which prove beneficial to an economy at large; that for every mutation that fails another succeeds. In sum, having the innovations constantly emerging is what sets the economy as a whole apart from others where such adventurousness is more cramped. At the level of the firm, however, if new investments become capricious, the danger to that firm is great, and the possibility of succumbing to such risks is a weakness in such personality-dependent structures.

A second major weakness in the sphere of adaptiveness is the possible diffraction of the organization as its efforts become scattered, and it loses its traditional concentration. This is not a normal process as the tendency to "stick to the knitting" is deeply inbred, but it can and does occur in second and third generations, and is often the cause of decline if talent and experience among the heirs is not evenly available. The likelihood of such a tendency to bring down a firm is clearly related to methods of financing and to where the risk is underwritten. Where it remains underwritten centrally, the firm is in danger as various sons and nephews rush off into the economy to do their own thing with the firm's money. If on the other hand control is tight, and risk is dispersed, the core firm remains protected.

The likelihood of such ventures coming under tight control is low, given the tendency in the Chinese family business to manage things personalistically rather than by formal system and procedure. It is thus possible for much to be going on at the periphery of the firm for which no account is given to the center. Although finance itself is traditionally managed very tightly, financial reporting systems in a decentralized organization can be used to delay bad news to a point where matters are beyond repair.

The main weakness in the attempt by many Chinese firms to grow by creating a conglomerate is one of control, and this breaks down into two components: the lack of bureaucratic objectivity, and the lack of a professional managerial cadre.

These points have been discussed earlier and will not be repeated now, but the outcome is that few firms are able to transcend these barriers and still remain intact. Instead, the tendency is towards constant break-up, much of it acrimonious when it occurs between relatives. Although this may still be done in such a way that the core business is protected, it nevertheless robs the firm as a whole of the kind of gravitas which it might benefit from to enhance its standing for financing, joint-venturing, or employing skilled people.

A more subtle final weakness affecting the firm's capacity to adapt is the lack of creative tension and debate on strategic issues. As markets become more complex and as firms move into new technologies, the intuitive skills of the chief executive, even though deeply informed over decades of experience in an industry, may still be inadequate to comprehend all the issues of strategic significance to the company. Other forms of expertise need to be incorporated. Technologists, finance specialists, executives close to the market, have valuable contributions to make, and unless there are means for their incorporation, the quality of a growing firm's strategic thinking must inevitably decline.

Footnotes

[1] Private comment to the author by one of the largest property dealers in Hong Kong, describing the normal way of dealing.
[2] The exception that, until recently, always proved the rule was Wang, but its loss of momentum has now provided indication that it too is following the same apparently inexorable track.

Chapter 10
The Significance of the Overseas Chinese

The central purpose of this book is to put the Overseas Chinese on the map. They have for too long been acknowledged as intriguing, seen as possibly powerful, but never really been understood outside their own sphere. Even inside their own sphere, remarkably little scholarship has addressed the question of their economic life. And yet they are clearly significant. As actors on the world scene they cannot be ignored.

In a sense, they are also moving inexorably towards center-stage. At first, this drift towards the spotlight was because of their dominant influence in the little dragons of East Asia, only Korea in that set being non-Chinese. More recently, their significance has taken on a new aspect and that has emerged because the possibility has dawned that China might finally be moving into a position to realize its quite awe-inspiring potential. That capacity to inspire awe, however, when applied to something so hypothetical, must be seen in context. It may well have been a false dawn. China's potential may always be just that. The performance may never be delivered. If it ever is, it is more than likely that the Overseas Chinese will have had a great deal to do with it. Their role may be only grudgingly acknowledged, but China has no more significant set of catalysts waiting to be added to its mixture of material and human resources, land, ideologies, and ambitions.

To understand the implications of what has gone before in this book, and thus to consider more carefully the significance of the Overseas Chinese, requires some breakdown of the interests for which such significance finds meaning. The world of Western business could be argued to be one of these, as it has a powerful and little understood competitor invading its traditional preserves at a time when it is still bewildered by, and licking its wounds from, the onslaughts of Japan. China is clearly another, as it would appear to have much to learn from its adventurous and experienced compatriots. In a quite different sense, the world of those thinking about the nature of organizations, the teachers of management theory, and the practitioners of consultancy might also be expected to ponder carefully the importance of a powerful form of organization playing by rules not found in the textbooks and not found either in the literature on that other compelling Asian phenomenon, Japanese management; something in fact a very long way removed from Japanese management in the way it works.

Finally, and also at the level of concepts prior to practice, the study of economic development, already now so concerned with re-adjusting to the unarguable realities of the last thirty years in East Asia, needs to come to terms with the particularly Chinese cultural component of the miracle of the little dragons.

There are then four constituencies where implications may be held to be important: the world of Western business, China, the world of organization and management theory, and the world of those trying to understand the economic development and modernization of societies. This final chapter will address the issues relevant to those four blocs of intellectual and practical interests.

The Overseas Chinese and Western Business

Western businessmen who might have on their agendas questions relating to Overseas Chinese are those who might be doing business against them as competitors, such as an American shirt manufacturer, or those who might be working in collaboration with them, such as an international distributor of brand name toys. Viewing them as competitors or collaborators naturally provides very different perspectives, as fundamental organizational characteristics come into the account as weaknesses to be exploited or strengths to be built on.

The Overseas Chinese as competitors bring to the arena a number of specific advantages, all of which are related to production efficiency, and one major disadvantage which is related to marketing.

When observing the range of manufactured goods now extensively available in Western markets, and originating in areas of Overseas Chinese dominance, their common denominator is price advantage. For price to be an effective advantage, certain minimum quality standards must also be adhered to, and in consequence it is normal for the items to be able to "perform," to have the same functions as their competitors. They may lack the glamor, the brand identity of the functionally equivalent Western-derived item, but Overseas Chinese strategy has normally been to say, in effect, to the customers, "we do the same basic job without the frills at less cost." Leaving aside, for the moment, the question of the Overseas Chinese manufacturing of Western brand-name goods (such as the Christian Dior shirt made in Hong Kong which I wear as I write), and concentrating on items sold in Western stores carrying a little-known brand name, their market penetration is based on perceived value for money. This in turn rests on a low landed price, and that in turn on a low factory production cost, and efficient long-range transport.

The sources of the productive efficiency lie only partly in the kinds of technology used. They lie in the workforce's quality of diligence, in the intensity of managerial effort devoted to the firm in the eventual pursuit of the family fortune, in the financial shrewdness and the efficient use of money, in the flexibilities possible within a network of companies allied by ties of mutual obligation and shifting easily to match market needs. There is much borrowing, and there is careful selection of areas of focus. Research and development is borrowed; design is borrowed; in a sense, the process of marketing is borrowed, or at least linked to in ways which reduce the Chinese need for deep involvement. Concentration is on the core operations of producing the goods, areas where the balance of risk against value added can be made very favorable, given long production runs and the safety of making to order.

Production ability, then, is a strength. Marketing, as already hinted, is a weakness. That is, if one sees the firm through Western eyes. The most noticeable characteristic of Overseas Chinese companies is their apparent reticence to enter the world of mass marketing of brand-name goods. In reality, this may be less a reticence than a result of the size limitations of the family business form and the consequent restriction of the range of activities which can be managed inside its boundaries. Once there are executives in other continents, analysing consumer needs and concerned to influence policy, once an international brand name is created which requires large-scale co-ordination of research, production, quality control, distribution, marketing techniques, public relations, then the strains on a core group, which insists on centralized decision making, are immense. The Chinese appear to sense these hazards and avoid them. They appear to know that they cannot thrive in such endeavors like the Japanese do.

Marketing, of course, takes place, but it is collaborative and it is in this field that possibilities exist for fruitful cooperation with Western firms. Given the Chinese sense of wishing to work within their own restricted organizational boundaries, this brings to a cooperative venture two benefits: firstly, a Chinese partner does actually need the marketing or design services which a Western company can offer as a bridge to Western markets; secondly, the Chinese partner is not likely to be harboring ambitions about extending its activities forward or backward into the areas which the Western firm sees as its own preserve. Partnerships of this kind can be genuinely beneficial to both sides and can become long lasting and stable. In the Japanese case, by contrast, the Western firm is often dealing with a monolithic corporation well able and anxious to take over the full set of operations in the Westerner's traditional preserve; collaboration in those circumstances is inevitably more circumspect.

Creating successful collaborations between Western firms and Overseas Chinese firms requires the acknowledgement of one important caveat. This is that a mismatch may easily occur if the Western firm is highly bureaucratized, a normal feature of any large organization. This introduces requirements for systematic behavior and neutral rationality which the Chinese firm is commonly unable to deliver. Such collaborations are rarely stable unless the relations between the firms are genuinely hands-off, a feature only attainable in certain industries. What appears to be more effective is the connection between firms where the Western half of the link is a firm with an understanding of, acceptance of, or sympathy for, the kind of personalism and informal structure used quite appropriately and normally efficiently by the Chinese firm. Such Western firms tend to be small and may also be family dominated, or have a personalistic, informal culture.

Thus the Overseas Chinese can and do link their economic activities efficiently and effectively into the Western economic system. They carry out the manufacturing component of a longer and more elaborate total system linking ideas to customers. This is also extendable into service fields such as typesetting, programming, transport, and communications. They can also deliver directly into Western markets goods which can satisfy the needs of customers emerging in the base layer of the mass consumption markets of prospering economies.

Western firms looking at Asia must also come to terms with the fact that on their own "home" territory of East and Southeast Asia, the Overseas Chinese in business are a force to be reckoned with. Doing business in that region, particularly if it means marketing into the region, but very often also if it means manufacturing or commodity extraction, is a matter of doing business with the traditional Chinese "middlemen" whose grip has grown increasingly strong. Finding a local distributor, an after-sales service agency, a transport company, an intermediate processor, an insurance agent, an accounting firm, an advertising agency, a warehousing company; all these searches will lead regularly to the Overseas Chinese sector. Similarly, the filling of executive or professional positions, and the hiring of professional services, will lead an outside company again to the diligent Chinese who have managed their education with the zeal necessary to place them in large numbers in such categories.

Such East–West linkages are normally fruitful, mutually respectful, and stable, but there is one over-riding issue which comes to affect the otherwise apparently placid scene, and that is the deep-seated desire of most competent Chinese to own their own company. This will regularly cause the employment bond to be broken, as a person leaves to set up on his own, and may introduce rivalry as the Westerner sees, in his terms, a cuckoo leaving the nest. This does not, of course, affect all cases, but it is sufficiently prevalent to cause a degree of wariness to enter into the Westerner's calculations as his or his firm's experience accumulates.

If a large Western corporation employs Chinese executives in the region, some other trade-offs may be anticipated in addition to the risk of being an entrepreneur's training ground. These stem largely from contrasts in behavioral norms and expectations, and it is not difficult to sustain the view that the contrasts have cultural origins. The point commonly at issue is the taking of responsibility on behalf of the organization, a perceived Chinese weakness which is a source of regular lament by senior executives of Western companies. There are, of course, many exceptions, but the comments, and presumably the reasons for them, remain widespread.

To understand this contrast in perceptions, it is necessary to enter into the mental world of the aspiring executive brought up in Overseas Chinese culture but now working in a non-Chinese multinational, typically the child or grandchild of immigrants, educated towards a career, brought up in an atmosphere of Confucian order, deference, and vertical authority, disciplined, hard working, and dedicated to upward mobility. He or she enters the multinational, sometimes after experience in a Chinese company, or if not, then with expectations, especially about the nature of authority, which have created a predisposition to understand paternalism as the normal mode of handling power.

Such a person looks upwards for guidelines and is prepared to accept and follow them. There are understandings that more senior people in the hierarchy will hold responsibility and will expect an exchange of obedience upwards for a degree of protection downwards. It is a context in which initiative from below is something of a deviation. Expectations are high about the boss doing his job by giving orders.

With this set of ideas about how the core process of organizing should be conducted, the Overseas Chinese individual enters a non-Chinese organization which is publicly owned, and where managers are professional administrators on behalf of a system which, while it may have developed a corporate culture and an organizational soul, does not normally have in it the kind of symbols around which the Chinese organizational soul is constructed, namely its owners. Nor docs it have a counter-attraction to the Chinese person's family as a source of psychological belonging. Unlike many Chinese companies, the multi-national is rarely familistic despite attempts often to be so; its countervailing pull is inadequate to win the battle of divided loyalties going on in the heads of many of its local members. In the end, their own families, and whatever best serves the fortunes of those families, will determine their behavior. This opposing pull against the organization's attractions has a dampening effect on loyalty, and the creation of the "organization man," so much a part of the Western and even more so the Japanese tradition of creating cooperative systems, is very much more difficult when an alternative organization of family dominates consciousness.

The Overseas Chinese and China

Perhaps the most significant thing to be understood about China today is that it still displays most of the elements of a pre-modern form of society. It is still in essence patrimonial. This is somewhat similar to saying, of a Western society, that it is still feudal. It does not contain the feudal structures typical of past European societies in which ties of allegiance to a local land-owning aristocracy were the basis for stabilizing order and providing security. Landowners in traditional China were normally not motivated by ideals of *noblesse oblige*, nor were they permanently ennobled by family to perpetuate their ascendancy. Instead, authority resided in the state via the mandarinate which became the focus of an alternative and unusual form of what could still be argued today to be state patrimonialism. Dependence on aristocratic protection and favor of the kind found in Europe was instead represented in China by dependence on the favor of personified officialdom, and this is still the key to fostering any important activity in China today. Without using the networks of *guanxi*, nothing significant can happen. The communist party has replaced the mandarinate and replicates its functioning, in that (a) it represents central authority, (b) it extends its influence into all areas of Chinese life, (c) its power derives from an ideology which although enshrined in a literature can nevertheless only be legitimate when interpreted by the power holders, (d) it has state military backing, (e) its source of influence at the center is a specific person with an emperor-like role, a change of person bringing a potentially massive change in ideology.

Stemming from such a structure, in which official favor is a requirement for most significant activities, from giving birth to trying to get a pay rise, from buying a van to locating a factory, it is not surprising that the principal dilemma in the background of any attempt to improve economic activities in China is the problem of fostering decentralized decision making. Given the switches of ideology possible when central authority is so personalized, and given the ravages of the red guards in the cultural revolution, or the PLA in Tienanmen Square, it is not surprising either that the problem of decentralizing authority is compounded by a large element of fear, or at least anxiety. In a society which can kill, maim, or exile to an equivalent of the saltmines, millions of its *own* people, people learn to watch their backs. Risks are not taken. Being responsible for something has, in the past, not done many of their friends and relatives any good at all, and they may be next in some uncertain future.

To break down this barrier is proving very difficult. It requires some move away from the historical Chinese pattern of central control towards something never before experienced in the state of China, namely real decentralization of authority. Given the massive complexity and sheer size of China, the danger of things getting out of control is severe, and always has been. Attempts in this direction have consequently only been tentative and partial.

Two further and related requisites exist which will have the effect of barriers if they are not available. They are developed property rights, and bureaucratic order.

When a system of property rights has become elaborated and stable, it has commonly been given much of the credit for a society's capacity to mobilize motivation to perform in the economic sphere. The psychology is simple. A person who can secure his prosperity, and can keep the fruits of his labors, will try harder. The development of property rights in China is still at a very rudimentary stage, and although movement to improve is discernible, the lack of the second element, bureaucratic order, is acting as a brake on progress.

To say that China lacks bureaucratic order when a claim could be made that China invented the classic government bureaucracy is a reflection both on the decline of government quality in the last two centuries, and also the highly limited sphere within which the mandarin bureaucracy operated. What is meant here by bureaucratic order is a set of organizing principles and their resulting institutions which provide the average individual with certain predictable frameworks. In a crude sense, a person knows where he or she stands, and can make decisions accordingly. The ability of people to operate within areas of discretion such as choosing where to live, what work to do, what prices are appropriate, can only take place on a large scale if other areas of life come under some form of accepted order: where a deal is a deal to be relied upon; where what is legal or illegal is clearly understood and respected by all; where the allocation of scarce resources is handled openly according to agreed principles; where seniority in terms of power is accorded to those judged worthy of exercising it; where systems of redress are open. For most societies which have achieved this condition, the major institution on which the structure rests is law, and the most effective source of its maintenance and protection is an incorrupt civil administration, preferably dedicated to the public good.

In the case of China, the traditional and still prevalent means of attempting to establish order is to rely upon a plethora of authority figures imbued with an ideology, each of whom has the power to resolve a dispute. Its resolution becomes a matter for that individual's judgement, and the framework within which such judgements are arrived at, although well intentioned, is still nebulous. There is no parallel authority enshrined in codified or precedent-based definitions. There is little redress. Dependence on the superior individual is still very high indeed, for most crucial issues. Hence the patrimonial state. Hence also the extreme dependence of the average individual on authority figures, and hence also the obsession with cultivating connections, the national pastime of *guanxi*.

It is in this context that the position of the potential entrepreneur may be viewed, and it is a position of extreme disadvantage compared to that of his cousins in Hong Kong, Taiwan, Singapore, or most of ASEAN. The surrounding order in which he attempts to make decisions is still highly contingent on "currying favor." The identity he can have with ensuing rewards is still much looser than it could be. Risks are higher than they might be, rewards are lower.

Seeing the two centuries old question of comparatively slow development in China in this light, in other words from the perspective of power relations and social order, reaches down to the fundamentals of the problem but takes no account of more tangible aspects lying nearer the surface. These must be considered briefly.

The Overseas Chinese make up one of the world's most effective economic cultures. Always seemingly capable of being successful middlemen, they have blossomed in the last thirty years, within certain political and economic circumstances, to transcend dramatically the restrictions of that earlier role. The organizational combinations made possible in the conducive climates where they flourish allow them to create economic systems of world significance. It is necessary to note how this is done and to point out the contrasts in China. In saying this, acknowledgement must at the same time be given to the essence of China's difficulties which is that, compared to most states, and certainly compared to all those inhabited by the Nanyang Chinese, the sheer scale of China, and the consequent difficulties of managing and controlling its life, makes its governance more challenging than for any other political body. One should never forget the weight of a fifth of the world's population.

Many of the key components of the state superstructures in East Asia imply a political philosophy supportive of capitalism and thus present a substantial ideological challenge to China but they are nevertheless considered here for what they are worth as key determinants of progress and leaving aside their political implications. Their common denominators are *laissez-faire*, export-oriented capitalism, based on stable, absolutist but decentralized government, using systems in tune with the specific cultural tendencies towards vertical order, contingent cooperation, and pragmatic motivation.

Laissez-faire capitalism is the precise opposite to the communism which so permeates Chinese economic life. Despite a clear move towards a softer version of the creed, and despite the replacement of references to communism by the somewhat more flexible socialism, still the demands of a totalitarian state conspire to undermine the three components of this general category, namely (a) a free enterprise environment, (b) developed property rights, and (c) efficient transaction costs.

An environment for free enterprise has been recently visible in China in family-based agriculture and in small-scale trading. The reforms of the 1980's have indicated both the ease with which this tendency comes to the surface, and more pointedly the completeness with which it may be blocked out by a regime obsessed with control. It can only be said at present, however, to be in a very fragile condition, and much else will be needed in the way of support and reassurance if a robust environment for enterprise is ever to emerge.

Property rights are a function of law, and particularly in the field of commercial law, China's condition can only be judged as primitive. Again the drift towards more predictable frameworks is visible, but it is tentative and slow.

The efficiency of transaction costs achieved by the Overseas Chinese is largely based on the use of interpersonal trust bonds as replacements for more formal contracts. These bonds, however, only work well between people who can genuinely control events under their discretion, in other words, people who have the power to keep promises. In the totalitarian state by contrast, the layers of overlapping authority are such as to reduce the average person's discretion substantially. He has to consult more people, and his commitments are far less reliable. Transaction costs are thus swollen by the need to negotiate a labyrinth of entanglements and clear a morass of official channels.

Entirely predictably it may thus be seen that China is not fertile ground for *laissez-faire* capitalism, and that despite the occasional surfacing of a will to change, the obstacles are deep-rooted, ideological, and require many years of consistent adjustment in one direction.

Export orientation is a clear feature of China's present industrial strategy, and most outsiders going into joint ventures are encouraged to produce for export. There is, however, a wide gap between wanting to export and knowing how to do so effectively. The latter requires a willingness and capacity to understand the foreign customer, something which the isolation of China, the disparity in living standards between it and its markets, and the persistence of a tribute mentality, have done nothing to foster.

The availability of capital, although often helped by inputs from foreign sources, must, in a healthy economy, eventually rest on internally generated surplus. Assuming the eventual growth of such a surplus, this in turn will only work for development if there are mechanisms for channelling it. Assuming property rights, such mechanisms are typified by the highly developed Japanese and American linkages between the citizen's savings and the stockmarket. Without such channels, the surplus will continue to flow into the traditional Chinese *culs-de-sac* of owning gold or property.

The question of the intensive use of labor as it applies to China evokes the old dilemma of the high level equilibrium trap: the intensive use of labor is inhibited by the sheer volume of labor available, and compounded by the poverty of capital investment in labor-efficient productive systems. Moreover, progression towards a highly paid and productive labor force must rest on a free labor market, free that is from the viewpoint of both employee and employer, a feature only emerging recently, partially, and experimentally in China.

When considering the institutions of government, under the overall requirement that administration be stable and (at least in Asia) can apparently also be "absolutist," certain subtle differences emerge between the case of China and those of its prosperous neighbors. There is a deceptive stability to the government of China which conceals the fact that it is fundamentally inconstant. Dependence on highly personalized political strategies, such as Maoism, Dengism, anti "gang of four"-ism, bourgeois liberalization, anti-bourgeois liberalization, leave the country to swing, occasionally literally violently, from one side to the other, each strategy emerging as an unpredictable outcome of the play of individual power politics from which the leaders emerge. Stability is thus an illusion, and although absolutism abounds, of itself it is inadequate to make the kind of business-like government, lean, disciplined, flexible, strong but fundamentally benevolent, under which the Chinese flourish overseas.

The inability to decentralize decisions has been remarked upon earlier as possibly China's most crucial weakness, representing as it does so much else in the way of mistrust and potential disorder.

The subtle influence of the "need to strive," noted by so many as a contributor to the success of the little dragons, finds little in the way of an echo in China. Very few people there are aware of how relatively backward the country is, even fewer have personal knowledge of conditions elsewhere, and even if they did, mobilization of the will to improve which is feasible in a small country, such as Taiwan, Singapore, South Korea, is immensely difficult over the huge scale of China. Moreover, the all-embracing support of the communist state, reducing all to more or less equal poverty and removing most incentives to strive, is the least appropriate context in which to try and replicate the competitive spirit of the overseas compatriots, honed as it has been on the twin challenges of deprivation and opportunity.

It was observed in chapter 1 that the cultural elements were more deep-rooted than the rest and by nature largely immutable. If that be the case, then the communist state might be argued to have produced a temporary distortion in their manifestation but not to have altered them radically. The unit of cooperation, the most natural collectivity, remains the family, and it would appear to be returning to its traditional centripetal role, as communes are dismantled, as the success of family-based agriculture provides vindication, and as small production and trading units proliferate again.

Cooperation through personalistic networking appears not to have changed at all in structure or process, but simply in the identifying of appropriate members. *Guanxi* is as essential as it ever was.

Vertical order is still visible in the patrimonialism of China, and the old Confucian order uniting relatives lies not far below the manifest surface.

Deep-seated cultural features remain, and are available as contributors to the overall mixture. Their potency remains, however, dependent on what they are mixed with, and this is nowhere more evident than in the cases of the work ethic and entrepreneurship. Both of these crucial ingredients lie dormant until incentives emerge to bring them to active life. Such incentives lie in the economic and political domains, in such features as property rights, free markets, and decentralized decisions. For these combinations to begin working, China has still a very long road to travel.

Implications for Organization and Management Theory

The success of Japan has already alerted the largely Western world of management theory to the need for an understanding of alternative organizational principles. The movement for instance towards a more people-oriented managerial approach evident in the corporate culture movement suggests that lessons are now being transferred from East to West, even though many such ideas were realized by Westerners years ago but not implemented widely.

This occurs in the absence of indigenous Asian management theories as such, as the whole notion of having a social scientific framework for the study and improvement of forms of economic cooperation is itself peculiarly Western, and derives from a non-universal tradition of scientific rationality. There are of course principles which lie behind the efficient business practices of East Asia, but, as is evident from the interviews in this book, they are articulated in terms of long-standing humanist traditions, pragmatism, response to societal circumstances. They are not argued out against a theory *qua* theory of organization *qua* organization. Our focus must then be on the implications of Overseas Chinese management *practice* for the world of management theory.

Two things are striking in considering such practice. In the first place, we observe another variant in Asia on the theme of releasing what Pye (1985) sees as the efficiency of benevolence. In other words, paternalism, in certain cultures, appears very suitably tuned to local expectations and able to provide an atmosphere conducive to effort by the average worker on the shop floor. In the Overseas Chinese case, however, the normal vehicle is a small organization rather than the large one used so commonly in Japan. The principles are similar, but the practice comes to look very different. A jeep and a Rolls Royce are not the same, but each has an internal combustion engine.

The second striking feature of the Overseas Chinese organization is that, in terms of the creation of goods for a market, the firm normally takes only a small part in the total process. Although this is common in other economies also, it seems particularly prevalent and characteristic for the firm to be part of a network. Coordination is via the interpersonal trust bonds of key individuals and exhibits the rare combination of flexibility and reliability, but it is not the coordination of a hierarchy. These markets are not built of hierarchies but of horizontal networks. The economic actor is not so much a vertically and horizontally integrated legal structure called a firm, gathered together under a unifying name, but more a loose and shifting pattern of mutually beneficial (because mutually exploitative) linkages. The understanding of economic action requires a shift from the traditional notion of the firm in economic theory if it is to make sense of the economies of the Overseas Chinese.

It would be a distortion to say that Western management theory has ignored the kind of organizational dynamics able to be released by the Overseas Chinese. There is a large literature on small business and a flourishing interest in entrepreneurship. Small is beautiful, has been argued cogently by Schumacher (1974), and diseconomies of scale have been understood for years by organization theorists who have observed the demotivating nature of increasingly machine-like bureaucracies. Corporate culture has brought back to the center of the arena the question of senses of belonging and identity, explicated by Barnard (1938) in the 1930's, and studied originally in depth as far back as the classic Hawthorne studies in the twenties.

It is as if the world of Western management theory knows what needs to be done but needs constant reminding from teachers and consultants that the core lessons should not be forgotten. The rational search for efficiency through systems, and the resultant danger of dehumanizing the organization, presents a permanent challenge to the advocates of the power of "good human relations."

In the Far East, for the Overseas Chinese and arguably the Japanese and Koreans also, there are no indigenous textbooks, no recognizable management theory, and the Western textbooks penetrate hardly at all. Nor are there consultants on the human subtleties of organization. The design of organizations is more instinctive, less openly discussed, somehow more natural. The organizations are cultural artifacts just as are their Western equivalents, but in the search for productive efficiency, they appear to have found a formula closer to the needs of their participants. The organizations are fundamentally humanistic, even in a hard competitive world, and the edge that gives them is changing the balance to their advantage. It is an old lesson. For the Overseas Chinese, it is some thousands of years old.

Economic Development and the Role of Culture

Given what has happened in East Asia over the past thirty years, an increasing number of development economists have come to see that culture must be included in explanations of why some economies have grown fast and others have not. The reasons why academic disciplines can go for decades without building bridges to other disciplines, which might have something to contribute, are doubtless best left to the sociologists of knowledge who can account for such intriguing resistance to understanding (e.g. Whitley 1984a, 1984b), but at least now some progress is discernible.

The shift, however, should not be allowed to produce a further distortion in attempts to understand. The cultural argument is persuasive and seductive, as it taps deep instincts of individuals who understand that they are different from others, and who want to know how and why, and because of this it is possible to err by running to the opposite end of the explanatory spectrum. If traditionally minded economists such as Samuelson stand at one end saying culture does not count, it is equally unwise to stand at the other end and say it is all that does count. The argument of this book is that culture does matter; it is a determinant of economic behavior, but it is by no means the sole determinant and may not be the prime determinant of the results of that behavior. The critical point is that it deserves a place. No explanation of the economic development of a country is complete without it. Although it is not sufficient for explanation, it is nevertheless necessary.

This book began with the Weberian theme: no capitalist development without an entrepreneurial class; no entrepreneurial class without a moral charter; no moral charter without religious premises. It has proposed that the Chinese capitalism now flourishing so impressively in a range of environments outside China has, as a key component, a class of entrepreneurs whose roles overlap extensively with that of the family father-figure, and whose power is largely legitimated by the acceptance of paternalism and dependence which so typify vertical relationships in much of East Asia. Such paternalism has a distinctly Chinese flavor making its application more limited in range than its Japanese equivalent, and it thus displays how historical experience causes societies to diverge in the practice of shared principles.

That moral charter begins with essentially religious premises in that Confucianism is a religion working to stabilize and provide meaning for much Oriental life and society. Filial piety, human-heartedness, paternalism, reasonableness, compromise, propriety are, in the Chinese context, religious principles. They are essential to an understanding of the moral charter, and that in turn is essential to an understanding of the emergence of this particular class of capitalists.

The economic culture of the Chinese is the aggregate of the shared beliefs of the actors in the economic system, and especially the key actors, the entrepreneurs. It is the spirit of their form of capitalism, and the latter cannot be understood in isolation from it.

The question of *how* big a part it plays in explanation is in itself intriguing, as it raises the issue of whether culture is more salient in some economic systems than in others. In turn, this evokes the question of the convergence hypothesis and whether standardization of production technology is causing worldwide a homogenizing of organizational processes, managerial practice, and behavior in organizations. In this regard, it is noteworthy that one of the original proponents of convergence has two decades later observed that the similarities which appear are superficial (Kerr 1983). Underneath them, the cross-national variety in the world of the mind remains as undisturbed as ever. Economic progress does not appear to radically alter the original values which shape the rules whereby a person cooperates with others. Organizations which may look the same are not the same when you get very close.

For the Overseas Chinese, their normal and representative form of organization, although classifiable as a family business, is a family business of a special kind. Other family business types do not have Confucianism providing vertical stable order, do not have the particularly Chinese form of paternalism based in long-standing patrimonial tradition, do not have trust bonds reinforced by the Chinese versions of obligation and reciprocity, do not have the same psychological dependencies, do not have the intensity of identity with family accentuated by experience of Chinese social history. These forces have shaped a special kind of cooperative system, and they contribute significantly to its economic efficiency.

Such forces are necessary parts of the study of a phenomenon which, at a superficial level of analysis can simply be treated as a large number of small firms. If such collections of firms are analysed from the standpoint of economics, or of organization theory, or of certain positions in sociology, then something is missing in the analysis. What needs to be taken on board is the notion proposed by Granovetter (1985) that economic behavior is embedded in social relations and that these latter vary from one society to another.

Granovetter proposed that the study of pre-market societies by most sociologists, anthropologists, political scientists, and historians had been conducted on the basis that social relations were crucial to understanding. There has, however, been a large-scale tendency in such disciplines to see economic behavior as becoming more rational and more removed from its cultural roots, as modernization proceeds. As does Kerr, Granovetter disagrees and claims that the level of "embeddedness," although not as high as sometimes claimed for the pre-modern case, is nevertheless higher than much modern theory allows, and has not radically changed in its impact from one historical period to another.

This has always been a central issue for the social sciences, and has caused cleavages as various schools of thought have grappled differently with it. The greatest cleavage is visible in the materialism—idealism split, the opposing camps of which might be labelled economics and sociology. That some safe and fertile middle ground is now visible is worthy of remark, and worthy of a lengthy quotation from a percipient observer, Robertson (1988).

It is becoming increasingly clear that the pre-economic basis of "economic compulsion" is a very significant *Problemstellung* of modern sociology and anthropology. What seems to be emerging is a kind of solution to—better, a transcendence of—the old materialism—idealism dilemma which has in various forms plagued the history of sociology (and which has also facilitated the disastrous cleavage between the disciplines of economics and sociology). That "solution" centres on the idea of economic culture—the ideas, values, symbols and so on, which are more or less directly available for, and implicated in, economic action. While implied by Marx's concept of commodity fetishism, and even more clearly suggested by Weber devoting most of the last ten years of his life to the analysis of the economic ethics of the major religious traditions, the notion of economic culture has a surprising ring to many modern ears precisely because it puts together (again) that which had previously been emphatically rendered asunder.

This book is a study of one economic culture. It proposes that values and ideas in the heads of key actors have emerged from a specific cultural tradition, and it argues that those same ideas play a significant part in determining the economic behavior those individuals are responsible for.

It is a new slant on the understanding of economic development, and it contains lessons for theory and for practice. While the rest of us consider those lessons, doubtless the Overseas Chinese will continue the pursuit of their specially designed form of human happiness.

Appendix

Methodology for the Study

This book is based mainly on research via a series of interviews conducted in 1987, and this appendix sets out the basic rationale and methods used in the process of investigating what was hypothesized to be a shared ideology. It will proceed by considering the following topics:

(1) the object of study;
(2) sampling;
(3) method of data gathering;
(4) methods of research coordination;
(5) data analysis and form of presentation;
(6) confidentiality;
(7) limitations.

The Object of Study

As is indicated in the text, the focus of study is an "economic culture." Following a now reasonably cohesive tradition (Berger and Luckmann 1966, D'Andrade 1984, Hofstede 1980, Keesing 1974), although by no means a universally agreed one (for a discussion of the debate, see Wuthnow et al. 1984), it is taken that culture is a synthesis of (a) shared meanings which emerge from the social construction of reality, and (b) those meanings as they are reflected in things people do and make.

In the economic realm, the focusses around which meanings are expected to gather are cooperation, authority, acquisition of wealth, etc., and the areas of behavior in which the meanings may be expected to show themselves are the processes of organizing economic activities, i.e. managing companies, conducting transactions, etc.

This is not to contend that the expression of shared meanings in statements is necessarily a perfectly clear window on them, nor that the mental frameworks are perfectly reflected in behavior. It is simply to say that there is a reasonable match and that the congruence between expressed belief and behavior can be empirically analysed.

The object of study thus falls into two components: the verbal expression of beliefs, values, and meanings; behavioral manifestations of those mental phenomena. This appendix is primarily concerned with the former. The latter enter the text in many ways but principally via the Aston data on organization structures.

The study of beliefs and values about economic action requires an agenda, i.e. a theory, and a method. The agenda was finally agreed in a workshop held at the Institute for the Study of Economic Culture at Boston University. This was attended by Peter Berger (host), Laura Nash (Harvard Business School), Alan Kantrow (Harvard Business Review), Shelley Greene (consultant), Paul Pryde (consultant), and myself.

It was decided at that workshop to investigate beliefs as if they existed as a cluster of concentric circles. At the center is the self, surrounding that are relationships and in particular family, surrounding that is the organization, and surrounding that society at large. It was anticipated that people's perceptions about these four fields would emerge during discussions of a series of more pointedly focussed topics, each of which related to being a businessman. These themes are thus laid across the basic framework to produce a matrix.

It is important here to stress that the process did not rely on a questionnaire being answered and what now follows *is not a questionnaire*. For reasons which will be discussed shortly, conversations were pursued on a sequence of topics using a series of prompts, and this is a prompt sheet to guide a conversation between a small group of people over two hours. It makes clear the themes pursued.

Chinese Managerial Ideology Interview Schedule

Interview by: Date of interview:
Place of interview:
How was this respondent recruited?
Organization Details:
Organization's name:
Organization's address:
Organization's main activities:
Date organization founded:
Number of employees:
Most recent total sales turnover figures, if available, and date:
Respondent Details:
Name: Estimated age:
Address (Town or district):
Position in organization:
Shareholdings or ownership in organization:
Length of employment/ownership with organization:

Family relationships within the organization (e.g.: wife is also a director, etc.):
N.B. Throughout give examples, anecdotes etc. whenever possible.

Theme 1   Why be a manager?
This investigates the reasons why people go into managerial roles as owner/
managers, and what they get out of it.

(1) What are the three most important sources of satisfaction in doing your
    job? Possible probe: describe a recent incident/situation which has given
    you satisfaction.
(2) Are there any aspects of the work which cause dissatisfaction? Possible
    probe as above in reverse.
(3) What do you (would you) want your children to be?
(4) Why are you (not) an employee of someone else?
(5) What is the purpose of striving to accumulate wealth?
(6) Whom do you most admire and why? (This hopes to elicit role models and
    mentors who may be public figures or private individuals known to the
    respondent.)

Theme 2   Socialization
This investigates how the norms of entrepreneurial behavior are absorbed, how
and where the attitudes were learned. Thus we are hoping to explore not just
information on formal "learning" and conventional notions of how someone
becomes a business person, but the more subtle influences, in particular within
the family. It is anticipated that these may be so pervasive that respondents may
take such influences as a matter of course, e.g.: exposure throughout childhood
to business discussions over family meals, etc. and not readily identify them.

(7) Did you have a mentor? Encourage discussion of his/her influence, values,
    etc.
(8) How did you pick up ideas about business behavior? What formal or infor-
    mal training did you have? N.B. especially family influence.
(9) Are there any reference groups you identify with? (This may refer to mem-
    bership of formal or informal groups and is trying to elicit which groups of
    people the respondent identifies with and is influenced by.) Try to establish
    the number of groups, their name, and what is their common interest.
    (Also try to establish the nature of the respondent's involvement with the
    group, how often he meets with them, how important is membership to
    him and what does he get out of the group.)
(10) Were there any special support systems (e.g. revolving credit) which
    helped you get started? What support systems do you have now?

Theme 3   Perception of the organization
The attempt here is to find out how the respondent sees the organization, and
how he understands the way it works. (It is thought responses may be analysable

in terms of a continuum from legal/finite terms to emotional/subjective terms, but don't attempt to bias responses using these terms.)

(11) How would you define a successful organization?

(12) Who are the key people with a stake in the organization's survival? (The concept of stakeholders relates to the degree of managerial discretion. Stakeholders may include shareholders, employees, unions, customers, etc. *Do not* give these as examples to avoid bias, especially as it is anticipated that in this region the numbers of perceived stakeholders will be low.)

(13) Assuming no restraints, what would you like to do to improve your own organization (and why)?

Theme 4   Self
This attempts to understand how the respondent sees himself and his own role in a larger context.

(14) If your company went bankrupt, what would you do?

(15) What would you wish to be remembered for having achieved?

(16) How do you justify the fact that you can influence other people's lives and their livelihood?

(17) Do you have to make any particular sacrifices (now or in the past) to be where you are now? This question may reveal deprivations to achieve present status and also other goals or activities relinquished.

Theme 5   Relationships—Kinship
This attempts to map the important relationships in the manager's kinship network.

(18) Who do you feel responsible for? This may involve material and moral (e.g.: in giving guidance to) responsibility. Try to establish actual and possible responsibilities.

(19) Where would you go to for help? Possible probe: where have you sought help from recently?

(20) How far does the family network go?

(21) Do you have a regional or clan loyalty? Expand on type and extent of contact.

(22) Are such relationships used in the organization, how and why?

Theme 6   Legitimacy
This investigates the manager's attempt to justify the access to the power he uses.

(23) Where does your authority come from?

(24) Is business a respectable occupation? Are there some parts of it which are not? What are they?

(25) What other jobs carry more status and why?

(26) What are the most likely causes for a businessman to lose influence in this society?

(27) How is it possible to lose influence inside the company?

Theme 7   Decisions
This investigates the approach to making decisions; in the background is the idea of a continuum from rational/Cartesian to fatalistic/intuitive.

(28) Is anything written down when you are in the process of making a large-scale decision?

(29) Is there a guiding principle which affects your choice of what to do next with the business? (Here we are trying to determine to what extent decisions are "intuitive.")

(30) How important to you is luck?

(31) Are you normally in full control of events or do you have to make allowances for fate to play a part?

(32) Describe a recent business failure and explain why it happened.

Theme 8   Relations with the State
This investigates the connection with the State and its system of law, and tries to establish the closeness or otherwise of the dependency or obligation.

(33) What should government's role be, as far as business is concerned?

(34) What do you think is an ideal corporation tax rate and why?

(35) What does government do too much of and too little of?

(36) What is your view of insider trading? Taking bribes? Breaking a contract?

Theme 9   Asceticism
This investigates the view of self-denial and whether people are prepared to save over long periods to build a more secure future.

(37) Is there a history in your family of a long period of frugal living before success was achieved?

(38) Do you save any of your current income, if so, what proportion and why?

(39) What is your view of owning an expensive car and wearing expensive clothes? High-spending teenagers?

Theme 10   Religious (quasi-religious/folklore) influences
This investigates the respondents' core beliefs about religion or its equivalent.

(40) Are you a member of a particular religion (establish which and the degree of participation)?

(41) Does it have a direct influence in the work situation? How?

(42) Are there any other guidelines you use, such as good luck traditions, *feng shui* etc.

Sampling

The sample of businessmen was designed to reflect the distribution of Chinese family businesses in each economy. A study of the size of various sectors (e.g. banking, textiles, electronics, etc.) produced a pattern against which respondents could be chosen so that the total sample reflected the distribution of industries in each economy. In terms of company size, the total sample was stratified to represent equal numbers of small, medium, and large companies.

Obtaining respondents was then arranged by the use of a network of contacts and referrals. Interviewees numbered 36 in Hong Kong, 21 in Taiwan, 12 in Singapore, and 3 in Indonesia. (The small number in Indonesia was due to the sad and untimely death of the research collaborator there, but it was felt appropriate to leave it in the sample as it revealed certain commonalities in a different environment.)

Each respondent needed to have the following characteristics: (a) Chinese, (b) experience in running a Chinese family business normally as the chief executive. Approximately 20% of interviewees were not chief executives as such but were working in a senior executive group. They were predominantly male, but there were three females. Average age was 43, with 27 the youngest and 76 the oldest.

Method of Data Gathering

The key to gathering data of this kind is the winning of enough confidence to remove the barriers which people commonly erect. This requires:

(a) some equivalence of respect and status between researcher and respondent;
(b) enough time to reflect, ruminate, debate, consider alternatives;
(c) an atmosphere conducive to persuading people to give something of themselves.

These requirements were met by using the technique of the objectifying interview (Sjoberg and Nett 1968). For this the respondent and the interviewer engage in an exchange of views on a topic about which they equally have a right to an opinion, and about which they both have some experience. The object of study lies, as it were, between them, and they consider it "objectively" together. Opening gambits in such discussions are, for instance, "We've both been in situations where . . . " or "I've developed an interest in a particular aspect of X and you might have a view on it; my view is . . . " For this to take place, the interviewer has to have credibility for knowledge of the business world, either as a previous practitioner or a practising consultant, or active researcher, or all three. The hardest part of this method is for the interviewer to talk as little as possible, but as much as necessary.

It is also necessary for the researcher to create the atmosphere of a board-room, although not a formal boardroom, and for him or her to behave comfortably in that context. For most of these interviews, this was achieved by taking a private room in a high quality hotel and arranging a dinner party with a table for three or four people. Respondents were thus invited for dinner knowing beforehand that the research would be conducted as after-dinner conversation. This achieves a number of practical and psychological purposes:

(1) Busy people will under no circumstances provide the hours needed for this particular social chemistry during the working day. Evenings are much easier for them, and they are less prone to look at their watches.
(2) Norms of reciprocity, especially for the Chinese, are such that providing a person a good dinner in elegant surroundings is a suitable offering in the exchange of favors which is the hidden agenda.
(3) The giving of face in this manner helps to reduce a lot of barriers to the exchange of confidences.

The process would normally begin with drinks from 7 p.m. to 7.30 p.m. during which time respondents would be introduced and exchange notes. It is important in this context that their status levels should be matched. Dinner would be served 7.30 to 8.30 during which time the researcher would explain the reason for the research and, in simple terms, "sell" it. Questions and suspicions would be dealt with and the guarantee of confidentiality stressed.

During the last course, or earlier/later if the circumstances dictated, a small tape recorder would be unobtrusively introduced, excused on the grounds of obviating note-taking, and permission for it requested. In no case did anyone demur, and the strong impression was that its being there was very soon after ignored. It could run for two hours of recording, with one turn in the middle, and it would normally remain running to about 10.30 p.m. when the process would end. After 8.30, drinks continued to be poured but nobody actually got drunk.

The method of enquiry was to raise a topic, outline its meaning, and probe people's views. It was also valuable to encourage them to debate points with each other. Probes could go deep and judgement was needed to avoid offense. It was also necessary to move through the agenda and keep to some hidden schedule.

The speed of movement through the topics could vary, as often an apparent conversational *cul-de-sac* could turn out to be an interesting route to explore and would justify delaying to do so. Equally, on occasion, other topics could be dispensed with quickly if opinions were unambiguous and shared.

It is necessary in such a process to be constantly on the look-out for opportunities to corroborate statements, to check consistency of beliefs, to push for examples of behavior to "prove" their validity, to challenge them for justification, and also to sponsor debate in case new facets emerge. Boasting is unusual in this culture and did not appear to present problems, but there is always self-delusion and fantasy to guard against, as well as wishful thinking.

The interviews in Hong Kong were conducted in English, as all respondents were fluent in the language. In Taiwan, the language of the conversations was Mandarin but the reports were rendered into English by Michael Hsiao before being returned to Hong Kong for analysis. The Singapore reports were gathered in Mandarin and English and transmitted in English. Those in Indonesia were gathered in Indonesian and transmitted in English.

Research Coordination

Much background practicality was handled by my research assistant Monica Cartner. I interviewed the 36 Hong Kong respondents myself. The 21 in Taiwan were conducted by Dr. Michael Hsiao of the Academia Sinica. The 12 in Singapore were conducted by Dr. Theodora Ting Chau of the National University of Singapore. The three in Indonesia were completed by the late Mr. Lie Han Hwa, with some kind assistance from his brothers.

In preparation for this fieldwork, a workshop was held in Hong Kong in order to familiarize the team members with the methods and the reasons for them, and to conduct practice sessions with volunteer entrepreneurs.

Data Analysis and Presentation

The aim of this part of the exercise was to take the mass of statements and tease out the categories and the logics used by the respondents, in other words, to reconstruct the map of their beliefs and values using their reference points.

This was done in the following way.

(1) All tapes and interview reports were gone over word by word for statements, and each statement was then extracted verbatim. It was then placed in the sequence of interview topics in a collection of 136 pages of close handwritten notes.
(2) Within each interview topic, for example "relationships and kin." every statement was then re-categorized and defined in terms of its theme, for example "filial obligation," "family financing," "trust and dependability." These were then entered into the larger categories of self, relationships, organization, and society. Each statement was numbered, there being just over one thousand in all.
(3) It was then possible to examine the terms in which for instance "organization" or "society" was seen by the respondents, and more importantly to

observe the differences in emphasis revealed by the frequency of reference to a particular theme. The number of topics which emerged within each general theme was: self 25; relationships 24; organization 22; society 22. Within each of these topics, there might be anything from one to around thirty statements, the highest number being 33 statements about the urge to control.

(4) These "blocs" of opinion, containing as they did connections with other units of the belief and values map, were then drawn graphically to make a model of the connections and to indicate the major categories used by the respondents. It is these four cognitive maps which together go to make up Figure 4.2. The text of the book is an attempt to represent those cognitive maps as truthfully as possible and in the respondents' terms.

Confidentiality

The Overseas Chinese are notoriously guarded about their own companies, seeing them appropriately enough as private possessions. Above and beyond that, the respondents were being asked to talk about things which many managers, even the most neutral professionals, might be diffident about discussing. For those reasons, all respondents were guaranteed confidentiality and anonymity.

All names were disguised and a simple code developed by taking names from the telephone book. All Hong Kong respondents are given names beginning with H, Singapore S, Taiwan T, and Indonesia I. This alleviates somewhat depersonalizing and allows some continuity between statements for a particular person.

Limitations

The epistemological limitations of the study have already been acknowledged. We are looking at "espoused theory," and it may not be "theory in use." There is nevertheless an attempt to check the congruence of the two in the other organizational data supplied, and to challenge deception during the interview process.

Sample sizes in Singapore and Indonesia are too small, and this is freely acknowledged. They indicate similarities but are suggestive rather than demonstrative. The use of English in Hong Kong, although not ideal, was not apparently a serious handicap either, and was at least partially counterbalanced by the use of native language in Taiwan, Singapore, and Indonesia.

References

Amyot, Jacques (1973): *The Manila Chinese: Familism in the Philippine Environment*, Manila: Ateneo de Manila University Press.

Ansoff, H. Igor (1976): The Changing Manager, in H.I. Ansoff, R.P. Declerck and R.L. Hayes, *From Strategic Planning to Strategic Management*, London: Wiley.

Argyris, C. (1976): Single-loop and double-loop models in research on decision-making, *Administrative Science Quarterly*, 21, 3.

Armentrout-Ma, L.E. (1988): The social organization of Chinatowns in North America and Hawaii in the 1890's, in Lee Lai To, (ed) *Early Chinese Immigrant Societies*, Singapore: Heinemann Asia, 159–185.

Baker, Hugh R.D. (1979): *Chinese Family and Kinship*, London: Macmillan.

Barnard, Chester (1938): *The Functions of the Executive*, Cambridge, MA: Harvard University Press.

Barnett, Corelli (1986): *The Audit of War: the Illusion and Reality of Britain as a Great Nation*, London: Macmillan.

Barton, Clifton A. (1983): Trust and credit: some observations regarding business strategies of Overseas Chinese traders in Vietnam, in Linda Y.L. Lim and L.A.P. Gosling (eds), *The Chinese in Southeast Asia: Vol. 1, Ethnicity and Economic Activity*, Singapore: Maruzen Asia, 46–64.

Bellah, Robert N. (ed) (1965): *Religion and Progress in Modern Asia*, New York: The Free Press.

Berger, Peter L. (1986): *The Capitalist Revolution*, New York: Basic Books.

Berger, Peter L. and T. Luckmann (1966): *The Social Construction of Reality*, London: Pelican.

Bergere, Marie-Claire (1984): On the historical origins of Chinese underdevelopment, *Theory and Society*, 13, 327–337.

Bloom, Alfred H. (1981): Language and theoretical vs reality-centered morality, in R.W. Wilson, S.L. Greenblatt, and A.A. Wilson (eds), *Moral Behavior in Chinese Society*, New York Praeger.

Boisot, Max and J. Child (1989): The iron law of the fief , Working Paper, China-EC Management Centre, Beijing.

Bond, Michael H. and Hwang, Kwang-kuo (1986): The social psychology of Chinese people, in M.H. Bond (ed), *The Psychology of the Chinese People*, Hong Kong: Oxford University Press, 213–266.

Braudel, Fernand (1984): *Civilization and Capitalism 15th to 18th Century: Vol. III, The Perspective of the World*, London: Collins.

Capra, Fritjof (1975): *The Tao of Physics*, New York: Bantam.

Carmody, D.L. and J.T. Carmody (1983): *Eastern Ways to the Center: An Introduction to Asian Religions*, Belmont, CA: Wadsworth.

Chan, Wellington (1977): *Merchants, Mandarins and Modern Enterprise in Late Ch'ing China*, Cambridge, MA: Harvard University Press.

Clammer, John R. (1978): Sociological analysis of the Overseas Chinese in Southeast Asia, in P.S.J. Chen and H.-D. Evers, (eds) *Studies in ASEAN Sociology*, Singapore: Chopmen Enterprises.

Cohen, Myron L. (1976): *House United, House Divided: The Chinese Family in Taiwan*, New York: Columbia University Press.

Coppel, Charles A. (1983): *Indonesian Chinese in Crisis*, Kuala Lumpur: Oxford University Press.

Creel, Herrlee H. (1987): The role of compromise in Chinese culture, in Charles le Blanc and Susan Blader (eds), *Chinese Ideas About Nature and Society: Studies in Honour of Derk Bodde*, Hong Kong: Hong Kong University Press, 133–151.

Crissman, L.W. (1967): The segmentary structure of urban overseas Chinese communities, *Man*, 2, 185–204.

Curtin, Philip D. (1984): *Cross-cultural Trade in World History*, Cambridge: Cambridge University Press, ch. 8, Bugis, banians and Chinese: Asian traders in the era of the great companies, 158–178.

D'Andrade, R.G. (1984): Cultural meaning systems, in R.A. Shweder and R.A. Le Vine (eds), *Culture Theory: Essays of Mind, Self and Emotion*, Cambridge: Cambridge University Press.

Dannhaeuser, Norbert (1981): Evolution and devolution of downward channel integration in the Philippines, *Economic Development and Cultural Change*, 29, 3, 577–595.

de Bary, W. Theodore (1959): Some common tendencies in Neo-Confucianism, in D.S. Nivison and A.F. Wright (eds), *Confucianism in Action*, Stanford, CA: Stanford University Press, 25–49.

Deyo, Frederick C. (1978): Local foremen in multinational enterprise: a comparative case study of supervisory role-tensions in Western and Chinese factories of Singapore, *Journal of Management Studies*, 15, 308–317.

Deyo, Frederick C. (1983): Chinese management practices and work commitment in comparative perspective, in L.A.P. Gosling and L.Y.C. Lim (eds), *The Chinese in Southeast Asia; Vol. II, Identity Culture and Politics*, Singapore: Maruzen Asia, 215–230.

Doi, Takeo (1973): *The Anatomy of Dependence*, Tokyo: Kodansha International.

Elvin, Mark (1973): *The Pattern of the Chinese Past*, Stanford: Stanford University Press.

Fairbank, John K. (1987): *The Great Chinese Revolution: 1800–1985*, New York: Harper and Row.

Fairbank, John K., E.O. Reischauer, and A.M. Craig (1965): *East Asia: The Modern Transformation*, Boston: Houghton Mifflin.

Fei, Xiao Tung (1939): *Rural China*, Shanghai: Guancha She. Transl. G.G. Hamilton and Wang Zheng, Institute of Governmental Affairs, University of California, Davis, 1990.

Feuerwerker, Albert (1984): The state and the economy in late Imperial China, *Theory and Society*, 13, 3, 297–325.

Ford, David et al. (1986): *Export Development from the Third World: a Structure for the Analysis of Buyer-Seller Relationships*, Washington, DC: National Center for Import-Export Studies, Georgetown University.

Freedman, Maurice (1979): The handling of money: a note on the background to the economic sophistication of the Overseas Chinese, in M. Freedman (ed), *The Study of Chinese Society*, Stanford, CA: Stanford University Press, 22–26.

Geertz, Clifford (1973): *The Interpretation of Culture*, New York: Basic Books.

Godley, Michael (1981): *Mandarin Capitalists from the Nanyang*, Cambridge: Cambridge University Press.

Graham, A.C. (1971): China, Europe, and the origins of modern science *Asia Major*, 16.

Granet, M. (1920): Quelques particularités de la langue et de la pensée chinoises, *Revue philosophique*, 101–102.

Granovetter, Mark (1985): Economic action and social structure: the problem of embeddedness, *American Journal of Sociology*, 19, 3, 481–510.

Hamilton, Gary G. (1977): Ethnicity and regionalism: some factors influencing Chinese identities in Southeast Asia, *Ethnicity*, 4, 337–351.

Hamilton, Gary G. (1984): Patriarchalism in Imperial China and Western Europe: a revision of Weber's sociology of domination, *Theory and Society*, 13, 393–425.

Hamilton, Gary G. and N.W. Biggart (1988): Market, culture and authority: a comparative analysis of management and organization in the Far East, *American Journal of Sociology*, Special Supplement on the Sociology of the Economy, 94, S52–94.

Hewison, Kevin (1985): The structure of banking capital in Thailand, Symposium: Changing Identities of the SE Asian Chinese since World War II, Australian National University, Canberra.

Hicks, George L. and S.G. Redding (1982): Culture and corporate performance in the Philippines: the Chinese puzzle, in R.M. Bautista and E.M. Pernia (eds) *Essays in Development Economics in Honor of Harry T. Oshima*, Manila: Philippine Institute for Developmental Studies, 199–215.

Hicks, George L. and S.G. Redding (1983): The story of the East Asian economic miracle, *Euro-Asia Business Review*, Part 1, II, 3; Part 2, II, 4.

Ho, Ping ti (1976): The Chinese civilization: a search for the roots of its longevity, *Journal of Asian Studies*, 35, 4, 547–554.

Ho, S.P.S. (1980): Small Scale Enterprises in Korea and Taiwan, Staff Working Paper No. 384, The World Bank, Washington, D.C.

Ho, Yau Fai and Lee Ling Yu (1974): Authoritarianism and attitude toward filial piety in Chinese teachers, *The Journal of Social Psychology*, 92, 305–306.

Hofstede, Geert (1980): *Culture's Consequences*, London: Sage Publications.

Hofstede, Geert (1984): The cultural relativity of the quality of life concept, *Academy of Management Review*, 1, 3, 389–398.

Hollows, Judith (1989): Technology transfer and East Asian business recipes: the adoption of Japanese management techniques by the Shanghai cotton spinners and their use in Hong Kong, Colloquium of Australian-Pacific Researchers on Organization Studies, Canberra.

Hsieh, Jiann (1978): The Chinese community in Singapore: the internal structure and its basic constituents , in P.J.S. Chen and H.-D. Evers (eds), *Studies in ASEAN Sociology*, Singapore: Chopmen Enterprises.

Hsu, Dau-lin (1970): The myth of the "Five Human Relations" of Confucius, *Monumenta Sinica*, 29, 31.

Hsu, Francis L.K. (1971): Psychosocial homeostasis and Jen: conceptual tools for advancing psychological anthropology, *American Anthropology*, 73, 23–43.

Huang, P.C.C. (ed) (1978): *The Development of Underdevelopment in China*, Armonk, NY: M.E. Sharpe.

Jacobs, J.B. (1982): The concept of *Guanxi* and local politics in a rural Chinese cultural setting, in S.L. Greenblatt, R.W. Wilson, and A.A. Wilson (eds), *Social Interaction in Chinese Society*, New York: Praeger, 209–236.

Jacobs, Norman (1958): *The Origin of Modern Capitalism in Eastern Asia*, Hong Kong: Hong Kong University Press.

Jesudason, James V. (1989): *Ethnicity and the Economy: The State, Chinese Business and Multinationals in Malaysia*, Singapore: Oxford University Press.

Johnson, Chalmers (1982): *MITI and the Japanese Miracle*, Stanford, CA: Stanford University Press.

Johnson, Chalmers (1985): The role of Japan in the Pacific Asian region and Japanese relations with the US, PRC and USSR, Conference on the Pacific Asian Region, Shanghai Institute for International Studies.

Jones, E.L. (1981): *The European Miracle*, Cambridge: Cambridge University Press.

Kahn, Herman (1979): *World Economic Development: 1979 and Beyond*, London: Croom Helm.

Keesing, Roger M. (1974): Theories of culture, *Annual Review of Anthropology*, 73–97.

Kerr, Clark (1983): *The Future of Industrial Societies*, Cambridge, MA: Harvard University Press.

Ketcham, David (1987): *Individualism and Public Life*, Oxford: Blackwell.

Landa, Janet T. (1981): A theory of the ethnically homogeneous middleman group: an institutional alternative to contract law, *The Journal of Legal Studies*, 10, 349–362.

Lau, Siu Kai (1982): *Society and Politics in Hong Kong*, Hong Kong: Chinese University Press.

Lee, Lai To (ed) (1988): *Early Chinese Immigrant Societies*, Singapore: Heinemann Asia.

Li, Lillian M. (1981): *China's Silk Trade: Traditional Industry in the Modern World*, Cambridge, MA: Harvard University Press.

Limlingan, Victor S. (1980): The Chinese "Pakulo": project management in an Asian setting; The Chinese walkabout: a case study in entrepreneurial education, Working papers, Asian Institute of Management, Manila.

Limlingan, Victor S. (1986): *The Overseas Chinese in ASEAN: Business Strategies and Management Practices*, Manila: Vita Development Corporation.

Lin Yutang (1977): *My Country and My People*, Hong Kong: Heinemann.

Lodge, George C. and E.F. Vogel (eds) (1987): *Ideology and National Competitiveness*, Boston, MA: Harvard Business School Press.

Lubman, Stanley (1983): Comparative criminal law and enforcement: China , in S.H. Kadish (ed), *Encyclopaedia of Crime and Justice*, New York: The Free Press.

Lui, Adam Y.C. (1979): *Corruption in China During The Early Ch'ing Period 1644–1660*, Hong Kong: Centre of Asian Studies, Hong Kong University.

Mackie, Jamie A.C. (ed) (1976): *The Chinese in Indonesia*, Sydney: Nelson.

Mak, Lau Fong (1988): Chinese secret societies in the nineteenth century Straits Settlements, in Lee Lai To (ed), *Early Chinese Immigrant Societies*, Singapore: Heinemann Asia, 230–243.

Marshall, G. (1982): *In Search of the Spirit of Capitalism*, London: Hutchinson.

Morawetz, David (1980): Why the emperor's new clothes are not made in Colombia, World Bank, Staff Working Paper.

Morishima, M. (1982): *Why Has Japan Succeeded?* Cambridge: Cambridge University Press.

Nakamura, Hajime (1964): *Ways of Thinking of Eastern People*, Honolulu: University of Hawaii Press.

Needham, Joseph (1956): *Science and Civilization in China*, Cambridge: Cambridge University Press, Vol. 2.

Needham, Joseph (1969): *The Grand Titration: Science and Society in East and West*, London: George Allen and Unwin.

Nivison, David S. (1959): Introduction, in D.S. Nivison and A.F. Wright (eds), *Confucianism in Action*, Stanford, CA; Stanford University Press, 3–24.

Northrop, F.S.C. (1946): *The Meeting of East and West*, New York Macmillan.

Omohundro, John T. (1981): *Chinese Merchant Families in Iloilo*, Athens, OH: Ohio University Press.

Osgood, Cornelius (1975): *The Chinese: A Study of a Hong Kong Community*, Tucson: University of Arizona Press.

Pelzel, J.C. (1970): Japanese kinship: a comparison, in M. Freedman (ed), *Family and Kinship in Chinese Society*, Stanford: Stanford University Press, 227–248.

Poggi, G. (1983): *Calvinism and the Capitalist Spirit: Max Weber's Protestant Ethic*, London: Macmillan.

Popper, Karl (1957): *The Poverty of Historicism*, Boston: Beacon Press.

Pugh, Derek S. and D.J. Hickson (1976): *Organizational Structure in its Context: The Aston Programme I*, Farnborough: Saxon House.

Purcell, Victor (1965): *The Chinese in Southeast Asia*, Oxford: Oxford University Press.

Pye, Lucian (1985): *Asian Power and Politics*, Cambridge, MA: Harvard University Press.

Redding, S. Gordon (1980): Cognition as an aspect of culture and its relation to management process: an exploratory review of the Chinese case, *Journal of Management Studies*, 17, 2, 127–148.

Redding, S. Gordon (1982a): Cultural effects on the marketing process in Southeast Asia, *Journal of the Market Research Society*, 24, 2, 98–122.

Redding, S. Gordon (1982b): Thoughts on causation and research models in comparative management for Asia, *Proceedings, Academy of International Business Asia-Pacific Dimensions of International Business Conference*, Honolulu: University of Hawaii, 1–38.

Redding, S. Gordon (1986): Developing managers without "management development": the overseas Chinese solution, *Management Education and Development*, 17, 3, 271–281.

Redding S. Gordon and Michael Ng (1982): The role of "face" in the organizational perceptions of Chinese managers, *Organization Studies*, 3, 3, 201–219.

Redding, S. Gordon and S. Richardson (1986): Participative management and its varying relevance in Hong Kong and Singapore, *Asia Pacific Journal of Management*, 3, 2.

Redding, S. Gordon and R.D. Whitley (1990): Beyond bureaucracy: towards a comparative analysis of forms of economic resource co-ordination and control, in S.R. Clegg and S.G. Redding (eds), *Capitalism in Contrasting Cultures*, New York: de Gruyter, 1990.

Redding, S. Gordon and G.Y.Y. Wong (1986): The psychology of Chinese organizational behaviour, in M.H. Bond (ed), *The Psychology of the Chinese People*, Hong Kong: Oxford University Press, 267–295.

Robertson, R. (1988): The sociological significance of culture: some general considerations, *Theory, Culture and Society*, 5, 3–23.

Robison, Richard (1986): *Indonesia: the Rise of Capitalism*, Sydney: Allen and Unwin.

Rodinson, Maxime (1974): *Islam and Capitalism*, London: Penguin.

Ryan, Edward J. (1961): The value system of a Chinese community in Java, Unpublished doctoral dissertation, Harvard University.

Samuelson, Paul (1979): *Economics*, New York: McGraw-Hill.

Schumacher, Ernst F. (1974): *Small is Beautiful*, London: Abacus.

Schwartz, Benjamin (1959): Some polarities in Confucian thought, in D.S. Nivison and A.F. Wright (eds), *Confucianism in Action*, Stanford: Stanford, University Press, 50–62.

See, Chinben (1985): Chinese organizations and ethnic identity in the Philippines, Symposium: Changing Identities of the Southeast Asian Chinese since World War II , Australian National University, Canberra.

Shiba, Yoshinobu (1970): *Commerce and Society in Sung China*, translated by Mark Elvin, Ann Arbor, MI: Center for Chinese Studies, University of Michigan.

Silin, Robert H. (1976): *Leadership and Values: The Organization of Large-Scale Taiwanese Enterprises*, Cambridge, MA: Harvard University Press.

Sit, Victor F.S. and S.L. Wong (1988): Hong Kong manufacturing: growth and challenges of an export-oriented system dominated by small and medium industry, Working Paper, Dept. of Geography, University of Hong Kong.

Sjoberg, Gideon and R. Nett (1968): *A Methodology for Social Research*, New York: Harper and Row.

Skinner, G. William (1957): *Chinese Society in Thailand*, Ithaca, NY: Cornell University Press.

Skinner, G. William (1958): *Leadership and Power in the Chinese Community of Thailand*, Ithaca, NY: Cornell University Press.

Skinner, G.W. (1964): Marketing and social structure in rural China, *The Journal of Asian Studies*, 24, 1; 3–43; 195–228; 363 399.

Spender, Jason C. (1980): Strategy in business, unpublished doctoral dissertation, University of Manchester.

Sterba, Richard L.A. (1978): Clandestine management in the Imperial Chinese bureaucracy, *Academy of Management Review*, 3, 1.

Strauch, Judith (1981): *Chinese Village Politics in the Malaysian State*, Cambridge, MA: Harvard University Press.

Tang, Sara F.Y. and P.S. Kirkbride (1986): The development of conflict-handling skill in Hong Kong: some cross-cultural issues, Working paper, City Polytechnic of Hong Kong.

Thomlinson, Ralph (1972): *Thailand's Population: Facts, Trends, Problems and Policies*, Winston-Salem, NC: Overseas Research Center, Wake Forest University.

Thubron, Colin (1987): *Behind the Wall*, London: Penguin.

Tu, Wei ming (1984): *Confucian Ethics Today: The Singapore Challenge*, Singapore: Federal Publications.

Vleming, J.L. (1926): *Het Chineesche Zakenleven in Nederlandsch-Indie*, Weltevreden: Landsdrukkerij. Translated by Lie Han Hwa.

Wang, Gungwu (1981): *Community and Nation: Essays on Southeast Asia and the Chinese*, Singapore: Heinemann.

Wang, Yeh-chien (1973): *Land Taxation in Imperial China 1750–1911*, Cambridge: Cambridge University Press.

Ward, Fred (1987): Jade—stone of heaven, *National Geographic*, 172, 3, 282–315.

Weber, Max (1951): *The Religion of China*, Glencoe, Ill.: The Free Press.

Weightman, G.H. (1960): The Philippine Chinese: a cultural history of a marginal trading community, unpublished doctoral dissertation, Cornell University.

Whitley, Richard D. (1984a): *The Intellectual and Social Organization of the Sciences*, Oxford: Clarendon Press.

Whitley, Richard D. (1984b): The development of management studies as a fragmented adhocracy, *Social Science Information*, 23.

Whitley, Richard D. (1987): Taking firms seriously as economic actors: towards a sociology of firm behaviour, *Organization Studies*, 8, 125–147.

Wickberg, Edgar (1965): *The Chinese in Philippine Life*, New Haven, CT, Yale University Press.

Wiener, Martin J. (1981): *English Culture and the Decline of the Industrial Spirit, 1850–1980*, Cambridge: Cambridge University Press.

Wilhelm, R. (1982): *Chinese Economic Psvchology*, New York: Garland Publishing. First published as *Chinesische Wirtschaftspsychologie*, Leipzig, 1930.

Willmott, D.E. (1960): *The Chinese in Semarang*, Ithaca, NY: Cornell University Press.

Wilson, R.W. (1970): *Learning to be Chinese: The Political Socialization of Children in Taiwan*, Cambridge, MA: MIT Press.

Wilson, R.W. and A.W. Pusey (1982); Achievement motivation and small business relationship patterns in Chinese society, in S.L. Greenblatt, R.W. Wilson, and A.A. Wilson (eds), *Social Interaction in Chinese Society*, New York: Praeger, 195–208.

Wolf, Margery (1968): *The House of Lim: A Study of a Chinese Farm Family*, New York: Appleton-Century-Crofts.

Wong, Gilbert Y.Y. (1989): Business groups in a dynamic environment: interlocking directorates in Hong Kong 1976–1986. Conference on Business Groups in Economic Development in East Asia. Centre of Asian Studies, University of Hong Kong.

Wong, Siu-lun (1988): *Emigrant Entrepreneurs: Shanghai Industrialists in Hong Kong*, Hong Kong: Oxford University Press.

Wright, A.F. (1962): Values, roles and personalities, in A.F. Wright and D. Twitchett (eds), *Confucian Personalities*, Stanford, CA: Stanford University Press, 3–23.

Wu, John C.H. (1967): The status of the individual in the political and legal traditions of old and new China, in C.A. Moore (ed), *The Chinese Mind:*

Essentials of Chinese Philosophy and Culture, Honolulu: East-West Center Press, 340–364.

Wu, Yuan li and Wu, Chun-hsi (1980): *Economic Development in Southeast Asia: The Chinese Dimension*, Stanford: Hoover Institution Press.

Wuthnow, R. et al. (1984): *Cultural Analysis*, London: Routledge and Kegan Paul.

Yang, C.K. (1959); Some characteristics of Chinese bureaucratic behavior, in D.S. Nivison and A.F. Wright (eds), *Confucianism in Action*, Stanford, CA: Stanford University Press, 134–164.

Yang, C.K. (1961): *Religion in Chinese Society*, Berkeley CA.: University of California Press.

Yang, Martin C. (1945): *A Chinese Village*, New York: Columbia University Press.

Yoshihara, Kunio (1988): *The Rise of Ersatz Capitalism in Southeast Asia*, Singapore: Oxford University Press.

Zinoviev, A. (1979): *The Yawning Heights*, London: Bodley Head, 1979. reported in Clive James, *From the Land of Shadows*, London: Pan Books 1983, 255–263.

Zukav, Gary (1979): *The Dancing Wu Li Masters: An Overview of the New Physics*, London: Rider/Hutchinson.

Index